# FLIGHT FROM PARADISE

Atray Vishal Lakshman

© 2021, Atray Vishal Lakshman, Brisbane *All rights reserved.*

# CONTENTS

**CHAPTER 1: A REFLECTION ON MY REFLECTIONS** ............ 1
**CHAPTER 2: COLONIAL RULE IN FIJI** ........................................ 4
The Indian Slaves on the Little Ship *Leonidas* ........................................ 5
No Rights under the Indenture System ................................................. 8
My Illustrious and Legendary Paternal Grandfather ........................ 9
The Early Reformers, Educators, Gurus and Scholars ...................... 11
Meeting the Prince of Wales ................................................................ 12
Indians in Politics in Fiji ...................................................................... 13
Life in Colonial Fiji ............................................................................... 19
The Mahatma Gandhi Memorial College ........................................... 23
Our Printing Press ................................................................................. 24
Button Industry in Lautoka .................................................................. 24
My Early Life in Fiji: Hell on Earth for the Elders,
Paradise on Earth for the Children ..................................................... 25
Food in Fiji .............................................................................................. 29
Memories of Our Primary School ....................................................... 30
Early Image of Fijian Village Life ........................................................ 35
Our Island in the Sun ........................................................................... 35
The War in the Pacific ........................................................................... 38
Hindu Swastika in Fiji .......................................................................... 40
Indian Women in Fiji and Religion .................................................... 42
Influence of Gandhi on Children ........................................................ 46
Infinity and Ramanujan ........................................................................ 48
European Contacts ................................................................................ 48
Indian Weddings in Fiji ........................................................................ 49
The Indo-Fijians ..................................................................................... 51

**CHAPTER 3: THE LIFE AND TIMES OF AN INDIAN
TOM SAWYER AND HUCKLEBERRY FINN** ........................... 53
The Arrival of the Americans in Our Paradise ................................. 53
    Ring the bells! Ring the bells! The Marines are coming! ............ 53

Our Adventures with the Americans .................................................. 60
    Raid on American supply dump: foreign aid for
    poor starving children ..................................................................... 60
    I brought dishonour to my family ................................................... 61
    Bicycles for hire for drunken soldiers ............................................. 66
More Childhood Adventures ............................................................... 71
    A hapless gardener ......................................................................... 71
    The joy of the cinema ..................................................................... 74
    Gautam, the innovator .................................................................... 75
    Comics and things comical ............................................................ 76
    Nature lovers .................................................................................. 80
    Peep show for children .................................................................. 81
Sympony on the Ocean ....................................................................... 83
    Bakana Island ................................................................................. 84
    Vomo Island, near-drowning experiences, and little truants ......... 86
    An Indian chief ................................................................................ 92
    Jean Simmons ................................................................................ 94
    Symphony on the ocean blue: how the ocean sang and danced ...... 96
A Reflection ......................................................................................... 99

**Photo Gallery** ................................................................................... **101**

**CHAPTER 4: COMING TO AUSTRALIA** ............................... **119**
My Experience .................................................................................. 119
Life at Grammar School .................................................................... 124
Love of History .................................................................................. 127
Young Bachelors Learn to Cook ....................................................... 128
    Important hints .............................................................................. 130
    Dhal ............................................................................................... 131
    Tinned Salmon Curry .................................................................... 132
    Tinned Corned Beef and Potato Curry
    (a starving student's delight!) ....................................................... 133
    Hot Easy Tomato Chutney ............................................................ 133
    Hot-Sweet Pumpkin Curry ............................................................ 133

General note .................................................................................. 134
How to use alcohol in good Indian cooking ................................. 134

**CHAPTER 5: MY LEGAL CAREER** ......................................... 136
Called to the Bar and almost Deported ......................................... 140
Asian and Polynesian Women Deemed Prostitutes ....................... 145
The Justice Department .................................................................. 147
English Our Mother Tongue and Scotland Yard .......................... 151

**CHAPTER 6: LEGAL CASES** ..................................................... 165
*The Southport Betting Case and Herbert's Trial* (1975) ................ 165
*Japanese Victim* (1976) .................................................................. 205
*The Queen v Julie Anne Wright* (aka Julie Cashman):
Angel of Death (1985) ................................................................... 207
*R v Knibb*: Murder on the beach in Cairns (1987) ....................... 210
*The Queen v Huirua Hoana Harding*: A child
witness (1988) ............................................................................... 219
    Hypothetical circumstantial evidence cases ............................ 287
*R v Barrie John Watts*: Murderous husband and wife
team (1988) ................................................................................... 289
*R v De Jackson*: Headless body (1991) ........................................ 295
*R v Meninga*: The sadistic killing in the park (1991) ................. 305
*R v Weissensteiner*: Bodies never found (1992) ......................... 314
*R v Stafford*: A controversial case (1992) ................................... 339

**CHAPTER 7: A FINAL REFLECTION** ..................................... 363

# CHAPTER 1: A REFLECTION ON MY REFLECTIONS

I once promised to share my story with my family, friends, and compatriots, and here it is.

My small shadow on the fabric of Time begins with some reflections and stocktaking of who I am and where I came from. The story is not rigidly chronological, and no doubt there are many repetitions, as must happen when recounting long-ago experiences. It deals with the perennial questions of human existence, with why most of us aspire, perspire and expire without leaving any footprints on the sidereal dust of Time and Space. Essentially, these questions deal with the why, when, where and what of our existence.

*Why* I write is to connect with you, my family, friends and readers. *When* I write is now. *Where* I write is here on these pages and on the slate of posterity. *What* I write is the history of my childhood in a paradise that was then under the oppressive colonial boot. It is a story of my struggles, trials, and ordeals, of my successes and failures in my new adopted land. I hope to give some glimpses of my philosophy and reflections on my toil and endeavours. It is the sum of who I am and why I tell my story about my past and present; perhaps it may predict my future too. In many ways, this is really Everyman's Story.

In my experience, there is one eternal truth about any reflection on the past: such reflections meander and are not like a perfectly structured novel or work of fiction. Reflections are not designed to suit the dictates of a coterie of literary critics who come and go and whose penchant for a particular structure and style vanish with them in a blink of a few centuries, leaving no trace behind.

The only true lesson is that most lives are disorganised, and the meaning of life is deeply subjective; memory is a cacophonic concoction of chaos and confusion. A search for meaning is a lonely journey in the existential sea of chance and happenstance where serendipity reigns supreme.

Experience teaches us that the past is a journey through a minefield of raw material still being processed and reprocessed. It is an exercise full of avoidance and explanation since recollection is a continuous mental digestive process akin to 'chewing the cud'. It is a regurgitation process through which raw material is refined and redefined by the very act of recollection.

The belief that the past can be accessed as something pure and unadulterated and untouched by the present must remain in the realm of imagination and fiction. The present infuses and informs the past, and the past is the foundation of the present. The past is kaleidoscopic; each separate attempt in life to visit the same set of events will bring a different result. Even a tilt ever so slight will change the tone and pattern. Alas! Such are the problems of writing about the past.

The artificiality of the exercise called writing is daunting because a single life is one long, seamless process with the past, present, and future all flowing and interacting. Definition and classifications are artificial constructs created by the mind.

I share the sentiments of those who say that to make sense of the past one must travel in Time through narrow labyrinthine passages of human thought, traversing many unsheltered, unprotected pathways of missed opportunities, regrets and longings, of lost and now forgotten love, and deep abiding hatred. It is an experience of illusion and a sense of propinquity; we feel we have been there and experienced something.

This mental recovery is like slicing through a multi-layered cake with a sharp, penetrating and searching mind; a glimpse of the past gives the illusion of closeness. Events that appear close-knit may be separated by months, years and even decades. We are in a house of mirrors experiencing mere glimpses, tangential kisses with fact and fiction.

# CHAPTER 1

We see only tiny slices of things long forgotten and sometimes subconsciously suppressed. These fragments of remembrance are sometimes clear, sometimes kaleidoscopic, sometimes comic, sometimes surreal. However, once the mind is stoked, these events arise like moths in the bright glare of a searchlight; memory is porous, tattered and shrouded in doubt. It is all these things and more.

I am writing mostly to my friends, relations, children, and grandchildren. I am old now, and most of my friends and older relations, with whom I would have loved to share my memories, are dead. Many problems come with ageing, none more problematic than that of memory. I must repeat that this is when we experience confusion, cacophony, and chaos and must deal with shattered memories.

There is also the additional problem of cynicism and sarcasm. When combined, this combination is the brine that pickles the mind. In the distant past it may have been respectable to be cynical and sarcastic without some pejorative connotation being attributed to it; in fact, these were seen as valued tools of a critical and searching mind, commanding the respect of scholars and thinkers. All this changed with the arrival of the social sciences and we no longer pass the 'correctness' test in this new civil society dominated by the keepers of correctness.

In outlining events we all want to be truthful. But truth is merely a perception, sometimes raw and unedited and untrammelled by logic.

I will endeavour to give my childhood stories, sentiments and philosophy but with the caveat that at this stage of my life memories are Time Perforated. Time Punctuated. Time Distorted.

The story begins, permeates and finally ends with the story of my father because in giving a personal account we cannot escape our past. In Australia, we live in a new age where it is fashionable for people to reflect on their convict past; now we all proudly proclaim where we came from.

# CHAPTER 2: COLONIAL RULE IN FIJI

My father was one of the direct descendants of those who lived under the colonial indenture system introduced in the Fiji Islands. The salient features of this system will be the background of the whole story. He was a child of a new post-slavery system, which was different from the classic form of slavery practised in America. The latter system involved the abduction and enslavement of African natives who were called Negros by the Americans. I am talking about the modern form of slavery introduced in many British colonial territories from the mid-nineteenth century.

The story starts in the colony of Fiji with the arrival of a motley collection of peasants from India in 1879. The European contact with Fiji was much earlier than the nineteenth century. We were taught at school that Abel Tasman sailed, and perhaps chartered, parts of the area in 1643, followed by Captain Cook in 1789 and then Captain Bligh, who chartered parts of Fiji. Some historians say that the white settlers first arrived with the idea of doing business sometime in the middle of 1850.

It is recorded that the Americans sent gunboats to Fiji because the Fijians had destroyed some American property in Fiji. This happened several decades after the visit to Japan by Admiral Perry with some 44 battleships, apparently on a courtesy call to open Japan up for trading in coal with the American ships. I mean who could refuse a courtesy call when a visitor arrives with that many battleships? The Fijian Paramount Chief, Seru Epenisa Cakabau, decided to cede the Fiji Islands to England in 1874 and this was due to the American threat. This was a wise decision. I mean there is only so much you can do with armed canoes!

In any event, shortly after the arrival of the white traders and sailors, the Fijian natives began dying like flies. The whites had a monopoly over medicines and modern diseases, and the Fijians could not barter their way out of dying from diseases brought by the white settlers. The spread of malaria, measles, chickenpox and other contagious diseases depleted the native population. The white settlers proved to be contagious in many ways from early times.

## THE INDIAN SLAVES ON THE LITTLE SHIP *LEONIDAS*

In 1879, some five-hundred, half-starved rural peasants in India sought a new future in a distant land, which prophetically was called the Cannibal Islands. There were still cannibals eating each other at this time, and inland in Viti Levu cannibalism was still practised. These miserable souls thus transported knew that—as is written in many accounts and as recited to me by my parents when I was a child—there was little or no prospect of ever seeing their motherland again. They knew that this was a forlorn journey into a form of bondage in perpetuity and that they were being transferred to an alien land far, far away.

These rural toilers had signed an agreement, and so some have argued that it was not slavery because those who put their mark on an agreement (mind you, most could not read or write) were free agents. These agreements were couched in the language used in contract law, which was familiar only to lawyers. The agreement was for a renewable five-year period with the right to return to India after the expiration of the term. So, they had the right to return but lived in such a state of destitution and poverty that they could not pay their passage back home; and this fact was known to the British masters and recruiters. We know how good they were with legal documents.

These are some salient background features in my story, which will be developed later. My father, Brahma Das Lakshman, was born in 1900 in a little village of Walia near Nausori in Fiji. He was born in abject poverty, which was the fate of the enslaved class. But he was very intelligent and hardworking.

As a recently married young man, he went to India to study in 1927, leaving my pregnant mother behind with her parents. He met Mahatma Gandhi and Jawaharlal Nehru and joined the Civil Disobedience Movement, which was Gandhi's quest for freedom. He went on the famous Salt March with them in 1929 and was imprisoned with them. In prison, he was physically tortured and punished, carrying the scars of his whippings till the end of his life. After he was released from prison, the British Government incarcerated him again and attempted to prohibit him from returning to Fiji because he was a revolutionary. His supporters appealed to the British High Court, which ruled that he had a right to return to his land of birth.

He returned in 1933 and went on to be instrumental in transforming Fiji's rigorous labour laws. He was a member of the Fiji Legislative Council on several occasions and even then he continued working as a headmaster. He was one of the founders of the first secondary school for Indian children in 1918 and he taught there as the headmaster for many years. This was the Gurkul School in Saweni, Lautoka. I was born in Saweni.

He also established the first (unauthorised) college for adults, both Indians and Fijians. This was revolutionary because the Indian community had only a restricted right to secondary education in Fiji; few were permitted to have a secondary education. I did not attend any secondary school in Fiji. My father educated his children with these adult students. He was prosecuted by the colonial government for this, but that failed to stop him. He founded the Fiji Industrial Workers Congress and was regarded as a great orator by even his worst political rivals.

He also raised eleven children. I was one of them. He died in Brisbane in 1981. I was with him. He had lived in Fiji all his life and was only in Brisbane for medical treatment. As he lay in the hospital dying, he regretted that he was not able to meet Mrs Indira Gandhi, who was at the time on an official visit to Fiji. Mrs Gandhi was the daughter of Nehru, who my father was in prison with. (In the photo gallery, you can see a photo of my father as a young man with Nehru when he attended a meeting of the Indian National Congress.) Mrs Gandhi presented him with a special award for his contribution to the Indian struggle for independence. This award was granted posthumously.

His struggle was like that of the other indentured labourers who were transported and used by the white settlers. The white races were intended to be the only beneficiaries in the British Empire, which some expected to last a thousand years. I have not read any other story from other parts of the world where a son of the indentured, as a very young man, returned to India during this slavery to struggle and fight for the freedom of Mother India.

When he went to India, my mother, who was expecting their first child, stayed with her parents. He told us that he came from a very poor family and this was the only way he could get higher education. This is a singular story of how people valued higher education. The Indian families were prepared to make great sacrifices to better the lot of the community. My eldest brother, Vidya Sagar, was born in my father's absence and was seven years old when he saw his father for the first time. The rest of us were born after my father's return from India.

I have searched but have not found any other story of a son of an indentured labourer, anywhere in the British colonial territories, who returned to India and marched with Gandhi in the famous Salt March in 1929 or stayed with Gandhi in the struggle for independence. No doubt, countless in India joined the movement, but I am talking about the poor indentured in the colonies.

At one stage, my father lived with Mahatma Gandhi at his Sabarmati Ashram to learn about the Civil Disobedience Movement, and he joined Gandhi's Satyagrah (Truth-force) Movement in 1929. He also joined the revolutionary Indian National Congress. Gandhi wrote to my father on several occasions, but these letters were lost, save for one tattered piece in Mahatma's handwriting. My father kept it as part of his precious memory of his association with him. It was printed in a booklet someone wrote about my father.

Mahatma Gandhi, Jawaharlal Nehru and Vallabhai Patel (known as Sardar Patel) and other Indian leaders were arrested and jailed at Yarwada

Central Goal, and their followers were also arrested. My father, who was then a student at Benares University, was also arrested and jailed in the same prison. He suffered heavily in prison; he was put in solitary confinement and made to make munj ropes. He also broke boulders with a heavy hammer. He had to run a *chukky* (stone mill) for grinding wheat into flour. He resisted some harsh orders and was whipped unmercifully until his back was deeply lacerated and he spat blood.

I have a vivid childhood memory of my father showing his children the deep marks of laceration on his back. I remember that on one of his early visits to Brisbane when he met my wife, Rosemary, and my children, he showed them the lashes on his back, now somewhat faded. Even after all that time, the long streaks were still visible.

The British Government declared his activities dangerous. Mahatma Gandhi and Nehru and other followers were released in 1930 under what was known as the Gandhi–Irwin Pact, but the British Government did not wish to release my father, transferring him from Bombay Province to Benares Central Goal in the United Provinces. He was eventually released in 1933.

## NO RIGHTS UNDER THE INDENTURE SYSTEM

The indenture system in Fiji lasted from 1878 to 1916. This was a time when India was still under the colonial yoke and the Indians in Fiji seemed indifferent to their condition, or just too feeble and helpless to intervene. The sense of being forgotten and abandoned created the most pervading and gloomy atmosphere, and the beauty of the deep blue Pacific did nothing to alleviate or soothe their pain. It was the tyranny of distance, being so far away from home.

Ironically, barely half a century after the abolition of the indenture system, which was about the time I came to study in Australia, most Indians eligible under that system declined to return to India and chose to remain in Fiji. This was now their home, and their future was in Fiji. I was part of this new change. I never longed to visit India, and it was only in 2006 that I went to India to attend the wedding of a granddaughter of a friend from India. The wedding was in Rajasthan.

# CHAPTER 2

When my father was born in the year 1900, it was only twenty years since indentured labourers had begun migrating from India. So, the accounts he gave had the benefit of immediacy, not tarnished by time. There is little doubt that the underprivileged and the dispossessed who entered contracts to be slaves for a period of five years knew that they would never return. I know that some say that they were free to sign the contract or not to sign. This is an argument about 'free will'. It may seem cliched to say it, but it is nonetheless true that the rejected, neglected and dejected throughout history had no free will. They did not have the benefit of philosophical contemplation or the ability to engage in didactics. These illiterate peasants from rural India whispered about the agreement they had signed and complained about British colonial bastardry. The agreement is now called *girmit*. (The word *agreement* sounded like that to the illiterates.) There are now societies and foundations around the world that commemorate and celebrate their triumph over adversity. This too is the reason I write. This is my somewhat belated salute to my ancestors. We, the remaining progenies of these Indian slaves, have come a long way since that little ship *Leonidas* came to Fiji in 1879. The Indian diaspora is now a success story.

The brutal treatment of the indentured labourers, which included women who toiled in the hot tropical sun in Fiji, has received attention worldwide but especially in India. The indentured system was abolished in 1916. However, by this time, some 60,000 men, women and children were already there. My grandfather was one of them.

## MY ILLUSTRIOUS AND LEGENDARY PATERNAL GRANDFATHER

There are few people on planet Earth whose grandparents are not illustrious and legendary in some way. I am determined, in my old age, to tell you about mine. My paternal grandfather's conduct explains why my father was different and destined to fight for the ordinary men struggling for survival in Fiji. He was an official in the British Indian Army and was stationed in Cawnpore. He came from Baraely, a town unknown to me. He was only sixteen years old when he entered the

British Colonial Army. During the Indian Mutiny of 1857, he decided to join the rebels fighting for Indian independence. This is now considered by many to be the first significant struggle for independence in India. It was the first major fight for the freedom of the whole of India.

The rebels were winning when they laid siege to Lakhanau (sometimes spelled Lucknow) where the British were holding out. Their fortune changed when the Punjabi troops joined the British. This led to the defeat of the rebels. There are no traitors greater than those found within one's own community. The freedom fighters retreated but were finally defeated.

My grandfather feared for his life and could never go back to his village or his people because the British were hunting down and executing the freedom fighters. He laboured for many years on a wharf near a beach and finally came to Fiji. My father told us that his dad did not talk much and would sit and stare at the Rewa River for long periods as he smoked his pipe. My paternal grandfather was married when he came with our grandmother. They had eight children and my father was the youngest.

My dad remembered that his father spoke mostly to his mother, who could recite from the Hindu sacred texts, and it was his mother who inspired my dad to work for the poor. My grandmother came as an indentured labourer too and toiled hard on Fijian plantations. She came in 1888 from Chapra a district in Bihar.

When my father left Fiji and boarded *SS Ganges* in 1927, he was dressed in the garb of an indentured labourer. I have a photograph of him boarding with a ticket around his neck, and with a *lota* (a special jug) and a tin *tasla* (see photo gallery). He has his ticket around his neck! I also have an old photo of him bathing in the sacred Ganges River, with a boatload of people behind him.

When I learnt about my grandfather's contribution to the Indian Mutiny of 1857, I realised that the British were cruel. I suppose the British did what the British did well during colonial times. They butchered the rebels in cold blood in the old-fashioned British colonial way. All without any trials. Many innocents were butchered, but the

British had a well-tested British defence: 'They were all killed because we could not tell the difference—they all look alike.'

My maternal grandfather, Gopal Sadhu, was a Holy Man. When there was a strike in 1920, he led a march from Nasinu to Suva. The army fired on the whole crowd of men, women and children, and many died. Their bodies were removed, and many families had no idea what had happened to them. My grandfather rushed to help the injured on a bridge and was shot down. As he fell, he tried to attack the army with his stick! He was very seriously injured but lived to tell what happened.

## THE EARLY REFORMERS, EDUCATORS, GURUS AND SCHOLARS

I am writing this in tribute to some highly educated Indians from India who came to Fiji under conditions I have described, leaving their families behind. Some never went back. I am reminded of this whenever young Australians leave the comfort of their homes and travel to remote parts of the world where they engage in the arduous and thankless task of helping people. Some get killed for their efforts. What is there in our human condition that we produce such amazing people? It is rare to see these Australians recognised or rewarded.

This happened in Fiji when a motley collection of Indians formed a committee to establish Gurkul in Saweni, Lautoka, where I was born. It was one of the first schools set up by the Indian community in Fiji. It is still there, and it was here that my father taught for many years before entering politics. The founding fathers belonged to Arya Samaj. They had vision.

I will speak only about one or two great men of influence who were contributors to the development of Gurkul, our schools in Fiji. I remember one who made a difference to the Lakshman clan. He was Pundit Gopendra Narayan Pathic, a distinguished scholar and one of the main shapers of our educational destiny in Fiji.

I remember him as a child because my father admired him, and we used to go to his home and eat everything they had in the kitchen!

He was truly a very learned man by any definition in modern times. He came from a wealthy family in India, and he was the one who selected groups of students and took them with him back to India for higher education. My father was in one such group.

It is a measure of this great educator and thinker's vision that he saw merit in selecting a young married man, despite many unmarried students thinking they were more deserving. He influenced my father, who shared his vision regarding higher education. In her old age, my mother paid tribute to him in these words:

> ... his sweet and tolerant nature, the way he kept his family like pearls threaded in a necklace ... cleverly showing others the way, truly supporting the powerless; and did many things that still inspire us today.

One of his sons went on to become a judge of the Supreme Court in Fiji. The other one of immense influence in the field of education was Pundit Amichandra Vidyalanker.

## MEETING THE PRINCE OF WALES

In his early years, my father taught at a Marist Brothers school in Suva. It was in this period that he addressed the then Prince of Wales, who was in Fiji with his current mistress. All the salacious details of the Prince's mistress were in the newspapers.

His brief encounter with the Prince was notable. I wondered how many children of labourers in Australia met the Prince of Wales when he visited Australia in 1920. I have an abiding memory of this because when I went to a Garden Party at Buckingham Palace many years later in 1991, I savoured and shared the occasion with one of my younger brothers, who was living in the East End of London. I knew my father would have loved to hear that I was at Buckingham Palace, the hallowed ground that would have been forbidden to the children of the indentured labourers in the past. I knew that in the early period only notable princes and princesses from the colonies would have been invited.

In his early period of teaching in Suva, one pupil was Mutyala Satyanand, who was a good student. Mutyala Satyanand eventually went to New Zealand and graduated in medicine from the University of Otago, where he settled and had a thriving practice. I met him in New Zealand and met his son, who was later appointed Governor-General of New Zealand. We still occasionally have lunches together when he visits us in Brisbane, and we communicate from time to time. I recall on one such occasion taking him to my local pub for lunch and telling some of the waiters that he was a recently retired Governor-General of New Zealand. I do not believe that too many Governors General go out for lunch in a pub. The waiters all surrounded him and wanted to be photographed with him! He is an excellent example of a descendant of the indentured going on to serve with distinction in many countries around the world.

## INDIANS IN POLITICS IN FIJI

I have not followed politics in Fiji since leaving in 1956 and have no intention of entering this minefield. It was said that in Fiji it was never necessary for our colonial masters to divide and rule because the Indian politicians did the work for them. The Europeans never ceased to be amazed at the constant internecine war between the Indian political leaders and parties. Political parties shuffled and changed positions like in a deck of cards. A politician who retired in Sydney said to me recently that Indians were divided and hated each other from the moment they were born! It has never been possible to make an objective judgement on these feuding politicians. However, feuding and division is in the very nature of politics, and one need look no further than the United States under Trump.

I wanted to discuss politics because the subject of Indian politics came up recently. I have already referred to the terrible living conditions of the indentured labourers and their children. After the abolition of the indenture system, there was a flood of migrants, mostly Gujaratis (shopkeepers and traders). The Gujaratis had never shared in the misery of the Girmitias (indentured labourers) and some, not all, made a living out of extorting high interest when the poor and illiterate needed to buy things from their shops. I know because my father used to write letters for these poor people to complain about these unscrupulous traders. He always threatened to expose them. I was told very recently by someone my age living near me that his parents were still paying debts to these kings of usury right up until they died!

The exploitation of these deprived poor people by the depraved Gujarati merchant class took a new turn when they wanted to buy the small holdings of these framers for a pittance and make large profits. These Gujarati shopkeepers did this with the connivance and support of a Gujarati politician known widely as 'A.D.'

Now, I warn you I am about to do something that I do quite a lot in this writing: digress. And I make no apology for dwelling on my own opinions. So, I will share with you my thoughts about AD Patel, a politician described by a local historian Brij V Lal in his book called *A Vision for Change: AD Patel and the Politics of Fiji*. Patel is described as the 'the greatest leader of the Indo-Fijian community in colonial Fiji and, arguably, one of the country's most brilliant public intellectuals'. With no disrespect to the eminent historian, it would be truer to say that Ambalal Dahyabhai Patel—who arrived in Fiji in 1928, some 12 years after the end of the indenture system, and died in 1969, one year before Fiji cast off colonial rule—had little regard for the well-being of the poor. No doubt at the behest of the traders, this man mounted a sustained attack on my father and told everybody that BD Lakshman never went on the Salt March and that he had never met Gandhi or Nehru, despite evidence to the contrary. Yet there is a photograph of Nehru with my father and one of Mrs Indira Gandhi presenting my family with a special award for his contribution to the struggle for freedom in India (see photo gallery). This proves that AD Patel was not a man inclined to let the truth get in the way of his agenda.

Why do I say he had little regard for the poor? Perhaps because I frequently saw Patel driving around in the backseat of a shiny, chauffeur-driven car, always in a fancy suit and chewing betel nuts—an image that seared itself on my young brain. More to the point, he never mixed with the Fijians and never attempted to speak their language, treating them with open contempt. Sir Ratu Mara, a highly respected Fijian leader, thought so little of him that he wanted A.D. deported! Patel called Sir Ratu Mara 'a crow among swans' and said Mara was a swear word in Gujarati. He called the Chinese people 'eaters of cats, rats and bats'. Not a way to win friends among the local communities. One report said that this attitude 'dissipated much of the remaining goodwill that the Fijian and British leaders had towards him'.

There were Indian leaders, including my father, who thought that Patel was a divisive, manipulative and unscrupulous person. His liaison with a divorced Englishwoman (whom he later married) did not endear him to many and was why his parents and clan did not want him back in India. It is with some reluctance that I introduce this sordid detail. It is no crime to fall in love with an Englishwoman, married or not, and our perception of morals has changed. The marriage did not last, and although that too is not necessarily a reflection on him, it did not raise his standing in the eyes of the locals, who referred to him as 'a white sahib'. Some highly educated Indians who held him in open contempt used to call him 'that randy dandy from Nandi' (Nadi).

Far from seeing him as a 'brilliant public intellectual', some of his critics called him 'just another garden variety solicitor and politician', who never appeared in many really contested cases and who spent most of his time manipulating the population. Many regarded him as a man with no vision and as someone who would latch on to any idea floating around when it suited him; for example, one of his ideas was to build a university—well, just about everyone had the idea to build a university on a suitable site. There was nothing original in that idea.

Patel's attitude was important because it was one of the reasons the Fijians did not want the Indians to be in control of their country. Accordingly, they overthrew a legitimately elected government, which caused much suffering to the Indian community. The official story is that the Fijians were tribal and would never have accepted Indian domination, no matter what the Indians did for the welfare of Fijians. At least, that is the view of Brij V Lal in his glowing biography of Patel. I make no complaint about Lal's view, except to say that when I sought to discuss the matter with him, I received no response to my emails.

Lal builds a picture of Patel as a moral equivalent to a saint and as a man 'steeped in the Gandhian tradition of politics at whose dawn he came of age'. Now, I know a lot about Gandhi through my father's stories (as mentioned elsewhere, in 1947 my father opened a college, which I attended, called 'Mahatma Gandhi Memorial College'). I never heard of Gandhi being accused of womanising or driving around in chauffeur-driven cars in dandy clothes or Gandhi castigating his political opponents as consumers of rats, cats and bats, nor did he support corrupt exploiters of the poor. So, what sort of Gandhian tradition of politics was Patel steeped in?

I have read some of the other works by this historian, and there is a consensus that he is a good historian. But his writings on Patel are so myopic that some of the Indians of my generation who have read his book have commented that it sounds like the work of a party hack or party apparatchik or some lickspittle. At the very least, it lacks objectivity and balance.

Lal said in his writings that he first heard of Patel from 'an illiterate but wealthy cane farmer' in 1959 when he, Lal, was attending school. However, in 1959 Patel had already been active in politics for three decades. I wondered which school Lal attended that he had not heard of Patel, the politician. He never met him. I knew about Patel from the early forties.

His description of Patel as 'the greatest leader of the Indo-Fijian community in colonial Fiji' is nonsense. I think that there should be more said about those who fought and struggled for the Indo-Fijians before Patel arrived in his light suit and with his predilection for fancy cars. Some suspected that perhaps the first thing Patel did was to look around for a polished car with a chauffeur! That is the image most early farmers and workers had of him. Lal compares Patel to Sir Ratu Lala Sukuna, a legendary political figure in Fijian politics, and says: '... Sukuna is honoured in public memorials and a national holiday is named after him' and bemoans the fact no such honour is accorded to his hero.

## CHAPTER 2

He found it even worse that, as he put it, Patel's influence had 'receded as a result … of a deliberate policy of manicuring reputations and accentuating things Fijian …' This is a bit rich coming from someone who himself engaged in similar acts of manicuring and preening the image of Patel! Lal rues the fact that Patel is 'now a forgotten figure' and is remembered 'if remembered at all in a few primary … schools that bear his name'. Some people are forgotten because they did little of substance for society. It is a fact that politicians in many countries are indeed forgotten with the passage of time. I think there may be good reasons for Patel to be forgotten much sooner.

My father, one of the founders of the first Indian secondary school (Gurkul School in Saweni Lautoka) and headmaster there for some years, never complained that nothing was named after him. As Patel's work did not involve teaching children, I think he was fortunate to get some schools named after him.

It appeared that the Denning Report on the sugar industry was regarded as a success for the farmers; naturally, all Indian parties represented in the Denning Arbitration in 1969 claimed sole credit for the result. This too is a common experience: success has many fathers, and failure is an orphan!

It appears from a cursory study of the political events that the Alliance Party not only claimed credit but won an election by excoriating the Federation Party and Patel who appeared before the Denning Arbitration. It should be noted that Patel was regarded more as a cunning politician than a forensic specialist lawyer. I do recall that at some stage he mentioned to me that some of the younger lawyers appearing before the Arbitration were very good, but he described Patel's performance as ordinary; that would not surprise many people familiar with lawyers.

This final political success claimed exclusively by the Alliance Party in its campaign during the ensuing elections was due in no small measure to the brilliant performance of a distinguished barrister, Gerard Brennan QC. I had known Brennan QC for decades, and my wife knew his sister—the two had studied together at the University of

Queensland. Both graduated with bachelor degrees in social studies and worked in the same field and were very good friends.

When Brennan QC was appointed to the High Court of Australia, I was appearing before the High Court as counsel for the Crown in an appeal against a conviction for murder. I had the conduct of this lengthy murder trial and had appeared for the Crown before the Court of Criminal Appeal in Queensland, so I was very familiar with the evidence in that case.

I have mentioned that background because of what I am about to relate. Now, in 1990, several decades after the Denning report, Brij V Lal wrote to Lord Denning about Patel and got a response that said Patel was the best lawyer to appear before him during the Arbitration and that he was better than the Chief Justice of the High Court in Australia!

This historian is an extremely good researcher and accurate on detail, so I do not doubt the accuracy of what he says as coming from Lord Denning. I have no idea what the good lord might have said in his dotage! Even this historian said that when he wrote to Lord Denning, he had no idea whether he was dead or alive! I also have no idea why this historian was wanting such an opinion after two decades had passed. I knew he had written Patel's biography and one possible unintended consequence would be a need by some to read this book—good press for the book.

I have no idea what he said in his letter to Lord Denning, but I did wonder, in a light vein, whether he said something like: 'My hero is dead. Please, sir, say something good about him. There are no public memorials in his name.' I have no idea, but I cannot imagine that Lord Denning awoke one morning and, completely unprompted, said something like: 'My God! For two decades I had forgotten to tell the world how brilliant this man Patel was, and I must correct all this now for the benefit of posterity.' The good historian should release his actual letter to Lord Denning so we can read it too. What prompted Lord Denning to respond?

When I read this, I spoke to Mr Brennen QC and related what I had read. He did not seem very interested in the matter, but he did say that he knew Lord Denning well enough to visit him on his trips to London. He met Lord Denning many times and spent some time with him at his home. I wanted to know what Lord Denning had to say about Patel's performance because of what I had read in this historian's account.

I made no notes because friends do not make notes when talking, but he told me that the only occasion was after the conclusion of the Arbitration hearing when it was possible that Lord Denning might have adverted to this subject and Denning might have said that most of the lawyers who appeared before him were competent and good. I mean, can you imagine a judge, after some hearing saying in the presence of all the lawyers: 'By the way, X was the most brilliant counsel to appear before me today'! I had the impression that on the occasions Mr Justice Brennen was staying or visiting Lord Denning at his home, there would have been no discussion about Patel. The historian's account of what happened in 1990, some twenty years later, seems to be the next time this matter was raised.

I cannot imagine (although I do not know) that during their various encounters the Chief Justice of Australia and Lord Denning would have discussed Patel. It would be like saying that the Law Lords in their esoteric discussions on Law would seek the opinions of their cleaners and gardeners! In the big league of eminent judges, lawyers like Patel would be in the category of cleaners and sweepers, the 'garden variety of lawyers', and this would be true about most ordinary lawyers.

When you compare AD Patel, who never got his hands dirty, with the constant struggle by my father, including how he fought for the Indians, then you can see why this Patel did not have a monument erected to him.

## LIFE IN COLONIAL FIJI

The general population mostly looked untidy and dishevelled and wore tattered and ragged clothes. Even those who came from relatively more affluent families rarely wore shoes. My brother and I never wore shoes until we came to Australia. Generally, Indian people wore leather sandals and long garments like those worn by Buddhist monks. The sadhus, clad in dhotis with white chalk-lines on their foreheads, moved exactly like those seen in Indian movies, completely oblivious and immune to fashion changes over several millennia, with their staves and bronze ablution lotta in hand. There were cane knives and spears and walking sticks everywhere, and there were wretched-looking children and flea-ridden dogs and cats everywhere too.

The animals and pets were neglected and generally uncared for. If these creatures could have spoken, they would have tried to migrate or go on boats to Australia where animals and particularly pets are not just looked after but pampered. In Brisbane, Australia, when I go for walks very early in the morning, I see serious-looking men and women in a deep meditative mood taking in the fresh morning air and walking behind their dogs, collecting dog poo in plastic bags. Pets are always keen to please their masters and sometimes they try to please them three or four times in quick succession. I am sure this is all good for their souls. For my part, I try not to look, although there is nothing more nourishing and uplifting for the soul than to see man serving animals. It probably prepares them for the drudgery of the rest of the day when they finally get to work after cleaning up after their dogs.

We do many strange things for the good of our soul. We sometimes are keen to serve nature and animals but have no time for humanity. Pet food and manicuring of animals in America is a billion-dollar industry, but there is never enough money for the starving and dying children in Africa and Asia.

When I was a child, Fiji was a very small British colony in the Southwest Pacific. To give you some geographical background, Fiji consists of a group of islands, an archipelago surrounding the Koro Sea, with a total landmass of about 18,000 square kilometres. It has close to one thousand specks of islands including islets and coral atolls; only 320 of these islands are of any significance. Even on maps, they look like tiny pimples on the torso of our vast Pacific Ocean.

We could never find Fiji on any map available to us. I recall that as a child, with the imminent Japanese invasion, the elders whispered that although the colony had no protection, the safety of the population was assured because they felt that the Japanese could never find these islands.

While the conditions for the Indian community in the early 1900s was utterly miserable, by the thirties they were making some visible advances in education and commerce. People conversed in English and discussed mundane subjects such as food and beverages. I was particularly interested in bacon and eggs, the smell wafting from little Chinese cafeterias. At the time, we Indians did not eat much pork; however, there were no religious restrictions on eating pork. We were told by some that Buddha died after a good meal of pork!

By the late thirties, the air was thick with confidence, which was partly due to the breaking of the shackles of the indenture system, which had been abandoned in 1916 after an extensive and worldwide condemnation of the treatment of Indians in Fiji. And there were also enormous changes in perception among the Indians about their own self-worth and of who they were, and these changes came thick and fast, always reinforced by deep and long-held cultural and religious convictions.

There was a renewed determination to succeed, and this came with the growing realisation that they were, after all, a race of people with a deep and long past, which could not be easily swept away by what the community saw as the savagery of the white colonial culture. There was a distinct new pattern in the general attitude of the people; from the thirties on, for the first time, there were stories of personal successes of traders, workers and teachers.

There were now a very small number of politicians, trade-union leaders, lawyers, doctors, accountants and administrative officers. When I left Fiji in 1956 there were only about ten lawyers. The people were more comfortable with the sudden arrival of articulate and able revolutionary leaders. They were prepared to confront the colonial government and demand changes. Not all Indians read from the same song sheet, but the general chorus was the same: a demand for better conditions for the workers and farmers and some representation in government.

The progress of individual businessmen in the community was discussed and related with obvious satisfaction and there were stories of commercial and business successes by Indians who were competing and succeeding against large European businesses. This was a harbinger of things to come. Like the soothsayers in other times, even the uninformed and uneducated, indentured workers were predicting that the future was going to be good. There was a gradual and detectable tectonic shift in power relations between the rulers and the ruled.

In my family, my father's background as a young revolutionary in Gandhi's civil disobedience movement and his deep engrossment in local politics ensured that we children grew up and heard many inspiring stories about early times. My father was a highly educated man and by any definition an influential social and political community leader in Fiji. I was inspired by him in my later struggle in Australia with the racist official mentality that led to an attempt to deport me, and he inspired me in the tenacious way I conducted criminal trials before numerous juries.

This was the general backdrop in Fiji when, at the age of eight or so, I witnessed the sudden arrival of New Zealand and American Forces. It was the early forties, and the interaction with the Americans especially gave a new boost and impetus to the local population, in business and other ventures.

In the forties, the local town council was near our home and the white town clerk lived a few doors away from us. He was suddenly very busy. It is true that he was mostly plastered and drunk by lunchtime, but that too was part of the civil service culture in colonial times. No one minded or seemed to take exception to it, probably because the community was in no position to mind or take exception to the activities of white colonial civil servants.

Lautoka exploded with activity; the local council began tar-sealing a few miserable pot-riddled streets and a few more lamp posts suddenly appeared in town. These activities went mostly unnoticed by the community; the lamp posts may have pleased a few stray dogs but did not impress the community, which wanted more rights and greater representation in local government. However, the appearance of benign neglect pervading the town was slowly yielding to change with small pokey construction sites springing up in some areas, and modest little houses with tin roofs instead of thatched cottages were springing up in surrounding areas, and there were now more commercial buildings made with concrete blocks. I have a memory of these activities because we children had nothing else to entertain us. We saw that concrete poured and poured; it rained and rained, and the little town mushroomed.

Sometimes, through ignorance or design, the people built first and got the planning and building approvals and paid the bribes later. Occasionally, they followed the more acceptable convention and paid the bribes first and then got their plans approved. The emergence of bribery as a necessary social tool for advancement had a murky past and one could never be sure whether the British introduced this custom to the Indians or vice versa.

I have a vivid recollection of when, at the age of eight or nine, after leaving school permanently, both my younger brother Gautam and I used to help make concrete blocks for building our home in Drasa Avenue in Lautoka. We would get up at six in the morning, take our bundle of roti and curry all wrapped up, and go to the building site to help.

## THE MAHATMA GANDHI MEMORIAL COLLEGE

There was only one government-approved secondary school in our district, and so many children had to leave school after primary education. My brother and I had to leave. It was only the exceptional students or those who could pay very high fees who made it to secondary school. The government prohibited the Indians from opening schools for higher education. So, without a government licence, my father opened a college for uneducated adults, both Indians and Fijians. Appropriately, he named it in memory of his hero Mahatma Gandhi, calling it the Mahatma Gandhi Memorial College. Classes were held during the day and at night. Most adults were in their twenties and thirties.

The government decided to prosecute my father because it had refused permission to Indians to open schools for higher education, but he fought back. That is another story. Some magistrates refused to issue proceedings against him because young Fijians who were unemployed and causing a disturbance were now seen to be attending school. There was a reduction in petty crimes. You can see in the photo gallery a photo of these young-adult Fijians, some of whom went on to become eminent leaders in Fijian society. One became a senator, and another became President of Fiji!

## OUR PRINTING PRESS

After leaving school, we made building blocks and learned some sort of trade. My father also had a printing press and published an Indian newspaper for the farmers and workers. I think he wanted us to work in his printing press as compositors, and we did. In fact, we worked in his printing press after leaving primary school until about the age of nineteen. We were mostly educated at home. My brother and I never attended a proper secondary school and never sat for any formal examinations until we came to Australia in June of 1956. We were not qualified to enter any university.

## BUTTON INDUSTRY IN LAUTOKA

The first industry in Fiji was my father's button industry in Lautoka. We worked in his pearl-shell button factory, but there was not much market for these things. He lost a lot of money.

We had ready access to pearl shells because of my father's frequent trading with Fijians to get the coconut to make copra and sea cucumbers for the Japanese market. This happened immediately after the war. I, with my brother Gautam, worked there making buttons and carving out pendants on machines. He gave work to unemployed Fijians, who were very creative. I have kept some of these creations for sixty years, recently giving a few pendants to our children, grandchildren and great-grandchildren.

## CHAPTER 2

# MY EARLY LIFE IN FIJI: HELL ON EARTH FOR THE ELDERS, PARADISE ON EARTH FOR THE CHILDREN

It is true that the account I give here may also reflect the ageing process. A reflection is a journey through the tunnel of time, sometimes running parallel and sometimes intersecting, squeezed out like toothpaste.

Traversing time to re-visit childhood unclouded by the present is difficult. It is difficult to leap through time without leaping through imagination. Even to those unaware of the meaning of introspection and contemplation, the question always is: how acute is the observer and how genuine and untarnished the recollection? This lack of purpose and will to deal with little flakes of events and doings that seem to count for little—and deciding which flakes should be treated as an important part of life—is a problem. I am dealing with it now as I write. Surely it matters little if the past events in a single life are never recalled and broadcast.

Also, sometimes old age makes for a brazen, boastful and garrulous rendition. The descent into details and particulars in examining a life is a bit like sharing the experience of ablution and personal hygiene for entertainment.

The problem with recollection is real and must be tackled before dealing with childhood matters. Some recoil and find it distasteful to read about those who claim to recollect things whilst still in their mother's womb and then proceed to tell us about the taste of milk and baby food and discuss embryonic intelligence—it is not exciting to delve into the nappy state! There is no need to be so detailed and so nostalgic.

A friend cautioned me that too much detail may put readers off biographical crap forever. Time distortion is even worse. The feigned or real feats and deeds at the age of two or three must tax the imagination of those who care. I have no inclination or taste for that! How early is early childhood? I will start at the age of five or six.

Lautoka was then a small, mosquito-riddled and neglected town on the western side of Viti Levu. I remember spending a lot of time pumping a detergent called 'Shelltox' on food and objects around the house. We knew little about detergents, or perhaps people thought that dying of toxic material was preferable to being part of the food chain for mosquitoes and insects.

The little town was surrounded by farming areas, mostly small sugarcane farms. I grew up there and knew our small town well; no matter what you did, you had to walk in the very hot sun and for miles. Lautoka was virtually on the waterfront. The main feature for us children was the wharf for loading sugar and berthing the occasional steamship that came on lazy early mornings. From home, we could hear when these massive steamers arrived in town, bellowing a long 'mooo' as if the company had stuck a cow in one of the chimneys.

There was the usual sight of passengers disembarking from steamships and approaching the town, and they were greeted with garlands and flower petals. On such occasions, even the sugar-mill complex near the landing area bellowed its horns. The tall chimneys appeared to us to reach a few hundred feet and were seen spewing and belching thick black smoke and looking like giant, freshly lit cigars.

Lautoka was hardly a tourist town; the seashore where visitors were greeted looked drab and bleak. It had mineralised grey-bluish sand, an eyesore made worse by the corroded and wasting metal and tin structures piled on the beach by the mill. The surrounding areas had tin shanties housing people, and there were parts of mill machinery and twisted railway lines around the sprawling mill complex. Some of these structures stuck up like dirty fingers in a rude gesture to the heavens, as if heaven cared.

A cacophony came from mettle on mettle, and the workers seemed to be simply bashing steel for the hell of it. This picture would not be complete without reference to the abandoned vehicles and tyres all dumped on the waterfront, sometimes by the sugar mill and sometimes by the millworkers. There were beer bottles everywhere despite valiant efforts by the council to collect them.

Then there was the presence of occasional drunk sailors and locals leaning on lamp posts. These activities increased when the Americans arrived to save us; unfortunately, there were just not enough lamp posts.

## CHAPTER 2

So many beer bottles and canned food surrounded the Americans that the locals wondered when they would find time to fight a war!

There was no electricity available in most parts, and so we children studied and did our homework in the light cast by hurricane kerosene lamps. Adding to the gloom was the absence of white sandy beaches in town or the immediate vicinity for recreation and swimming. Looking out to sea from the shore, instead of a blue sea, the eyes were greeted by the unattractive muddiness of the sea. We saw this every day from our primary school.

Bakana, a low-lying, nondescript, long and narrow strip of an island, was just across from the school, obstructing a view of the distant open sea or most of it. It rained and rained most of the time. It drizzled or poured on whim. Water everywhere, pouring, seeping or streaking and going into the sea from little creeks and numerous manmade drains. We experienced sullen changes of mood in the rain god, and we saw dark and angry clouds. The sky was the slate on which the gods delivered their messages.

Lautoka town was really meant to be a depot and dumping ground for the Colonial Sugar Refining Company (now better known as CSR), which was a pillaging and plundering Australian enterprise. It dominated everything that happened there. Not noted for contributing to cleaning the town, it was devoid of aesthetic taste in architecture and design.

The main street in town had a railway line with railway trains snaking through the town day and night loaded with sugarcane, spewing smoke and dust from dawn to dusk, and it got worse during harvest time.

When on shore, the tourists from the steamers would be faced by choking soot and dust and by coughing, sneezing children who, despite all this, happily played rain or shine. The tourists surely must have noticed that the place was designed to disappoint: a place dilapidated in shape, form and spirit. Or perhaps not, because they invariably rushed to the line of little shops to bargain for gems, trinkets and shell jewellery.

We children loved and liked our little town. We were born there, and all our friends were there. A place is the people and we had loving and caring people around us. I also remember our dirty, muddy feet because we seldom wore shoes. Children had soggy wet clothes when playing for hours in the rain; slosh and dirt were just part of us, and we were at home with it. There is no point in telling happy piglets that they live in a pigsty; and after all, we now know that life itself emerged from a dirty primordial soup or a cosmic primordial pigsty.

It is universally true that parents with eleven children have more to cope with even in more affluent and sophisticated societies. I must say at this point that I did think of starting the whole book with the words: 'It is a truth universally acknowledged that …', but I knew that some ardent followers of Jane Austen would accuse me of borrowing those immortal words without her consent!

Families with many children had very little in the way of social services; and life was a constant struggle against the poverty, disease and hardship found in most early colonial settlements. Fiji was full of conflicts and contradictions. The popular image of the Fiji Islands as a magical Pacific paradise with dancing palms and lovely sunsets was tarnished with squalor and misery.

The earliest recollection I have is of children peeing and peeping out of the little bedroom windows at dawn and seeing workers and labourers on their way to work; these workers laboured from dawn to dusk with no future before them, save toiling for a pittance surrounded by little children.

To flip Tolstoy's famous opening line from *Anna Karenina* ('All happy families are alike; each unhappy family is unhappy in its own way'), I say that happiness may need an explanation, but misery is universal and needs none. The plight of most Indians in Fiji in those early days was no exception and in many respects was even worse than those of the early settlers in Australia. The Indian people in my parents' time were mostly the children of the dispossessed and geographically displaced, but surprisingly they were relatively intact culturally and religiously.

## FOOD IN FIJI

Our childhood in Fiji at the end of World War II (1945), when I was aged nine, was radically different from the time of the first arrival of the indentured labourers. At the time of my writing, some seventy-five years have passed since the end of the war.

The original indentured suffered from starvation, disease and hunger. They were told that part of the reason for their malnutrition was their failure to adapt to the Fijian diet. Fijian food, such as dalo and taro and other root food, was new to them. For some time, the Indians had no access to Indian food such as lentils to make dhal or to most ingredients to make curries and other items of Indian origin, and this made life more difficult. It took several decades for things to change. (I have some original ideas for authentic Indian curries—see 'Young Bachelors Learn to Cook' in Chapter 4.)

It was the lack of supplies and services in processed food such as flour, sugar, salt and other ingredients (and sometimes even curry powder) that made it hard for the very poor. The means of exchange was money and that troubled them the most. The barter system failed in a society suffering from an increased level of sophistication and greed. It was difficult to offer a few bananas or a handful of vegetables or a spoonful of lentils to get on a bus or buy sugar and salt or modern medicines.

We were mostly unaware of these early conditions. In our recollections, we felt that we grew up during the times that can truly be described as idyllic and magical. We experienced no ravages of war that devastated other parts of the world and no famines like that experienced earlier in Australia during the Great Depression.

But tropical fruits were something else. Fiji had tropical fruits, such as bananas, oranges, mangoes and pineapples, in abundance, and by the time I was a boy, we had a veritable feast of vegetables and lentils of every variety to make dhal, including some varieties unknown to us. How things had changed!

I still love vegetable curry made of dalo leaves. These were consumed and eventually became part of our staple diet. Vegetables grew everywhere and were cheap; the cost determined our taste. A staple diet is whatever nature provides in abundance.

The Fijians enjoyed a rich fare of nuts and tubers, with taro, cassava, tapioca, and breakfast fruit; also, dalo and ubi and you name it. Then there was the food from the sea in abundance; extensive large-scale net-fishing was not practised. And when it came to fish, there was nothing the Indians or the Europeans cooked that tasted like the fish cooked in the traditional Fijian way. Even the poor in Fiji were the least-starved people on earth. In my childhood, the poor luxuriated in the abundance and variety of fruit and vegetables. They had no excuse for not growing some vegetables in their yards. In the sub-tropics, the fecundity of nature knew no bounds, and in the ocean, life gushed with life.

## MEMORIES OF OUR PRIMARY SCHOOL.

St Thomas' Primary School was right on the beach in Lautoka and only several hundred metres away from our home. Each morning, we children had to cross just one street to get to the sprawling school compound, spread over a large area of perhaps three or four acres. I have no idea how large it was, just very large. The foreshore was muddy, and it was not a white sandy beach but covered with blue-black mineral sand. When walking on the sand, there was a sense that the ground below was pulsating with small yellow crabs and other creatures, and the whole place was itching with sand-flies.

Children never swam near the foreshore directly in front of the school because the water looked muddy. Sometimes after school, a whole line of boys stood in front of the beach to have a pee, but this was a disappointing exercise because the sea level never rose no matter how hard they tried. Several kilometres away from the school, there was a typical native settlement or village called Namoli Koro, and sometimes children went there for a swim. It had a nice, clean beach.

My school was run by Catholic nuns, who were mostly Irish, English or Scottish. They were always attired in their full habit and always seen hurrying from school to school between lessons, looking to us like penguins in distress. Their full habits were like that seen in the portraits of Mary McKillop. We had no real idea where these nuns came from, or how long they stayed or where they went when they left our town. We never ever saw them in informal dress and never met them socially.

## CHAPTER 2

In an area just beside and behind the church, there were the boarding quarters where the nuns lived a frugal life. Further down towards the beach was the exclusive school for white children. Some distance away from the entrance to the school compound was the school for the Eurasian children—the white people called them half castes. Just behind that school, close to the beach, was the school for the Indian and a small number of Fijian children.

So, there were three distinct and separate schools, and each had a different name. I now have no memory of what the other schools in the large compound were called. The three separate school buildings were not separated into distinct compounds, but each occupied its own space in the large school precinct. These were co-educational primary schools—girls and boys were not separated.

The sprawling complex was thus notionally segregated, although that term was never used. The children from the mixed races played with the Indian and Fijian children, but the European children did not mix or play with the other children in the school. By the time I came to Brisbane in 1956, I had never met or talked to a European boy or girl of my age save on rare occasions. I never had Europeans of my age as friends. We never mixed. Perhaps when they were older, they returned to Australia or New Zealand to attend boarding schools.

Christian missionary organisations, both Catholic and Methodist, provided education to children of all races and religions, and the Catholic schools were full of fee-paying Indian children. St Thomas' Primary School was run by a Mother Superior and the nuns were called sisters. Sister Jerome was the Mother Superior during my time at St Thomas'. We said the Hail Mary three times a day and did Bible studies.

At the front entrance of the school compound, there was a lovely church. On some evenings, it would be all aglow in candlelight for the evening service. We children would peer inside the church to watch the religious rituals and proceedings. When we were tired of that, we would leave early and go to a nearby cricket pitch that was brightly lit by the moon and stars. We would mostly run about in the field, which looked as if was lit with massive lights, the starlight was so bright. Then some adult in a house would call to us to 'pull up stumps' and we would be sent to bed.

On some evenings, the Magellanic Clouds pressed so low on the whole township that they seemed in touching distance, and the sky was brightly lit with starlight. This was a magical experience for the children. Just visualize. We seemed to play in cosmic dust until late into the evening. Our feet were visible from a distance, and our spindly legs made us look like we were floating on matchstick stilts. These tiny figures appeared to be thin shapes gliding on sidereal dust, like some lesser celestial beings. The biblical stories the nuns told us about angels with wings worked their magic in such surroundings. It was easy to believe that there were real angels in the sky as taught during catechism and Bible lessons. However, there were no angels among the children.

Education was neither free nor compulsory, and most Indians living in grinding poverty did not have the luxury of education. Life in grinding poverty was necessarily bound in shallows. The hackers of wood and drawers of water do not need and are generally not further burdened with education. In the thirties and early forties, compared with Indians, there were only a handful of native Fijians who went to school.

We children had nothing to do. Left to our own devices for entertainment, we mostly watched and emulated adults. I will give an account of what happened on countless occasions, and this story does come within the category of stories that could start with an opening like: 'It was a dark and stormy winter's night …'.

The elders, after a very hard day's work, huddled together in the evenings with one hurricane lamp hanging on a branch of a tree, some dressed in *dhotis* (loincloths) and a wide array of *pugrees* (turbans) in striking rich colours and of varying lengths and sizes, and some in trousers that looked no different from pyjamas. There were no electric lights in homes, and there were only a handful of streetlights in the whole of our little town. The evenings hummed with moths, insects, and mosquitoes which seemed to latch on to our faces. Mosquitoes mostly fancied children's earlobes, and that hurt a lot. All engaged in deep, animated discussions, mostly about politics and the evils of the British

# CHAPTER 2

Raj. We used to sit and listen because the speaking parts were strictly reserved for the elders. Rights for animals and children, in that order, were still decades away.

In eerie quietness and oppressive summer heat, misery descended like a thick cloud on whole communities living in unhygienic shanty towns; they lived in sheds and in the leaking corrugated humpies that were all around us. We could identify them from the flickering lights of the kerosene lamps. These are some of the memories veiled in the mists of time. These are the common memories of Indians plaintively looking to a brighter, better distant future.

We were often told as children that sweat and toil would lead to a bright future. Living in dilapidated conditions, we were told to work hard and study. Every child in the towns and villages was going to be a doctor, an engineer or a lawyer. We knew that this must be true because the elders said so; no child was going to work cutting cane or slaving for a pittance on the farms once they grew up. As I write, I can say that their prophecy did come true for many of these children.

In our spare time, my brother and I plotted the destruction of all colonial empires. We had no idea what these empires were, but we were taught by my father to hate all empires. It fitted in so well because children sometimes love hating things that they do not understand.

Gautam and I developed a taste for hating and decided to hate our father's empire too because he made us work, and sometimes we summoned enough courage to refuse to work for him and this lasted until we were hungry again. We found that sometimes we could do without food for as long as four hours, but that was the limit! We were told often that in India, Gandhi fasted for weeks and months. We had no stomach or intention to fast for that long for any cause, noble or not.

The men all engaged in deep animated discussions, mostly about politics and the evils of the British Raj. Kava was drunk at any time of day or night, and children at dusk and before bedtime would sit and listen to the elders just to avoid being put to bed. As children from the age of six to ten, we jockeyed for position, trying to get as close as possible to the turbans of those who smoked or chewed tobacco because some of the elders kept tobacco and sticks of matches in their turbans, and we just loved the aroma of tobacco.

Politics was of no interest to us but the cursing and cussing and choice obscenities that were learnt by children at the feet of the elders were later to prove valuable to me in my profession as a criminal lawyer. Such language is used frequently by criminals and faithfully recorded by police in most confessional material. The only handicap at these gatherings was that the speaking parts were strictly reserved to the elders.

Some of the elders kept their tobacco and sticks of matches in their turbans and as well as loving the aroma of tobacco we envied these elders who chewed betel nuts and could spit like some primordial monster a good distance of several feet in a straight line. For the children, this was more impressive than anything Americans could do with their much-vaunted cooing or yodelling. Australian cockroach and toad racing were not introduced in Fiji. Children were bored and would have liked something new and exciting borrowed from Australian culture.

As said earlier, the general population mostly looked dishevelled and wore tattered and ragged clothes. The whole place was littered with knives, garden forks and spears as if the giants we read about in Gulliver's Travels had just left after their hearty breakfast without doing the washing up!

Indian children were never taught anything in schools about the richness and vastness of our Indian culture and traditions. These schools were mostly operated and run by various Christian missionary organisations; there were hardly any true Indian schools in the early days. We were taught mostly about Western culture and traditions. However, in most homes, children were taught about Indian culture and traditions by our elders in the community and these included those who were illiterate but knew a great deal about the oral traditions.

By the time I was about fifteen, and mostly because my father had numerous history textbooks in his home-built library, I knew something about the other ancient civilizations, like the Sumerians, Assyrians and Egyptians, and much later about the Greek and Roman civilizations. I was struck by how these had vanished whilst the Indian civilization remained glued together by its culture and tradition and had survived some five millennia up to the present time.

The elders made sure that we knew and could recite verses from the Vedic tradition and the Upanishads. It was the easy familiarity with such teachings that gave solace to the displaced Indians. Gandhi had shown that it was easy to crush Indian bones but not the Indian soul or their will to fight and survive. This was the mindset of the indentured workers and their descendants. My father was a very important example of this Indian mindset.

## EARLY IMAGE OF FIJIAN VILLAGE LIFE

The Fijian people loved singing and dancing and being happy. In my town, we had Namoli Koro, a local classical Fijian village. It was right on the beach and, unlike the condition of the town, was clean and tidy. We knew the local Tauki or local village leader. Every morning he would speak through a loudspeaker asking the Fijian villagers to perform their communal duties, such as planting crops for the whole village and doing the lawns and doing their share of minding children when the womenfolk went out to fish and dig out shells for food. The whole community shared the work. Tauki Ni Koro's name was Amena. He loved my father because he helped him with money. Amena sometimes carried one of us on his shoulders when giving directions to the villagers. This koro (village) was close to the township.

Most Fijians were now Christians, and there was a church on the way to this koro. Early on Sunday mornings, we could hear them singing Christian hymns. The eerie quietness of our Sunday mornings was broken by a deep primordial sound booming and vibrating, rising and falling and seemingly shaking the ground. This was their version of 'a rumble in the jungle'! Those familiar with the beautiful singing voices of the Fijians would know that this is true even today.

## OUR ISLAND IN THE SUN

The real attraction for tourists and the locals lay in the pristine beauty of a string of outlying islands that could be reached from our locality. Our little township was blessed and bejewelled with tiny islands surrounded by coral reefs. These semi-circle islets looked from the air like a necklace with an opening at one end that allowed boats and canoes to reach the beaches on these mostly uninhabited tiny islands. Some were luxuriant, lavished with swaying palms and rich green vegetation. It was exactly as described in romantic fiction based on imaginary tropical islands.

The jewel in the crown was the tiny group known to us as the Yasawa, Malolo and Vomo islands. At one stage, we stayed at Vomo Island for several months. We stayed on Waya Island too. These were a part of a sprinkling of pristine islands. There were atolls and islets, all accoutred and attired in coconut palms and paw-paws as a small subtropical paradise should be. These islands remained painted and etched in our collective memory long after we left them. I have a vision of paradise virtually untainted by the passage of time and modernity.

There was no electricity in most houses, only kerosene lamps and candles; and in some villages and homes, the lights went out when the sun went down. The youth in Lautoka today would have no idea what it was like to live on these islands in an era not fuelled by electricity and untarnished by the current epidemic of information technology.

It was a time when there were very few opportunities for instant gratification of the senses, now found in computer games and other escapist pursuits so readily available on television. It is trite but true to say that every generation runs the gauntlet of an aging population that rues the passing of some real or perceived age and who rue that such good times will never return. We rue these things oblivious to the fact that each new generation discovers something new and better and does not mind the passing of the previous age. Such critical reflections come naturally to the ageing population in every generation without exception. I am now part of this last phase.

The environment and living conditions shape our destiny, and beauty is noticed mostly by those who are at least free in mind and have the time to stand and stare. The early indentured souls transported to Fiji were not known for extolling the virtues of living in this distant land. As a child, I spent a lot of time with the older people and seldom heard the old men in the district telling us about their fishing expeditions or the beautiful island life. Their life was bound in toil and misery, and there was harshness written on their old leathery and tired faces.

They spoke mostly about their work and the harsh living conditions and their poor health. The children of the indentured, such as my father, did not talk much about the beauty of the land either but were more relaxed than their parents. In fact, they were beginning to like their new land. The experience of the indentured was like the experience of isolated communities in other parts of the globe. They, too, describe their struggle with meagre resources and possessions and speak of their sense of denial, neglect and betrayal.

These old people, both men and women, repeated the stories of their sufferings over and over—that they were the sons and daughters of the indentured slaves abandoned in some alien land, far from their motherland, with no rescue or redemption in sight. Even settlers who came a bit later and not under the indenture system did not expect the terrible conditions that greeted them.

In comparison, Australia and New Zealand were seen as privileged and coddled societies, partly because the horrendous experiences of the early settlers and convicts in these lands were not widely known in Fiji. In relative terms, they seemed coddled and protected.

The Indians were landless and struggling for recognition and acceptance. They had no meaningful rights such as genuine and true representation in the running of the country or even in local government. Gautam and I, and many others like us, were fortunate because the children in my time were mostly coddled and protected by our parents. I was born in a period of hope and new beginnings, and the community was now alive with commercial activities. The siege mentality prevailing at the beginning of the twentieth century was now slowly yielding to new hope for the future.

Gradually, people spoke less and less of their past and more and more about how smart the children were in their activities, including schoolwork; and for the children, life was not all doom and gloom. We grew up with the usual mischief and disobedience required of children the world over. I can only remember all the good parts. We were generally happy living on a tiny smudge in the vast ocean and mostly oblivious to the true impact of the Great Depression of the early thirties and with no premonition of the pending disaster of the coming war.

## THE WAR IN THE PACIFIC

We were young and barely conscious of the death and destruction being wrought in the ocean during World War II. We lived unaware that some parts of the world were about to be ground and rendered by death and destruction.

The first indication of an impending war came with whispered talk by the elders and parents. We heard them saying late at night that we were right in the middle of a raging war in the Pacific and that the Japanese were expected to land on our shores. We knew something bad was happening but did not understand what the fuss was about. I was only five or six. The villagers, farmers and mill workers could not understand what could possibly attract the Japanese to our shores. The indentured especially could not understand what might attract the Japanese to the hellhole that they were experiencing.

The conditions in Fiji may not have been that bad, but the disenchantment was very real. Perception does matter. The people were cynical about many things and expressed it in cynical ways. Cynicism is really a valuable tool designed for the protection of the oppressed and a balm to the suffering soul. As such, it should not be treated with contempt. It is a protective sheath for the vulnerable in society.

It has been said that if God exists, he must be cynical. Creation is most likely a product of such a god. How else can one explain why the reputation of religious institutions is more important than the rape and sodomy of children. Or why it is more important to sell arms to feuding tribes than provide food to starving children. Or why tens of billions of dollars are spent on feeding and preening pets when millions of children are starving or are blind. The explanation may be that animals are pets, and children are pests; there are times when frustrated parents would agree with that sentiment. Our parents did!

# CHAPTER 2

It must be said that during the time of the Japanese attacks in the Pacific, the Indians preferred the British to the Japanese. All they wanted was a true partnership and a stake in the bounties of the British Empire. Indian anglophiles like Gandhi and Nehru, after securing independence for India, still could not let go of Mother England's petticoat. They wanted to continue the association in some shape or form; they supported the creation of a 'Commonwealth of Nations'. This was the prevailing sentiment in Fiji too.

The pervading climate in which we grew up was full of contradictions, and this was probably true for most colonial Indians. It is somewhat strange to me now that the global killing spree during the war was depicted as a battle between good and evil for the betterment of the generations to come. We were told that this was a critical war for the survival of liberty and equality for all.

Ironically, some nations were fighting for the perpetuation of the various colonial empires, which were only for the benefit of the white part of humanity. The result turned out to be a classic case of the ill wind of war doing so much good for the oppressed peoples.

The yellow, brown and black races were not aware that they were going to be the unwitting beneficiaries of a cataclysmic struggle in which the fascists were seeking to dismantle existing empires to create and carve their own. I think history will eventually record that there were no great moral issues at stake as far as the oppressed were concerned. The struggle was about sharing the booty of the planet, not about universal freedom and justice. The dismantling of the colonial empires and the emancipation of the downtrodden and the subjugated were not on the agenda.

Here's another irony: the vanquished won in the end. The ink on the surrender terms had hardly dried when Germany and Japan began to rise and flex their economic muscle. There was no such luck for the colonial empires. They collapsed absolutely. The French fought in Indo China to no avail. India was free. China asserted itself and today is flexing its muscles. The Germans and the Japanese went on to shape the economic history of our planet.

Churchill lived to witness the liquidation of the British Empire. He did not personally preside over the liquidation or discuss it further with the naked fakir (Ghandi, whom he never liked, and my father adored), but his immediate successor Attlee did. My father was the President of the Trade Union Congress when Lord and Lady Attlee visited Fiji just after the war. Lord Attlee was regarded as a hero in Fiji and elsewhere, just as Churchill was perhaps regarded as a hero in Australia. My father was so effusive, elated and even overwhelmed when he met Lord Attlee. I have a photo of my father with Lord and Lady Atlee (see photo gallery).

The other true winners were the Americans, who had no stomach for colonial empires but were busy creating a structure for their own Thousand Years of American Domination. An empire by some other name. So, in one sense, we as children were about to be the main beneficiaries of a new world order in which the official racial policies of Australia and South Africa could not survive. However, not all Indians in Fiji knew or understood the significance of all this immediately and generally struggled on as if nothing much had changed.

The American Empire is collapsing, as I write. Like Humpty Dumpty, the Great Empire has had a great fall. After Trump, the Deluge! So, I lived during the time when we were about to be the beneficiaries of a new world order in which the official racial policies of Australia and South Africa were doomed to fail. I made my little contribution when I was a student in Australia and was threatened many times with deportation back to Fiji.

## HINDU SWASTIKA IN FIJI

When the Americans came to Fiji, they were shocked to see swastikas everywhere—the sign of the enemy! Many did not realise at first that the swastika long predated Adolf Hitler. They seemed to be looking for Nazis under the bed (a precursor of Commies under the bed).

The word *swastika* is Sanskrit in origin and means 'conducive to well-being'. When we were little, many Hindu homes in Fiji were decorated with murals and paintings of the swastika, and Indian weddings had swastikas made of bright red or dark pink rose petals or with layered rich-orange marigold. Marigold is regarded as a sacred flower by the Hindus. These floral swastikas were lovingly prepared with rose petals or marigold and laid richly and thickly in the required pattern. They were created to give the impression that the swastika was embossed.

The swastika lies deep in the heart of Hinduism and is a symbol of such antiquity that even Hindus make no serious attempt to give a definitive view of its origin or attempt to trace the course of its migration into the Hindu religious consciousness. It is thought to arise from Sumerian times and is shared with several other cultures and traditions.

Like the wheel, its origin is claimed but not clearly traced to any one culture, save that it was deeply ingrained in the Hindu culture and tradition. The swastika was linked to Creation and, like Creation, required no further proof or justification for its existence. In Hindu consciousness, the swastika is in a sense a symbol of some eternal truth and second only to the other great Hindu symbol: 'OM'. Even in parts of the West, the swastika was well regarded as a symbol of good luck—until Hitler appropriated it and promulgated it for his racist agenda. Its beauty in the West is forever damaged, but in the East, it remains untainted.

I have mentioned how deeply the emblem of the swastika was ingrained in Indian consciousness and how these swastikas were lovingly created with petals of roses and marigold to cover some sacred area where the wedding ceremonies were conducted. I went to several weddings that were interrupted by the arrival of American jeeps with military police who trampled the swastikas with their boots and dragged away the uncomprehending village elders at the wedding for questioning. They wanted to know how the Nazi symbols had arrived in the Pacific before their landing. The villagers were grilled and released; the arrival of Nazi influence in Fiji confounded the Americans. They were searching for radios and other devices with which Hitler had penetrated the islands in the Pacific Ocean. The caustic comments by the elders at that time were unprintable!

# INDIAN WOMEN IN FIJI AND RELIGION

The cultural and social background of the observer is relevant because culture and tradition determine personal perspective and attitudes. This is really the story of my perspective, determined by my culture and background during World War II, which was the most important immediate driver of the change. These rapid changes included the collapse of colonial empires, and our perceptions and attitudes changed over time.

The inconvenient and unpalatable truth was that the real untouchables were the neglected women and children of the world. It was ironic that the West always lectured, preached and hectored the East on liberty, fraternity and equality when it had such an abysmal and sorry record on the rights of women and children. Churchill, the great champion of democracy, does not spring to mind when speaking about women's rights. Gandhi does. Most women's liberation models at the core are Gandhian. It is well known that Gandhi was greatly influenced in his thinking by Englishwomen, including Annie Besant and the suffragettes in England fighting for the franchise.

The other important factor in shaping the perceptions of men on the subject of women and their real status is to be found in some of the religions in India and particularly in the matrix and the architecture of Hinduism itself. There is a deep feminine aspect to the divine, which informed the Indian mind and influenced and dictated how men saw women. There is an array of gods and goddesses with immense powers. There are female goddesses such as Durga, Lakshmi, Kali and Saraswati to name just a few. These goddesses exerted their divine dominance over both men and women.

We all grew up with this constantly recurring feminine divine undercurrent in our consciousness. This was true from time immemorial. The Indian women always knew that there was gender equity, at least in the divine world if not on Earth. The male gods did not have a free hand in the cosmic universe, and the earthly women were never backwards in throwing a whole host of goddesses in the face of the males. Indian men would vouch for that: I was there and grew up with this.

## CHAPTER 2

In contrast, Europe seemed to stray from very similar ancient beginnings as those in India regarding feminine divinity. Europe then got God (we were told to spell the name of this divinity with a capital G) from the Middle East. The West gradually cast out the ancient goddesses and offered no equivalent substitutes for female divinity. So, they had no idea what to do with Mary, who was the Mother of the Son of God. The only goddesses we hear about now in the West are found in the film and fashion industry.

This is not a discussion about theology but an expression of my personal bias towards the Hindu religion. The Bible is chiselled on stone; nothing can be changed. The Hindu religious scriptures happen to be a sort of tabula rasa in that they can be written over, and what is erased and written over is still there to be seen and gleaned. Nothing is completely erased from our collective consciousness, assuming there is such a beast. The problem with reflecting on the religious past is that it does not make for good reading or sound reasoning.

We grew up in a remote colony in the British Empire, with perhaps a mangled, mingled, distorted and tortured view of our place in the world. We were taught that only the weak-minded would seek logic and science in religion. The atheists were tagged as religious and dismissed as 'children of God' too, like the rest of us. The atheists were treated as religious because they, too, had a deep belief based on nothing more than a deep conviction that there was no proof of the existence of God. It was their zeal and fervour, their deep conviction that made them religious. In Hinduism, you are judged by your actions, and good actions make you religious; an untold number of atheists come in that class of men of good action.

My mother was surrounded by goddesses in the sacred area where she prayed, but the Christian divine world was all about God the Father. In the Catholic school that we attended in Lautoka, there was no mention of where Mary sat on Judgement Day. Certainly not on the Left or Right Hand of God the Father. Not even behind God. My mother was shocked when, as schoolchildren, we told her that Mary, the Mother of God, was not a goddess herself.

The actual status of women in India was in many respects worse than in the West, but there were no mainstream Hindu religious texts relegating women to a subordinate role. Rather, as I mentioned, the Hindu teaching and mythology is full of goddesses. If the goddesses are anything like women on Earth, then I can imagine them pushing and shoving to get the upper hand to get into bed with some god and then fight over some divine real estate, exactly as they do on Earth. I imagine that the gods in the Hindu mythology had their hands full living in fear of property settlements in the divine world; it was some version of 'in heaven as it is on earth' when it came to divine property settlements.

The women in the West were seen as relatively more emancipated and had voting rights, but for some inexplicable reason, it was the less liberated world of the East that produced in our time the first elected female prime minister (Sirimavo Bandaranaike in Sri Lanka). A little later, one of the most powerful elected female prime ministers was Indira Gandhi in India.

It is easy to dismiss this as the result of a token concession on the part of men in the East, but it reflected a deeper reality. It is true that political power is only one form of power. In our home, we knew that women did not wield political power, but we were obliged to follow their rules at home. To my brother and me, it meant that we had no lunch unless we completed what our mother told us to do early in the morning!

It is difficult to understand why women were slower to get elected to the top positions of president or prime minister in the democratic countries of Europe. Why was the East setting the example? There may be other explanations, but the main reason is to be found in the denial of the existence of divine gender equality in Christianity. Women are still fighting to be accepted as priests, ministers and parsons. I cannot imagine a female pope (popess?).

Martin Luther King Jr and his followers, who were Christians, eventually followed Gandhi's method of civil disobedience before they got any action; he and his followers even wore Gandhi caps in their quest for civil rights.

## CHAPTER 2

I have not mentioned that in Australia the real shock came with various women's liberation movements, which produced new destructive goddesses; Kali clones like Germane Greer and many others out-thought and out-cussed men. Some men were unaccustomed to women bringing grace and charm to foul obscenities; men felt that foul language was strictly in their domain and found obscenity-laden female intellectuals very difficult to handle.

I remember Germane Greer's book *The Female Eunuch* was a shock to many, and some could not bear to see the emasculated figure of that female eunuch on the cover of the book. This was a period when the world was still some time away from the spitting, swearing, kicking females in schools that we see on the internet now. Men had rarely seen nicely dressed women falling in the gutter in front of hotels, but the best was yet to come. In earlier times, men would have paid to watch such a sight. The most shocking development was the female demand to invade and desecrate the exclusive male sanctuaries of men's clubs; and even worse, to raid the public bars and get drunk and lie in the gutter. But the writing was on the wall.

It must be said that the experience of Indians in Fiji was in stark contrast to the fate of some other native races transported from the African continent or other areas to the Americas. For those people, their spirit was broken, and they found solace in alcohol. Transportation destroyed their cultural and traditional patterns for survival as a community.

In contrast, the Indians in Fiji and other colonies carried with them a deep sense of being, a deep sense of who they were. They carried with them all their traditional values, and the most powerful were their religious beliefs as found in the Indian tradition, which did not acknowledge a hierarchical structure. To the Hindus, their body was their temple and events happened within the individual; they carried and orally conveyed, in perpetuity, these religious traditions and culture to their descendants.

The Hindus have massive oral traditions, and gurus and sages are sometimes just optional extras to our religion. Many of them are seeking their own spiritual salvation. The impact of sages, sadhus and saints is deep but also incidental. They grease the collective holy machine but do not create anything completely new. They mostly buttress and nurture the living soul.

The survival of the Hindu religion and traditions is seen as a collective responsibility. No one has an exclusive claim to the driver's seat in this religion; perhaps there is no driver's seat on planet Earth. There is no hierarchy, no driver and no driver's seat. Even the most illiterate indentured labourers knew and practised their religion and *dharma* (righteous way of life), and the discipline of mind and body was encouraged in every family.

Fracturing and dispersing the Indians to the various colonies did not destroy their inner being. Just as scattering rice seed in remote parts of the planet produced only rice, so Hindus produced Hindus and required no missionaries to show them the way. Regeneration came from a small group within each village community.

I must mention that one of the most amazing thinkers on the power of myth was Joseph Campbell. I read the transcripts of his 1988 conversations with Bill Moyers in an American television documentary called *Joseph Campbell and the Power of Myth*. In it he gives his global vision of the power of myth, a vision that has captured the imagination of the generations who have followed him. The Hindu and Buddhist visions on the practice and the power of myth permeate the whole structure of his thinking. Perhaps that is why I read it many times!

## INFLUENCE OF GANDHI ON CHILDREN

The admiration for Gandhi played no insignificant part as he was a dominant influence. We, as children, were spoon-fed Gandhian philosophy at every turn. This was when Winston Churchill was receiving bad press in the Indian community because Churchill had berated Gandhi, incensing the Indian community. It seemed that Churchill's main fault was that he vehemently opposed the very idea of an independent India and spent his spare time dreaming about a thousand-year British Raj or Reich and denigrating Gandhi.

## CHAPTER 2

Ironically, in several millennia Churchill may be a mere footnote to the writings on Gandhi because on that time scale the details fade and even vanish. Children never thought of Gandhi as a sage or the like. Gautam got into trouble when our mother told him to get dressed and he retorted with: 'How come Gandhi can walk around in his baby nappy and no one says anything?' Mum was furious and sent him to our Pitaji (father) for further education and indoctrination.

The importance of Gandhi to the oppressed Indians in the various colonies was that he both generated and unleashed a new and powerful source of energy, which typically the Indians regarded as a form of cosmic energy. We Indians are big on cosmic energy and super-consciousness! The civil disobedience movement not only fuelled and empowered the disenfranchised and the powerless but led to Indian independence.

Just as throwing Gandhi out of a railway carriage reserved for whites in Africa did not affect how Gandhi saw himself, so too the Indians in Fiji, no matter how miserable their life and how terrible the treatment and living conditions, never forgot or lost their pride in their culture and traditions and were proud of their origins now lost in the mist of antiquity. They knew that their religion and traditions had been there continuously since perhaps the Sumerian times.

In this long process, it was the oral tradition that lay deep in the heart of the collective consciousness of the Hindus. For the common man it was the oral tradition that accounted for the continuous, unbroken and almost seamless transition through some five or more millennia. Written material is only parchment-deep and a latecomer in the field of transferring information. To the common man, the oral tradition was etched and carved in their consciousness and very being. This was the traditional method of information gathering and sharing.

Thus, this rich religious and cultural tradition coursed through the veins of the mostly illiterate indentured workers in the field. However, the illiterates did not travel alone because in their wake came groups of cultured literate and learned Indian men, who, for various reasons, like in the case of other religious minorities, had opted to come to Fiji of their own volition.

These indentured received more moral and spiritual support with the arrival of men from India who were educated and could read and write and understood what was happening to the community.

## INFINITY AND RAMANUJAN

Let me digress to tell you something about Infinity. Infinity is at the heart of everything Indian. It is in our painting, in our religion, in our mathematics and in our philosophy. It is central to everything Indians do. In mathematics, the concept of zero, used in the way it is used, is all very Indian. I have always understood that when you count and march forward towards infinity, you are using Indian mathematics. Think of adding up to a million in Roman numerals.

Ramanujan is a prime example of the divine concept of mathematics, and Brahmagupta and others gave the numerals used in modern mathematics. The numerals are the alphabet used in the language for dialogue in mathematics. Many great mathematicians think that it is India that has produced the best mathematics in the last 2000 years.

## EUROPEAN CONTACTS

Indian children did have contact with the older European men and women through commerce and many worked in Morris Hedstrom or Burns Philips, which were large general-purpose stores owned by Australians. We spoke to them when shopping.

I must stress that the colonial government did not have an overt racial policy, but there was blatant discrimination against the Indians in employment and education. This was never seen as an official policy of segregation or a planned attempt to keep each community separate because each community seemed to function in harmony with the others.

The social, cultural and traditional practices were different, and that contributed to this sense of separateness. There was no sense of racial tension in the community, just an awareness that the communities belonged to different racial groups with different social and cultural habits. Ironically, the Indians wanted to be separate but equal. They shared very little in religion, culture and tradition with the Fijians and the white settlers.

I remember that the hotels in Lautoka had a separate section for the Europeans. The sign only said 'private members', but it was understood that it was a section reserved for the white races. The Europeans respected the Indian culture and tradition, and the relations were cordial and civil. It may sound strange, but the Indians preferred the arrangement too. The Europeans seldom, if ever, shouted at us in racial language. In fact, they were nice to us as children.

The manager of the Northern Hotels in Lautoka in the late forties was Sam Hollander, who came from Christchurch, New Zealand. He became the Mayor of Lautoka. I understood that he was a well-known chess player in Christchurch or Wellington. He taught me how to play chess and, after several years, gave me nice chessmen, which came to Brisbane with me and have remained in my possession for some sixty years. He sometimes borrowed books from my eldest brother, and we often discussed politics. Most Indians had good friends from England or other British colonies, and the tensions were not racially biased.

## INDIAN WEDDINGS IN FIJI

This is a description of Indian weddings in the early forties. There have been immense changes in the organisational and catering departments since. Thank God.

When we were little, the local Indian weddings were large affairs. Apart from the formally invited guests, the custom was to 'invite everybody' and so Indian weddings were expensive communal gatherings. The invitations were specific and general so that if a relative was invited he could come, sometimes announced but mostly unannounced, with all his relatives, and his relatives could come with some of theirs.

The rule of thumb was that if a hundred guests were officially invited, then the wedding reception required preparation of food and beverages for five hundred guests. Often, that was a conservative estimate. No one ever looked at guest lists to check who had been officially invited. It was quite common to go to an Indian wedding in Fiji in the forties and find in the middle of the festivities that the food for the guests was running out. Then, out of the blue, a dozen or two of the family members of the bride or groom, and sometimes even unfortunate guests, mostly women in all their finery, were commandeered to report for duty to prepare more food because an additional hundred or so guests were suddenly expected to participate in the wedding processions and festivities.

Sometimes when the bride or groom lived in another district, hired buses took the wedding guests to the reception. Again, matters were mostly determined by a rule of thumb. For example, if fifty guests had indicated that they required transport, three buses were necessary for transport. However, the host was required as a matter of custom to have another three buses for those who might suddenly decide it was a lovely day for a wedding and that they would attend after all. This was a general picture of an organised wedding. I am reminded of what a great American diplomat told Kennedy on his return to America—that India was the only functioning anarchy in the world. I suppose that is just another way of saying that India is a real democracy.

Children who attended these weddings hated being caught and directed to help, mostly by carting buckets of cordial drinks for the thirsty guests. The elders never looked fazed or worried about little hitches like these. These were Indian weddings, after all, and these developments were expected. That was the picture of organised weddings. Some weddings were not organised with that precision, including those in which the guests had forgotten the day of the wedding or turned up in the wrong district or sometimes at the wrong wedding.

Most Indian marriages were arranged marriages in which the parents chose the bride and groom, and the prospective brides and grooms were often barely acquainted before the wedding. With so much confusion, the children giggled at the possibility of the bride and groom waking the next morning and shrieking at finding they had married the wrong person.

There was even more teetering and giggling at the prospect that since the bride and groom would not have known each other, they would not have noticed the difference anyway. Indian brides in Fiji never wore veils but the traditional Indian saris were decorated and perforated on the wedding day with gold jewellery: endless bangles and finely filigreed earrings and nose rings. Their hands were henna-painted, and their body roiled in perfume. The Europeans in Fiji were not versed in Indian customs and traditions and so probably would have attempted to see these in terms of their own customs and jewellery, not that we had any idea what they thought. The Indian women, seeped in their culture and customs, would not have minded what others thought. The petite, adorned brides were like Christmas trees.

## THE INDO-FIJIANS

Those who grew up under the indenture system found that reflection on the past was not much of a problem. The oppressed and the downtrodden seldom had the time to stand and stare, and the poor and needy had no time to delve into the past. The luxury of reflection and reverie was thwarted or denied or simply relegated further down the list of priorities in the life of the common multitude in our society. The common multitude is the abode of the forces of fecundity and creation in nature.

When we were young, our lives were transformed with miracle cures. Antibiotics had arrived. Many children had died of tetanus and various other infections. Now we had more drugs, sedatives and injections.

The poor are often 'afflicted' with large families and encumbered with 'extended families', which really means that there were coteries of hangers-on called relatives, a class that was undefined. In Fiji, as in other colonies, there were no social services or good medical facilities.

There were very few schools, and education was neither free nor compulsory. Life for the indentured was misery writ large. It was said that sex was perhaps the only luxury there was for the indentured, enslaved classes. Once married, sex was for free. This may have accounted for the large families in those times. It never ceased to amaze that men who never seemed to amass large fortunes and who mostly lived in poverty, and in the fear of sin, had large families, for which they endlessly praised or blamed God. Very few thought that sex had anything to do with it. It seemed that women related to the idea of immaculate conception. There is religious support for that proposition.

The affluent in any society have an entirely different life experience and have better access to social and medical services; they have homes and secure retirements and the luxury of introspection, contemplation and reflection. Meanderings in the past belong to the class or caste who have the time to stand and stare. Thus, they are more likely to hanker for the past and the time for reflection. It is with such caveats and qualifications that I approach and revisit my childhood and my past.

# CHAPTER 3: THE LIFE AND TIMES OF AN INDIAN TOM SAWYER AND HUCKLEBERRY FINN

Our childhood was idyllic. We played the role of one-eyed pirates on some days; on others, we played the Pacific Island version of Tom Sawyer and Huckleberry Finn. There were no televisions, and the radios were battery operated and full of news and static.

We children were oblivious to the prevailing harsh conditions under which our parents toiled, blissfully unaware that the same fate awaited us down the track. We were busy being happy and playing games and just sitting and watching little things around us.

These stories recount some of the adventures I had with my childhood companion, Gautam, in our island paradise, with no mind to the oppression of the descendants of the indentured, who lived with no hope of a better future. They lived, languished and perished in an alien land—but to us, it was home.

## THE ARRIVAL OF THE AMERICANS IN OUR PARADISE

### *Ring the bells! Ring the bells! The Marines are coming!*

The Americans arrived in Fiji in 1942, just before the Battle of the Coral Sea or soon after. The purpose of their arrival was lost on us as children, and even the adults had no real idea even years later why the Americans came to Fiji. It so happened that the Americans were now engaged in serious military action in the Pacific.

Thus, came the projection of American power and culture in the Pacific. Power and culture were synonymous and interchangeable commodities because power was an essential part of American culture. The Marines always travelled with bazookas and tanks and left devastation in their wake, and that was the image and the impression created in the minds of most people in Fiji.

The United States provided a protective shield for the islands in the Pacific. But just like Goliath in the biblical tradition, America was not regarded as a repository of high culture. The thinking people had no high expectations of the Americans. However, the children did because the Americans came with Wrigley chewing gum and bottled soft drinks, which, in the eyes of the children, was high culture in any language. The adults who had seen the good movies with cowboys and Indians quickly concluded that the Americans had no respect for culture. This was the prevailing muddled thinking in a very muddled world.

The truth was that after the war, in a relative sense, the Americans were more sensitive to Japanese culture and more humane than the French and the British had been to a defeated Germany after World War 1. Ten years after World War II (by the time Gautam and I arrived in Australia in 1956), most shared the view that but for the presence and extension of American power in Europe, Britain and France would have made the Germans sign the Treaty of Versailles Mark II, laying the foundation for World War III.

Without the presence of the United States, Churchill, De Gaulle and Stalin would not have oozed with the milk of human kindness as far as Germany was concerned. There would have been no European equivalent to the Marshall Plan, even if Europe had the wherewithal. Festering hatred dies hard. The world owes gratitude to America for this foresight. Roosevelt, Truman and Marshall were giants compared with the pygmies in current American politics. In the time of Roosevelt, the current crop of politicians would have been hard-pressed to get a decent job.

The people in Fiji were preoccupied with the little problem of survival, and the general population was not very educated in the forties. They shared a distorted sense of history. And because the British and Americans were close allies, they saw the presence of the United States as a projection of British power in the Pacific and not the other way around. There was a seething undercurrent in Indian thinking because the struggle for Indian independence and Gandhi's dominance may have blinkered their perception of the world, particularly about the British.

Hindu mythology is full of demons and gods, and sometimes our goliaths and demons do good things—so the Hindus have nothing against them per se. America was our goliath, and people loved and appreciated the American presence in Fiji. Even the negative Indian sentiments towards the United States were confined to the perception that somehow the Americans were committed to maintaining the British Raj in India. But this did not blind them to the dire necessity of the American Alliance thwarting the designs of the Japanese in the Pacific.

That was the way most thought. They lived in a small, cocooned region of the Pacific, and there is a big difference between the perceptions of those who write or purport to write history and those who live it. This was the perception of those who were living history and not writing it. We in Fiji saw the American Alliance as an alliance of convenience based on necessity. Some Indians adapted and used the language attributed to Americans when dealing with foreign powers, declaring: 'These Americans may be bastards, but they are our bastards!' Some sections of the Indian community saw the Americans as the tool of the British Empire and continued to see Britain as the dominant power in the Pacific after World War II, despite evidence to the contrary.

The shared view by most sections of the informed community in Fiji, both white and black, was that British traditions and culture and British democratic institutions were superior to any professed by the Americans. They thought that the Americans were insensitive and had little or no understanding of the local native customs. All this without any reflection on the work of Margaret Mead!

The Indians did not expect the Americans to understand or care about the plight of the Indians who came under the indenture system or the oppressive conditions under which the Indian farmers worked and lived in the sugarcane industry under the dominance of the CSR

Company. It was well known that the Americans did not have much of a track record with the native American Indians. It is just that the Americans did not loom large in Indian consciousness.

The historical significance of the battles fought and won in the Pacific during World War II proved to be enormous for the people of the nations that lapped the shores of the vast Pacific Ocean, and even in the Indian Ocean, but this is a passing reference to the little people in Fiji. The decisive defeat of Imperial Japan and the frustration of Japan's ambitions to control and shape the destiny of the Pacific also shaped and determined our destiny in Fiji.

It meant that I did not have to go to Tokyo to seek further education. The victory of Imperial Japan would have sealed the fate of China, and that would have been only a beginning. The fate of India would have been uncertain with the rise of Japan. Given a choice of dealing with an obstinate and uncompromising Churchill on the one hand and Imperial Japan on the other, even those dedicated to the task of dismantling the British Empire preferred to deal with an obstinate Churchill and not Japan. Gandhi never thought of Japan as an ally, and Gandhi was the role model for Indians in Fiji.

There was no need for a leap of imagination to know that the British might beat you with lathis, but the Japanese had the habit of summarily executing opponents. The choice was easy. The more educated Indian politicians of all political persuasions in Fiji understood the significance of the contest, and there never was any support in Fiji for Japanese expansion in the Pacific. True, most of the population was oblivious to the long-term global issues.

I was only five years old when Pearl Harbour lit up the horizon in the Pacific in December of 1941, which was also the year the first Americans arrived in Brisbane. I was only six during the Battle of the Coral Sea (May 1942) and the Battle of Midway (June 1942). The Americans arrived in our little paradise in the Pacific at the start of the period of bloodletting on some tiny atolls in Guadalcanal (from June 1942 to February 1943). So, most of the stories dealing with the Americans happened by the time I was ten or eleven.

# CHAPTER 3

It was sometime in August of 1942 that the Americans landed in their traditional way with tanks, guns, bazookas, spirits, wine and beer cans. In another context, some little Corsican who became master of Europe said something about the army marching on its belly. The world could have scarce imagined that, hardly a hundred years later, the basic food rations for Marines during the war would be so lavish. It is now part of folklore. It was these basic food rations issued to the Marines—and not American foreign policy—that was most appealing. It was the American food rations that, according to the locals, later became the guiding concept of the great Marshall Plan; they were soothing and attractive to the pulverized cities in devastated Europe, including a defeated Germany.

We learnt quickly that the Marines could not move without chewing Wrigley's gum for traction and eating ice cream for motion. We had traces of chewing gum on our bare feet most of the time during the war. The children were at first very frightened of the Americans, but after several months they were elated by the discovery that the Americans never travelled without ice cream, lollies and chewing gum. Our attitude changed and we leaned towards the democratic forces when the rumour spread among the children keeping a close watch at the Lautoka Warf that spirits, wine and beer cans, followed by ice cream, chewing gum, biscuits and lollies were being unloaded long before the unloading of the guns and tanks.

We never paused to question the source of such rich intelligence reports but always accepted them as true. Sometimes the reports came from the labourers working on the wharf. The children thought that the Marines were sensible and had their priorities right! It seemed that throughout their relatively short history on the world stage, the Marines always had the same motto: 'NO ICE CREAM, NO WAR'. It was rumoured in those days that in every land battle where the Marines fought, the first things unloaded were the ice-cream canteens followed by tanks and guns. With priorities like that, the Americans were winning the hearts and souls of the future dole bludgers and baby boomers. The thoughtful, serious little children appreciated their logistic priorities.

The American presence in Fiji requires some explanation before dealing with the more serious matters that exercised the imagination of the children. Historians have dealt with the various naval engagements that eventually led to the collapse of the initial naval superiority of Japan and have described the intense combat in Guadalcanal, which destroyed Japan's image of invincibility. As the battles ebbed and flowed, the prominent features were the American retreat from the Philippines and the collapse of the British outposts in parts of Asia, including Singapore and Hong Kong. Guadalcanal was a defining moment and a turning point. But the Japanese losses were not so apparent in 1942, and Australia was expecting a full-scale invasion. Japan appeared unstoppable.

In 1942 the United States had already embarked on an ambitious plan to use the vast Australian continent and the deeply committed Australian population to stop any further Japanese incursions. The threat was real because, though badly mauled, the Japanese Army was still a formidable fighting machine that was sweeping aside colonial forces like flies. It was now that Japan was perceived as an imminent threat to Fiji too. In 1942, the Japanese were poised to take possession of key island territories, and their landings in the Solomon Islands and other colonial territories were deemed a signal of things to come.

The people in Fiji thought that the invasion was imminent, and this was seen by many people as a very real threat. The landing of some 30,000 American troops was mostly in the Nadi area at Lomolomo, a town next to Lautoka. The remains of the observation posts, with large, corroded guns pointing to the sea over Nadi, are still there. Nadi Airport was built by the Americans during the war. Strangely, considering the impact the Americans had on the people of Fiji, very little is said by the Americans about Fiji when dealing with the war in the Pacific.

Air-raid shelters were hurriedly built in Lautoka, and crude trenches dug. Whenever the siren went, we all rushed to and dived into these trenches, sometimes in drenching rain. The drill was that after about half an hour the siren would scream again, and we would all come out of the trenches. We were told to follow all instructions, and some labourers were charged for walking about after the siren went.

# CHAPTER 3

I remember one Saturday morning at about 11 am the siren went, and we followed the drill. The children dived into the trenches and waited for the bombing to start. Nothing happened. I really mean that nothing happened. We waited and waited for three or four hours. The stupid postmaster who was supposed to sound the siren to end the drill had gone up to the pub and got drunk and then gone home. The drunk was roused from his drunken stupor and brought back to sound the siren again so we could come out of the crude trenches.

When the war commenced, there was little protection or defence of any kind until the arrival of the American Marines and the troops from New Zealand. The wise elders, instead of being hostile to that idiot in charge of the siren, praised him and thought that in the event of a Japanese landing on our beaches, the whole population should follow his example.

It was feared that in the absence of American intervention, Japan would take Samoa, New Hebrides and Fiji as Japanese forward bases for launching attacks on Australia and New Zealand. New Zealand forces were already in Fiji, and this was followed by the deployment of American Marines. It was estimated that some 30,000 to 40,000 Americans descended on sleepy Fiji. Pacific Islanders loved tourists, but not like this.

New airfields and other military facilities were either planned or built. Fiji was to be a major supply depot, a forward base and a training ground for American forces, a vital transit point for allied troops rushing to other theatres of war in the Pacific. This then is the potted historical background to the children's adventures with the Americans in Fiji.

The early memory of childhood events, as already suggested, is a hazardous backward glance—a journey back in time in which memories come hurtling towards you like boulders in a heap of confusion. It is a journey through many tunnels, some running parallel, others intersecting. Some recollections must be dragged by the scruff of the neck and teased out of the tube of Time much like toothpaste, thus yielding a result that is convoluted, constricted, distorted, and tortured.

I must remind you again that recollection is a contrived and artificial exercise because of the intrusion of the present on the past. The present always infuses and informs the past. An unadulterated and pristine recollection of the past is fiction. Good thing too. Who would ever want to go back to a clear recollection of bedwetting, smelly napkins, and globs of congealed porridge dribbling down the neck and throat? Thank God memory edits the smell of the goo and poo and the toothache too.

Recollections without the benefit of diaries and records are often stultified and fail to capture nuances and feelings. I might remind readers that it is like being in a house of mirrors with mere glimpses, tangential kisses, tiny slices of things long forgotten and sometimes subconsciously suppressed appearing in flashes. However, once stoked, some events arise like moths in a bright flare or searchlight on some dark deserted night, darting in and out.

## OUR ADVENTURES WITH THE AMERICANS

We children found new opportunities when the Americans arrived sometime in early August of 1942. There was nothing much for us to do apart from the weekly cinema and sweeping out the house and yards and certainly nothing by way of plays, circuses or entertainment. The radios were battered, battery-operated gadgets that crackled and hissed all the time, and there were no radio programmes for children, certainly not for Indian and Fijian children. All we could do was watch and listen to what went on around us. Indeed, we were told to learn from those around us. We did.

I have said that the arrival of the American soldiers in Lautoka was something new with immense possibilities for children. We were now ready for action. Within several months of their arrival, we were in business. The first venture was a miserable failure, and no one claimed credit for the idea.

### Raid on American supply dump: foreign aid for poor starving children

At the time of the Americans arriving, the Lautoka wharf was being used exclusively by CSR for exporting bulk sugar to Australia, and this now became a hive of activity for the Americans. The ocean in front of our little township was cluttered with American warships, numerous landing barges and amazingly fast and very large speedboats with outboard motors. Seaplanes landed in the ocean from time to time. It was such an exciting experience for the children, who always gravitated to the wharf that was only a few kilometres from the centre of the township.

Sometimes we left home early in the morning before school, which started at 9 am. As the wharf was only a few kilometres away from our home, all we had to do to get there was to keep walking past the school. Some children went straight to the wharf and only went to school if they were caught and brought back, and sometimes children went to the wharf after school and stayed there till dusk. It was a case of total surveillance and absorption of details for further adventures.

In this episode, I have a clear memory of what the Marines looked like and how they dressed. I can visualise the large, grey-green army trucks and the seaplanes, and guns and bazookas and even the army boots and helmets too. But I lack the skill to describe shapes and sizes and colours of objects and creatures in detail.

It was the presence of the Americans that gave rise to our little adventures. There were almost as many troops from New Zealand, but they looked and dressed like the British and did not interact much with Indian children.

## *I brought dishonour to my family*

I was no slouch in planning new ventures. But in this episode, I brought dishonour and disgrace to the family. The community called my father 'Pundit' because they respected him as an able and learned man in the district. So, when I brought disgrace to the family, I lost all confidence in myself because dishonour to an Indian family is worse than death. I hated talking about the subject for years, and even now, decades later when writing I still have some hesitation in mentioning it. Surely, my children and grandchildren will understand. I wanted to forget about the whole thing just as much as Gautam liked to remind me of it, even years later.

When the Americans arrived, they came with a massive supply of jeeps and army trucks and weapons and ammunition. They had tractors and heavy machinery of every kind. They had a massive army dump, which was surrounded by a barbed-wire fence, and there was an armed patrol around it. Some labourers from the local village were paraded in court and sent to jail for stealing army equipment. Sometimes we heard rifle shots late at night and our mother, who pretended that she had reliable intelligence reports, never stopped telling us that the Americans would shoot us. Now, that is not a fanciful idea when one thinks about Vietnam and Afghanistan.

I was curious to see this well-guarded place and, after some surveillance, found that the barbed-wire fence was close at one point to very thick bushes, and there was a ditch or stormwater drain close to the fence. Heavy rain had scooped out the soil just under the barbed-wire fence, but you could see this only when you stood in the drain. In this way, I got into the compound where there was an eerie silence.

A heavy tarpaulin covered everything with green-grey netting. As luck would have it, I got under the heap closest to the drain near our shanty home. The tents had boxes and boxes of tins, which were round and coloured dark blue with writing on them that I could not read. The tins could be opened very much how we open corned-beef tins today, except these were round. I opened some and found meat, but as I was about to leave in disgust, I opened another one and struck gold. On the bottom was a layer of sweet biscuits, and on the top were lollies wrapped in silver paper. The meat tins were heavier. By rattling the tins, I could tell the light ones because they made a slight rustling noise. I quickly took three or four tins and all the open meat tins for Teeka, our dog.

Gautam was very impressed and accompanied me in a series of sorties foraging for food and sustenance as Roman armies did, and we shared our plundering with a motley army of children. I mean motley because we only had five or six children in this group. Mere numbers mean nothing. Remember the defenders in the Battle of Thermopylae? That too consisted of a small number of soldiers. I do not want my readers to treat my group with contempt and derision.

# CHAPTER 3

We were very careful to keep our trips secret and ate the evidence in the library, which was a free-standing building some distance away from the residence. My mother noticed some changes in our behaviour but had no idea what was happening. She noticed that instead of fighting over food at lunchtime we were generous with our shares and wanted the others to have some of ours. The truth was that we were chock-a-block with biscuits and lollies. We carried out three foraging missions, each time with our mother's warnings about what the Americans might do to us ringing in our ears. Eventually, it became too dangerous, at least in our minds.

There was no merit in dying, even on a full stomach. The next time we ran out of supplies, I simply refused to go, and Gautam threatened to go on his own. I threatened to report him and send him to jail. There was a stalemate. Gautam then came up with a brilliant idea. We called three of the toughest kids on the block to a special meeting under the tank and laid out some of the sweets and goodies for good effect, exactly like the Americans do today during G-7 meetings. Gautam laid out his plan.

We were going to franchise our criminal activity. For three or four shillings, each of the franchisees could go through our property to gain access to the supplies where they would take what they could carry. We would show them how to get in through the barbed-wire fence. They were to take all the risk and supply the village children and charge for it. There was much haggling, but we refused to give them any rights in perpetuity for a paltry three or four shillings and told them that they would have to pay something more, but we had no idea how much.

It is only the purists in morals and ethics who will quibble with this arrangement. This is exactly how international trade is conducted with no one knowing what they own or who they are selling to. American foreign aid is delivered with cuts for the warlords and the middlemen and the contractors, as in Afghanistan. I think we were ahead of our time when it came to price-fixing. So, as it turned out, we were probably doing the right thing. Except it took me some six decades to find moral justification for all this. I went through so much anguish and guilt for nothing.

The first sign of danger came when we ran out of our meagre supplies of biscuits and pleaded with these new merciless partners for some 'freebies' from the supplies they were taking, and they refused unless we paid like the rest of the children. The very cheek of these greedy monsters trying to extract money from the founders of the thriving industry! We refused. I would get the supplies myself, I thought. I asked Gautam to come with me, but he said no—not on any sound principle but because I had turned him down the last time.

I went on my own, and Teeka followed me. He had done this on three or four previous occasions. Teeka liked the army rations too, and he also got his cut. Teeka was an intelligent dog, and there was a chance that, unless his interests were looked after, he would squeal on us. Well, Teeka did squeal on me for no reason at all. When I got under the barbed wire and opened a tin and was enjoying the fruit of my labour, Teeka started barking.

Our dog may have heard something and was perhaps issuing a warning, but at the time, I thought he simply betrayed me for the hell of it. I had never thought that dogs were man's best friend. There were so many dogs in our town that, when little, I had been bitten twice. That is another thing worth recalling because it was shortly after I was bitten that I completely stopped kicking dogs when I walked past them. Kicking a dog, I must add, was not an act of cruelty. Sometimes dogs went to sleep on tracks and would get run over by cars or army trucks if not given a swift kick, and sometimes they just sat on footpaths asking to be kicked. Well, we used to nudge them out of the way rather than kick them. It is possible that dogs are stupid and can't see the distinction. Dogs have no horse sense.

The next thing that happened was that the whole compound was swarming with the Military Police, and I was caught. I had no idea where they came from. They had guns, and I screamed and burst into tears and screamed some more. It is difficult to frighten soldiers by screaming because they scream back. No one came to my aid. I was marched to army headquarters, which was about a kilometre outside the compound, wailing and hopping all the way, and no one came to my rescue.

# CHAPTER 3

There were men chopping trees on the roadside on our way to the American 'concentration camp', and I appealed to them, yelling to the kind people to tell my parents that I was being taken away to be shot. But they just grinned. The fact that on some days Gautam and I, with our mates, used to give a rude version of a Churchill salute to the cane cutters and poke faces at them while they were working in the hot sun, and then outrun those men when they attempted to catch us, may not have helped. Little children are not good in public relations in these circumstances.

This tough-looking American officer with some ribbons on his shoulder came out with a glass of whiskey in his hand, and my captors saluted him. He looked red-faced and bored. He gave orders to put me in a sort of solitary confinement, and I was left there for a very long time, some three hours. Then another, sharper, much more focused officer turned up with a mean, lean look, exactly the type seen in comic books in which gangsters belt innocent people.

He had with him an Indian interpreter, an Indian quisling as it turned out, trying to please his American masters. He was no bloody help to me. Just for openers, as if I had not suffered enough, he said in Hindi that if I did not answer all the questions, I would be kept there forever. If that was not cruel enough, he added that he knew my father well and no matter what happened he was going to tell him too. The unkindest cut of all!

I had been ready to confess all along, and if there had been any way I could have changed places with Teeka I would have done so. I loved Teeka, but what has love got to do with anything when your life is at stake? I answered all the questions, and the grim-faced officer remained grim-faced for most of the time until I told him how we had franchised the whole project to our friends and how our friends were trying to make us pay and how I thought that that was unfair. I also gave the details of how I got entry to the dump and how I got caught.

He seemed to grin a bit at this stage, although you can never tell what torturers are grinning about. I was slowly getting reconciled to being shot, but the threat by the quisling to tell my father was still worrying me. Half an hour later, I was released and told never to go near that compound again—as if I would ever want to.

A reception committee was waiting for me at home and Gautam was going to give the King's evidence. His theme was that this was all my idea, and he had nothing to do with it. So, I lost confidence in myself, and Gautam became the chief planner and architect for future operations, which explains why he oversaw the bicycle enterprise described below.

## Bicycles for hire for drunken soldiers

Our family's printing press for printing newspaper for famers was housed in a tall building made of corrugated iron with no insulation at all. It was a bit like mechanics garages in country towns in Queensland. Gautam and I would sit in front of the printing press and watch the American soldiers, some of whom were armed with rifles and automatic weapons. There were also American Military Police with red armbands emblazoned with 'MP' in large letters. During the day, we could see all the comings and goings from where we sat outside our printing-press building.

The Military Police went around in jeeps with pistols in holsters picking up drunken American soldiers. Sometimes they were lying in ditches, and sometimes we heard sharp echoes of rifle fire. We thought that probably it was the only way to wake up the drunk soldiers. I mean we were told many times that the Americans were very innovative. At first, we were terrified of the Americans, possibly because, to keep the children home and properly disciplined, parents would tell their children that if the Americans caught them, they would shoot them. This was untrue, but misinformation and propaganda were used not only by the nasty Nazis and nasty Japanese but by parents against their own dear little law-abiding and obedient children.

The children's rights movement was yet to come, and the right to abuse one's parents and to swear at them and punch them and report them to the police and to run away from home and become decent street kids, like we now have in affluent societies, was still decades away. But only

## CHAPTER 3

a few weeks after some Wrigley's chewing gum and lollies and biscuits were thrown at us from army jeeps and transport trucks trundling along, we began to love all Americans, and we began to follow them, though always from a safe distance.

It is interesting that as children we never saw the Americans giving silk stockings and perfume to women in Fiji. We thought they must have run out of silk stockings after spending time in Australia. The children would have known if the Americans were handing out silk stockings and perfume simply because they keenly watched everybody. Most of the children that I knew would have made very good spies during the war. We watched and watched. Watching was our entertainment and pastime.

Lautoka was a tiny township, which meant that most of the activities happened within a radius of ten kilometres. There were only a few tar-sealed roads. The rest were dirt roads pockmarked with holes filled with dirty water and suitably adorned with cow dung, dog poo and other rubbish. The little town was riddled with tracks made by foot traffic and bicycles, and these tracks crisscrossed sugar farms and other properties. So, the American soldiers were showing a mild interest in hiring bicycles to look at places not accessible in army jeeps and large army trucks.

There are many similarities between adults and little children when it comes to business enterprises under the capitalist system. We as children certainly did not have offices and board rooms, but some of the captains of industry amongst the children aged between six and twelve used to meet under a large water tank on our property, and we decided to go into the bicycle-hiring business. My father thought it was an excellent idea but would not let us have total control or all the profits from the business. He was, however, prepared to let us run this business and bought eight or ten clapped-out, second-hand bicycles to get us started. Gautam and I became experts in repairing bicycles and tyre tubes.

We parked the bicycles on a rack outside the huge printing-press building, and on a large blackboard, we erected the sign 'BIKES FOR

HIRE'. We used to write on slates with chalk when we were at primary school and had a lot of practice with blackboards and thick chalk. Once the business was in operation, we would sit there from morning to dusk waiting for American soldiers to hire our bicycles, but business was very slow. Then we noticed that one member of our group, Shiu Lal, who had only two bicycles, seemed to be doing better. One day Shiu Lal turned up with a wad of American dollars. We had never seen so much money before. Shiu had something like ten or twenty dollars in his pocket. He was spending his money and boasting about his business success but would not tell us how he got it. It is very typical of those with ill-gotten gains to boast and spend more than others. The only one I could think of in later years as matching Shiu was Christopher Skase in Australia.

Gautam, who was younger than me, was the resident self-appointed planner and thinker for new ventures at this time. I had been replaced because of the earlier failed venture mentioned above, and little brother Gautam muscled in as the chief planner and organiser. Gautam decided to spy on Shiu, a common business practice even here in Australia. When he got nowhere with that, Gautam did the next best thing and decided to blackmail Shiu. This too is a common practice in business the world over. He threatened to tell Shiu's father, who was a police officer. Now, there was nothing immoral or unethical in this because spying and blackmailing are common commercial practices everywhere.

However, Gautam came back after threatening blackmail and mayhem and told me an amazing story that I at first refused to believe. So, we summoned this enterprising little bastard to a boardroom meeting under the water tank so that he could be bullied under more rigorous conditions. This method is very similar to the police practice when a suspect refuses to confess on the spot. The police would politely ask the suspect to accompany them to the police station, and the suspect would obligingly follow them back to the police station where no other members of the public were present. The water tank was on our property, and this gave us more power.

I hated the very idea that someone like Shiu could cheat an innocent customer and compound it by not sharing the loot with us. There never was a sharp distinction in the capitalist system between profit and profiteering. We had seen Robin Hood in many movies and comics, and he always shared with the poor. What made it even worse in this case was that Shiu had kept the know-how as a trade secret unto himself. We all know from the scandalous price-fixing cases in recent years that failure to share evenly can lead to bad blood, claims and counterclaims, and public exposure. Much later in life, I learnt that the High Court of Australia, consisting of illustrious judges, had approved the bottom-of-the-harbour tax avoidance scheme, thereby giving moral justification for some of our actions as children.

What Gautam had found out was true. This conniving, sneaky little entrepreneur told us that one day a very drunk American soldier had turned up wanting to hire a bicycle and he had refused because his parents disapproved of drunks. There was some argument because the very drunk soldier insisted on his democratic right to hire a bicycle, and it was well known the world over that a drunk American insisting on his democratic rights is more forceful than a sober one. The boy's father told him to give the soldier the bike.

Lautoka is very flat in the centre of town, and Shiu sat there fuming at the way his father had sided with the drunken soldier as he watched the soldier pedalling away into the distant horizon. He then noticed that both the soldier and the bike had vanished out of sight. The soldier and the bike appeared to disappear into the ground. Shiu rushed over and found that the soldier had fallen in a trench or water drain. There were water drains everywhere in Lautoka because in the rainy season with storms and cyclones, most of the low-lying places flooded quickly. The soldier was lying in the trench in the blazing midday sun, turning into a beetroot. He was snoring with one leg wrapped around the bike. The boy was furious and pulled the bike away. After farewelling the Marine with a 'fuck off' and a 'you drunken bastard', he took the bike home and forgot about the incident.

Some days later, the American Marine, now sober, appeared at Shiu's home and apologised profusely for not returning the bike. He told Shiu that when he came around, the bike had vanished; it had been stolen from him. He gave a speechless Shiu a wad of American dollars to buy a new bicycle. Shiu Lal was shocked but took the money. Now, pilfering and stealing was so common in Lautoka at that time that if people left knives and plates in the yard or clothes on the line at night, these items would have vanished by the next morning; even plastic toys and plastic plates were not safe.

People were used to petty thefts, and the idea that someone would refund someone for stolen goods was unheard of. Shiu, now an astute tycoon, with eventually a total of thirty-odd dollars in his pocket through this enterprise over a period, saw the possibilities of a niche market and was going to specialise and deal only with drunks. He decided to cater to this new niche market. He would hire out the bikes only to soldiers who looked very drunk.

The problem was that, to children, there was no foolproof way of telling who was drunk. Shiu used the smell technique known to all children on the planet and that was the only technique known. He then followed the soldiers for long distances for many days, but not one fell off his bike, and business slowed down again.

To make up for the failure to tell us what had happened, Shiu said that he had no objection to our following drunk soldiers who hired bikes from him to see if we had any luck. Gautam rejected this outright. He liked the basic idea of a niche market for drunks but hated any suggestion of physical exertion in the hot sun. He was a thinker, not a worker. Gautam and I had always avoided hard physical work and were not going to be taken for a ride, even on a bicycle. We just went home.

Gautam spent the next few days in a sullen broody mood, and I could tell because he had the habit of copying our father, who used to sit sometimes with his hand under his chin. Gautam had a very chubby face, so when he sat like that, you could see a very slight drooping of his cheeks on both sides. He thought that he had a brilliant solution, so the next morning, on the large blackboard with the sign 'BIKES FOR HIRE', he added three more words so that now the sign read: BIKES FOR HIRE TO DRUNKS ONLY

The first sign that something was happening came when a couple of American army jeeps with the Military Police in them stopped to stare, and then they threw back their heads and laughed. This was not a laughing matter for us, and we could see nothing funny in it. This was followed a day or so later with groups of Americans standing around the sign, all laughing. We had never seen so many laughing drunks in our lives.

For whatever reason, the business boomed, and the Americans loved dealing with Gautam. Some of them, when hiring bicycles, actually said: 'Got any bikes for drunks today?' or 'Hi! Your drunk is here again'. Sitting on a little stool with a large drooping towelling hat on his head, Gautam would look up into the blazing sun and, squinting, nod politely and seriously before putting out his plump, sweaty little hand to collect the daily takings. Business boomed.

During business hours sitting in the blazing sun waiting for the American soldiers, we always wore towelling hats that drooped over our faces. I still tend to wear a drooping towelling hat when I go for a walk in the local district, even though our children, when little, used to refuse to walk with me unless I took off 'that silly thing'. Even now, I am told by some neighbours and friends to 'get a proper hat'. I thought the towelling hat was stylish, and this was confirmed later when I saw Gilligan in *Gilligan's Island* wearing a somewhat similar hat.

## MORE CHILDHOOD ADVENTURES

### *A hapless gardener*

I was only five or six when one day while working in the garden digging small plots for growing vegetables I was injured. Children were expected to do household chores, but there was no money in it, *and* it was boring. There was no money in cleaning, sweeping, washing, cooking and especially making the beds. Gautam and I thought that those sorts of tasks were for our mother and sisters; that was their job, as dictated by tradition. Who were we as little boys to change this tradition? And in the Indian community, there were ample oral traditions and precedents to back us up. Even our mum supported this tradition, which was always a big start for us when avoiding domestic chores.

There were also early signs that both of us had an instinctive attachment to capitalism and profit without doing too much work, capitalism being more a genetic disorder than anything else with Indians. This drove me to do gardening as we were paid two pennies for a bunch of anything we could grow. Two pennies were a lot to us, the penniless.

We had a stream of people coming to see our father day after day to deal with strikes and other disputes. So just as little children emulate their parents and pretend to be lawyers and doctors, Gautam and I had our own powerful trade union with two members. This was because of the frequent arguments we had with our father about the inadequate pocket money he gave us. So, we grew vegetables such as cucumbers, beans, lettuces and eggplants and tried to sell them to our parents. There were frequent trade disputes between our union (us) and management (father), mostly about what constituted a bunch of something we offered for sale. We wanted the same price he paid in the local marketplace.

We as little children thought that five or six leaves of lettuce or eight long beans constituted a generous clutch or bunch for sale, but management disagreed. My father wanted to do bulk buying and give us sixpence for it. He took the typical capitalist moral high ground and said that we were using his land for a vegetable garden without paying him rent, and that we were not paying for board and lodging at home either. And finally, as a crushing blow, that we ate everything he bought from us.

We found it difficult to respond to his persuasive logic. But what has logic and fairness got to do with little children! The idea of children's rights, including compensation for having to put up with parents and for being spanked, was virtually unknown to us in Fiji. This dispute continued for a long time.

As I said, my favourite pastime after school was gardening because there was a tiny bit of money in it. However, one day I was using a large and very heavy garden fork for digging. I had a tendency when using heavy tools such as a large hammer or spade to close my eyes. It was some sort of a squint to summon more strength. It was like what some people do when hitting someone—they close their eyes or bite their tongue when striking! I did this to make up for the fact that I was of slight build and very thin and found hard labour difficult.

I was digging and hit the ground very hard (with eyes closed), and the fork went right through my foot and into the ground. Not a bad hit for a weakling, but it was my foot. This was a terrible omen for someone who would later attempt to study law; we are trained to put the pitchfork into others, not into our own foot.

There were no children's hospitals, and the medical facilities were generally poor. In the ward where I was admitted, there were about fifteen men, mostly old, who had sustained injuries while working in the fields cutting sugarcane or chopping down large trees with axes.

My ankle was tied with a cord and this was tied to the frame at the foot of the bed in such a way to keep the foot on the bed and keep it stable, and perhaps also to prevent me escaping because I made two attempts in the first few days and was caught and brought back. I thought I had been tied up to keep me in the hospital because, as the police might say, I had 'form'.

I was terrified of these men coughing and moaning around me. They told my father that they had trouble sleeping because I was screaming most of the time. The nights were more frightening because these poor men, who were only hovering over me to make sure I was alright, were scary to me; so, there was more screaming. There were no sedatives for screaming children in those days. I was given injections several times as part of my treatment, but I thought these were more by way of punishment for screaming all the time.

The needles were very thick and looked more like knitting needles to the children. In fact, naughty children were told often by irritated parents that if they did not behave, the parents would take them to the hospital and make sure they got injections—that did little for my confidence in the medical treatment at the hospital. The burly Fijian nurses sat on me to give the injections and laughed and sang all the time, no matter what the task. It was certainly no singing matter to me. It was not even funny.

On the bed on each side of me was a thickset, very big Sikh or Rajisthanis wearing a bright red or purple turban. They both had thick beards and wild, piercing, penetrating large eyes. In the dark, their eyes appeared to glow, exactly like in the ghost stories we were told when we were little. It was a terrible sight to behold at the age of four or five and with one foot tied to the bed too.

I was reminded of their eyes years later in Brisbane when I read those immortal lines from William Blake: 'Tyger, Tyger, burning bright in the forests of the night. What immortal hand or eye could frame thy fearful symmetry?'

The older men in the community always looked angry and serious to us young children. When we were older, though, we found them to be our oral historians and storytellers, not to mention staunch guardians who protected us from being bullied or threatened.

My father put one of these men in charge of me, and he seemed to growl and roar whenever I cried! He hovered over me and stared at me like some animal about to pounce, the type that stands very still and stares at things. I was not game to cry any more, and when my parents visited me again, the men in the ward told them with much nodding of heads that I was such a sweet, lovely obedient little boy and so very quiet too!

## *The joy of the cinema*

There was always intense competition amongst the children to earn pocket money, and large families with a shortage of food and other material wants suffered the most. I happened to belong to a slightly more privileged family, but we all competed for pocket money like the rest. The children desperately needed pocket money because, from the age of four or five, we wanted to go to the cinema. These cinemas were at first crudely constructed sheds with corrugated iron roofs, which ensured marvellous acoustics when it rained. There were movie matinees for children, but sometimes during the week children sneaked in to see movies if they could avoid detection.

Our favourite movies were the Westerns with all the blazing gunfights, and war movies with battleships and air raids and soldiers in battle. I do not remember ever hearing any dialogue in these movies because of the whistling, clapping and shouting that started as soon as the heroes appeared on the screen and never stopped until the film was over. Any onscreen kissing led to a pandemonium of foot stamping and more wolf-whistling and catcalls. The older boys, who seemed to be wise and worldly, told us that these were real scenes of men and women making love and having sex. So, the earliest knowledge of sex education led some of us to believe that sex was all a matter of osculation. It did seem a more delicate and tasteful way of designing sexual contact.

This childhood version of what was happening on the screen was upstaged decades later. I chuckled when I read in a 'laughter' column in a newspaper about a little girl who saw a couple kissing in a park and asked her mother whether they were pollinating each other. We thought that something like that was happening on the screen. It was strange that a race of people who produced one of the most popular and authoritative books on sex (the *Kama Sutra*) never discussed sex with their children.

## *Gautam, the innovator*

In the forties, there were no modern contraptions to make life less miserable. The radios were battery operated and were mostly full of news and music that made no sense to children. The reception was sharp and punctuated with whistling and bursts of crackles on the airwaves.

We had no clue how the radios produced sound at that age or how these magic boxes operated. Sometimes Gautam, frustrated because he had no idea how this gizmo worked, used to kick the old radio. In those days, radios came encased in a large compartment like a desk or a fancy set of drawers. It was just a fact of life that radios in Fiji started again after being kicked. These may have been 'indentured' radios because they refused to work without being kicked. Who knows what motivated Gautam. He was an innovator and thinker and may have got the idea from the local homegrown and self-trained mechanics who repaired old cars. They could be heard talking about kick-starting cars, and we saw them literally kicking the sides of vehicles in frustration. Gautam probably had no idea what else it could mean. I would never admit to anything as silly as that, but from personal experience, we both knew that the technique worked with dogs and cats because these always responded quickly when we kick-started them. This practice stopped when I got bitten twice by some savage dogs. I still have the scars. Dogs had no sense of humour and knew nothing about equity and fair play when it came to a balanced response required by law when acting in self-defence. The force used by dogs in Fiji was always excessive.

Most children of that period would remember having some worn-out gramophone records with now-forgotten recordings, perhaps about Red Riding Hood, Old Mother Hubbard, or the Old Woman Who Lived in a Shoe. We played these on a rickety old gramophone that was cranked by hand. Gautam and I tried to improve the sound quality of our old gramophone, and Gautam suggested some advanced technology. Accordingly, we filed and sharpened the needles on a barber's sharpening stone, but there was no improvement in the quality of the sound. Worse, the new technology made holes in the records. This display of lack of skill and a natural talent for making holes may have convinced my father that the only course available to me was to study law: make holes in other people's pockets.

### Comics and things comical

Our childhood coincided with the golden age of comics and even with the passing of over six decades, a mere glimpse through the tunnel of time is likely to overwhelm people who grew up in this golden age of comics. Nostalgia has no meaning unless you grew up with, and were swept up by, comics. We grew up with the notion that eternal truth can only be conveyed to children through reading good comics, and good comics meant just about any comic we could lay our hands on.

Gautam and I suffered from being born into a biased family that rejected comics. Our eldest brother, Vidya Sagar, who was really in charge of what we could read and who was fond of English literature, thought that in comics you only have broken English. Gautam and I believed that in a democratic society, everyone was entitled to live in ignorance and speak in broken English. We had no objection to Vidya Sagar having such a biased opinion, but we objected to him telling our mother that comics were bad for us. My mother grew up without having the opportunity to read or write English, and she was not going to have her children speak broken English.

So, under her influence, our father decreed that there would be no comics in the house and told our mum to tear up any comics in our possession. It was like living during the Inquisition in the Middle Ages with us fearing that our comics, which were full of real persons to us, would be caught and torn limb from limb or be burnt at the stake. Tearing up comics is infinitely more damaging to the culture and traditions in the children's world than tearing up grammar books. It is far worse than tearing up textbooks because we did not mind if we were not allowed to read any books for school but could not get along without comics.

The mere prohibition on reading comics was serious enough but tearing up comics was far worse than burning schoolbooks because children never paid for schoolbooks. We had to buy our own comics with whatever little pocket money we had. Most children could not afford to buy comics. We had to make do by exchanging comics with other children. If the comics were destroyed by mindless adults, we were required to replace them. To us, this was an expensive exercise. And the withdrawal symptoms of drug addicts are nothing compared to small children denied comics.

As I write about some early events, I am again confronted with the problem of recollection; acute details present a problem most of the time. With age, the human mind sometimes recoils and avoids glancing back and at other times we relish and marvel at the daring and the cheekiness of our exploits as children. As I peer into the past, the half-forgotten memories take on a special glow and significance, all burnished by Time.

The comics we loved were harmless. We loved *Superman, Captain Marvel, The Phantom, Buck Rogers, Pop Eye* and *Tarzan*. We had never seen a movie with Superman or the others, but we saw some Tarzan movies and just loved Cheeta, the monkey. Cheeta had such charisma and personality and looked real to us.

We knew Cheeta had something special about him because Jane spent a lot of time hugging, kissing, cuddling and holding Cheeta close to her breast. Indeed, Jane spent more time with Cheeta for companionship than she did Tarzan. And, unlike in other movies in which the heroes used to punch the baddies if they tried to get too close to their girls, Tarzan did not seem to mind Cheeta monkeying with Jane.

Tarzan was our action hero, and he was certainly more photogenic than action heroes today. Although all of them were about equal when it came to grunting a few words occasionally, instead of having a normal conversation, Tarzan had much more to offer. His call shook the jungle and frightened elephants and lions a long way away.

He also impressed because, although a man of few words, he had a special way of sneaking up behind lions who were minding their own business to rip open their jaws with his bare hands, and children found this brave and exciting beyond belief. We hated 'Boy', that little son of Tarzan, because we were not impressed with a child of that age still wearing a nappy. Every time lions and crocodiles came near him, we used to cheer the animals.

Cheeta, too, was a real hero in many other ways. He used to steal the radio receivers from the German spies in Africa and confuse the Nazis who thought they were the master race, but whenever they matched their wits with Cheeta, the monkey always won. It took the whole length of a film before the Nazis could trace and find Cheeta's whereabouts, and by then, they had lost the war.

We thought that if our mother really understood how important the comics were to us, she would accept them. Accordingly, we showed her *Superman* and *The Phantom* and explained that when they repeatedly said 'pow' and 'wow' and the victims fell shrieking 'eeeek!', it was good for our English.

My mother could not read or write in English. So, we tried to make her understand by showing her the comics and explaining the good parts that appealed to us (these were mostly the punch-ups and animals

## CHAPTER 3

escaping Tarzan's grip and the heroic deeds of Superman as he flew through air and space in his underwear). But out attempt to educate her turned out to be a complete disaster because she scooped up all the comics we showed her and rushed to show them to our father. We could hear her shouting 'Look at this …. and … this and this … what possible good is there in the children seeing these naked men in underpants flying through the air with a towel hanging on their shoulders and not covering their bottoms and going 'pow' and 'wow' all the time?' The only comics she liked, although she would not allow us even these, were comics with Pop Eye because he ate spinach, and she was a lifelong vegetarian who was always pushing us to have more vegetables with our meals. But although our mother thought that Pop Eye had something to offer, rules were rules. This was a losing battle.

Gautam and I raved and raged under the large water tank because torn comics meant that we had to pay for any borrowed comics that were ripped—and, like drug addicts, we needed comics. Where there is a will there is a way. Gautam suggested that the best way was to buy torches and to read comics under the blankets when the kerosene lights went out at night. This worked well. We held the torch in one hand and the comic in the other under the blanket. The problem with this, as most lawbreakers know, is that you get caught sooner or later. Our tragedy was that we got caught sooner rather than later. It was Gautam's fault and I have no idea what made him do such a silly thing.

We all slept under a huge mosquito net to keep all the creepy crawlies out and there were many of these in Fiji. One night there was a large moth with a wingspan of many centimetres on the ceiling and Gautam took his torch out and shone it on the ceiling. My mother came storming into the room and said that she had seen a strange light in the room. Mum had seen some lights on the previous night, too, and she wanted to know whether we had seen someone shinning a torchlight from the outside into the bedroom.

I had not noticed anything during the previous night and truthfully said no. Gautam, who was the culprit shining the torch, feigned that he was asleep and had just been disturbed. A few nights later Gautam again got this urge to engage in his new hobby of moth watching at night. The stupid boy could have easily watched moths all day long. But no, he had to do this at night. We were caught with a bed full of comics. All comics were confiscated and torn up. For several months, we had to help the Fijian labourers making bricks after school.

## Nature lovers

It was a full six months before we recovered from the disaster of losing the comics, and relief came with divine intervention. We used to spend a lot of time in the detached library, which was near the residence but not very close to it. For some reason, our mother never went there except when she swept the place. It was clogged with books, encyclopaedias and history books, National Geographic magazines and Time magazines. There were even newspaper cuttings from the debates in the Legislative Council in Fiji.

My father was a member of the Legislative Council. At this time, he was mostly away in Suva, the capital of Fiji, on the eastern side of the main island of Viti Levui. Lautoka is on the western side of the island.

It so happened that the owner of the buildings leased by my father lived very close to the printing press. He was married to a Eurasian lady, a very beautiful and charming woman. He had studied law in England and had a habit of galloping around the district on horseback with saddles and all the fittings that go with horses, and he was always smartly dressed in what looked like jodhpurs. He did this every morning as long as we lived near the printing-press building. He knew that my father suffered from rheumatism and that he was also diabetic.

We used to see them talking quite frequently together over the fence. He was a wealthy lawyer and might have had a sailing boat. He, too, must have lived on some of the islands, but we had no idea about his other social habits apart from his horse riding. He may have lived on the outer islands for health and recuperation too.

But as children, we had little contact with him. I found out the rest of the story sometime later. He had told my father something about iodine in saltwater, which was good for rheumatics and told him of the healing power of the sun. He said that there was an enormous amount of literature on the healing power of natural remedies. He gave my father fifteen monthly magazine-type books. I think my father must have simply put them away with the other stuff in the library until Gautam and I hit pay-dirt.

## *Peep show for children*

One day with nothing much happening, we were going through his books and were shocked to see these magazines. These were nature magazines with nude males and females walking on the beaches, the photographs mostly taken from the side or back. It was a goldmine of fifteen magazines. These were not like models of today but mostly middle-aged, pot-bellied people. We had never seen any naked white people in our life. There were no swimming beaches in Lautoka, but the Europeans always went to a separate secluded beach at Koro-Levu, miles away from Lautoka. We had seen bare-breasted Fijian women swimming near the local koros but only from a great distance. The Fijians were deeply religious and did not encourage people to swim naked. The European children went to separate schools reserved for Europeans and so, as a child, I had never met and talked to a single white child and only saw them when we passed them in the streets. This was an age when some illiterates thought the European men were probably born in suits or in shorts with long socks on.

My mother was serene and happy because she had never seen me and Gautam so engrossed in our studies in this detached building, and this went on for many weeks. Gautam had another brainwave. I thought the idea was mine, but he always disputed this. It was probably his idea because it has his fingerprints all over it. He said that there was a market for all this and that we should organise peep shows for the children in return for comics to read, and since there were fifteen magazines, we could show them only a few pages at a time.

Soon children were lining up with their comics, including some children we had never seen before. My mother appeared pleased that there were so many children occupied in reading books and keeping us company. I feel nostalgic even now when I think about the golden age of comics. We were now reading them in the library and thought we really looked like students. The word spread because none of the children had seen naked white men and women at such close quarters. The main wonderment lay in the fact that the women had such large breasts and bottoms.

No one had seen naked people with such large bottoms. There were very intense discussions about the female breasts that seemed to cascade halfway down the stomach to the belly button. No Indian females could have competed with them, but that is hearsay only. The children had seen women with their mammary glands tucked in bras but had no idea of their telescopic or periscopic powers and potential.

No one seemed to know where these women tucked away their breasts once they had finished sunning them. The massive collection of National Geographics with prehistoric creatures like dinosaurs and hippopotamus never aroused as much interest as these nature magazines did. Word was passed in whispers, and we had comics everywhere. When we ran out of children of our own age, the older boys arrived, mostly fourteen and fifteen years old. For the first time, my mother thought there was something suspicious because we had never played or done homework with older boys before.

Then one day, my mother barged in unannounced and found a group of us ogling to our hearts' content. The only recollections I have are hazy but were of the shrieks and screams and the boys scattering in all directions. My mother grabbed us by the collars and wanted to know where we had got such filth. We were very quick to blame my father and told her exactly where he had hidden them. They were not really hidden, but it just came out that way, and it went well with our story.

Then, still shrieking and shouting, she reeled around and went out screaming and looking for my father. We could hear him speaking in a muted voice but had no idea what he said, and it really was his problem. After all, he was the one who had authorised the destruction of children's literature. My mother burnt them all and we took perverse pleasure in seeing the adults burning their own books for a change. We knew that the golden age of comics was over, and there would be no more comics while we were in Fiji.

## SYMPHONY ON THE OCEAN

I recall mentioning it before but would re-affirm in passing that in remembering the past, the ordinary becomes extraordinary, and the extraordinary becomes divine. I will give an account of our communion with the ocean and what is meant when we describe our now-lost paradise. This was a period when we doted on the ocean and the stunning sunsets, and I have tried to capture this in my remaining memories under the heading of 'symphony on the ocean'.

There is no denying that the remembrance of the many islands we visited or stayed on during holidays as children were perhaps as close as one can get to the never-never of the past. This then is a glimpse of the past, the residue that remains in the silence of maturity; somewhat tarnished but deeply ingrained. A remembrance of a time when we lived in blissful ignorance, a time before we were sent to Australia to be educated and civilized so that we could return and bring progress to other lives back in the colony. We were even then still in the quest for adventure; still seeking and finding fun in the sun. These were our defining moments and our idea of a golden age. These are my last memories before coming to Australia; and I had never relived them so intensely as I did when I began writing about them now.

Gautam and I were preoccupied and absorbed with the idea that we were some sort of sailors, although we had never learnt to swim, let alone to sail. My father had many small boats and engaged in island trading mostly for copra. Just after the war, there was a great demand for sea slugs. Our eldest brother, Vidya Sagar, would leave home on a motor-powered launch towing a barge to collect these from the various surrounding islands. The Fijians who sailed these boats and worked for my father were attentive to whatever we demanded, provided we told them that it was our father's wish and command. The Fijians treated my father as some sort of an Indian Chief and an equivalent of their own local chiefs or Ratus. My first adventure began in the middle of 1942 when we went island hopping on our little boats. I was about six.

## Bakana Island

We went to live on Bakana Island, which was several miles across the sea from our school in Lautoka. It was a time when my father was recuperating from an illness. He had suffered from rheumatism for years and sometimes felt incapacitated and needed rest. At the time, the cause of rheumatism was unknown, and little could be done to alleviate the pain. From all his readings, my father thought that there was some sort of iodine in the seawater that had a curative effect. He also needed to be away from all the pressures of work.

So, during our adventure on Bakana Island, our eldest brother, Vidya Sagar, was left to manage our printing-press business on his own as my father had decided to stay on Bakana Island for five or six weeks. We were attending school at the time, but my father saw no problems with that. He arranged for a boat to pick us up every morning for the next six weeks, leaving Bakana Island early and dropping us off just in front of the school. Every afternoon after school, we would go back to the island and our mum would be waiting for us on the beach.

Thus, it was that we went to school on a boat each morning, and in the afternoon the boat arrived on the beach in front of the school to pick us up and take us back to the island; and what made it so exciting was that virtually the whole school was watching us. Just imagine, a group of little children disembarking early in the morning and embarking after school. We were the envy of the other children. The boats, too, changed according to availability; sometimes it was a boat with a large sail and sometimes it had an outboard engine.

On Bakana Island, we lived in large army tents that had been transported there, and everything including drinking water had to be transported on boats. There was no water on Bakana Island. We had a power generator for electricity that travelled with us from island to island on our various trips, especially when we were expected to live

# CHAPTER 3

on an island for any lengthy period. When we were living on Bakana Island, there were several occasions when the boat nearly sank because in the rainy season with stormy weather and sudden gusts of gale-force winds, the little boat would be rising and falling like a cork, almost submerged in water. None of the little children (about six or seven out of the eventual eleven) had been taught to swim.

There was a white sandy beach on Bakana and a live coral reef very close to the beach. We just played on the beach and tried to learn to swim and made plans to avoid school on some days. The difficulty was that there was no point in pretending to have stomach-ache or the like because our mum used to produce castor oil or Epsom salt, two of the most-ghastly substances known to children. Sometimes she was surprised at seeing how quickly we recovered before she forced us to take our medicine.

We had many little boats, and at some stage, my father bought an old tugboat, the type that tugged large vessels to the ports and docks. This one had a massive engine for such a small boat; tugboats are notoriously small for the big tasks expected of them. It was sleek and extremely powerful.

The tugboat added to my father's collection of punts and other little boats for island trading. These came in very handy because, after the war, this tiny lot of wretched and battered boats, some with peeling paint and all tired and dirty-looking, went from island to island buying copra and trochus shells (used in the manufacture of buttons) and *nadri* (beach-de-mere or sea cucumber), which looked dirty and filthy to us but were a delicacy to the Japanese who were buying it. The Japanese arrived (peaceably) in Fiji sometime in 1948 and were looking for everything, including nadri, copra, trochus shell and scrap-metal. We dealt with a Japanese company called Bano Brothers.

There were many such little boats owned by the locals, some with little engines or tiny outboard motors and others were native sailing boats with little masts, some hired, and some bought and all going from island to island and trading.

## *Vomo Island, near-drowning experiences, and little truants*

Learning to swim on a beach is difficult, but Gautam and I decided to make a serious effort on a more distant trip to a more distant island, Vomo Island. We went there on several occasions in 1947. On two such trips, the boat struck a reef, and we all nearly drowned. I still recall many details of those trips with water bubbling and seeping around the engine, which suddenly stalled and stopped. The tide was going out rapidly, leaving us stuck in the middle of the ocean on an exposed reef—high but not completely dry!

There was no radio or other communication on little boats. The only safety net was the inter-island traffic with numerous small sailing boats passing each other. These boats were built more like large canoes than boats. The Fijians were always somewhere on the horizon but on this trip, no one came to our aid. We waved and screamed, and they waved back and screamed with cheering and laughter, not realising that we needed help. Perhaps they thought we had just stopped for fishing, and that too was a common sight. The more we waved, the more they waved and cheered.

Vomo Island was some twenty or thirty miles from us. In those days we thought that we were going very far away and the whole trip took almost all day. This trip was on a small launch with a small engine, and the boat returned about once every week with supplies that were not available on the island.

On a clear day, Vomo Island could be seen from our shores in Lautoka. As I remember, it was painted on the horizon and looked like a tiny toenail in the distance; and again, from some distance, one end of the island looked as if a tiny part on the western side had been nicked with a penknife and was floating in the air just above the horizon with the rest sitting on the horizon.

On this occasion, we were going to stay on Vomo Island for five or six weeks, and the near sinking of the boat was not an auspicious start because none of the eight or nine children could swim.

# CHAPTER 3

It was sometime before our trip to Vomo Island that our father had bought our aging but powerful tugboat with its massive engine. We were told that it was a 'pilot' tugboat because it was used to pilot other larger vessels to shore or to the docks; it was bought and brought from some other port, not Lautoka.

With nothing to do but go to school for boring classes when we lived in Lautoka, Gautam and I naturally opted to go on these trips; sometimes with parental approval but on several rare occasions instead of going to school Gautam and I would sneak out to the local koro where the boats were anchored and tell the local hired 'captain' working for my father and on his way to collect things from adjacent islands that our father wanted us to accompany him for the day trip and he never questioned us. Our father was regarded with respect by the Fijian chiefs who called him Ratu (chief) because he had taught some of the chiefs and their children. These children of the Fijian chiefs were much older than us; some were young adults.

We knew the consequences were dire if we were caught, but we never expected it to be so soon. On one occasion Gautam and I boarded a boat that was expected back in Lautoka at the end of the day, just in time for us to go home and give an account of our day at school! As luck would have it, the boat was late, and a reception committee greeted us. Every adult who came within range of my mother was abused for being part of a conspiracy to take us out to sea without her knowledge. She shouted that it was all the fault of the adults. We agreed.

Fortunately for us, our mother thought that Gautam and I were too little and too stupid to think of things like that. When this happened, our father, who was a member of the Legislative Council, was in Suva and Gautam and I were very lucky that he was not around because he had a different way of looking at our responsibilities and capabilities. There were only two unauthorised short trips like that. The price was too high. I mean for Gautam and me.

Sometimes we pretended to be real helpers and cabin boys for our eldest brother Sagar when he went to sea with the Fijian captain at the weekends to collect copra and shells. There were no regulations, and anyone could be captain and sail and drown as they wished. These were short daily trips or when Vidya Sagar was expected to be away buying and transporting small quantities of copra, nadri and trochus shells at weekends. He was seldom away for more than several nights.

But when on regular trips, we went as a whole family with our father and stayed on some of these islands on extended holidays when my father chose to get away from his work. These were the really memorable periods of our existence, and even more memorable when we recalled them, unglazed by distance and time. No one impressed on us to soak up and enjoy these moments deeply and intensely. We did not realise and were never told that we were not likely to go back to many of these islands ever again during our lifetime.

I never went back to these idyllic islands again, save on one occasion when the whole family was invited to Fiji by our parents, and we went to Mana Island. The occasion was our parents' fiftieth wedding anniversary in 1972. I went to Fiji with Rose and our children, who were little at the time. We went to Lautoka and stayed on Mana Island for a week. It was too expensive to show my children the other islands, including Vomo Island and Waya Island where Gautam and I had had most of our adventures.

Fiji in 1972 had changed. It was very expensive for the whole family to travel on tourist boats on my public service pay. So, I never took the children to those islands, although I pointed out some of them from a distance on our way to Mana Island; the children were very little, and one island is enough for little children.

But in the forties when on holidays we went with our parents putt-putting from island to island and sometimes stayed on these tiny islands for several weeks at a time. I remember some of the names of the islands, but we generally referred to them as part of Yasawa or Waya or Vomo or Malolo or Naviti and so on. As children, we took as much notice of names of islands as children in Australia might of the bus routes they travelled on. There was constant inter-island traffic, and the Fijians were natural sailors who crisscrossed and sailed the open seas without the aid of compass or radios. Sailing was not seen as high adventure or recreation but toil. It was just ordinary work for grown men and part of their daily life. They had no time to gawk and stare—that was for the idle tourists who had nothing better to do.

It is only when reflecting on the distant past that this period in life remains a period of extraordinary adventures for us as children; a golden age when we sailed from island to island and lived on that tiny smudge on the ocean that was our home, in a group of islands that lay like a misty spray in a forgotten part of the vast Pacific Ocean. The dreamers and romantic spirits from other parts of the world may have seen Fiji as an idyllic paradise but for ordinary people born and immersed in daily toil and blessed with a large, hungry family to feed, the romance was missing. But for us, the children, this was all a never-ending big adventure, and always extraordinary. We never worried about where the next meal was coming from—that was the responsibility of our parents and had nothing to do with us.

On more than one trip to Vomo Island we almost drowned. My father was the captain, and we had a Fijian helper, Lagi, on board, who was more a handyman than a mechanic; he would try to repair things when we were at home. These open seas were mostly unchartered with reefs that would suddenly pop out anywhere, and whilst the Fijians were deft sailors and knew what was what, the Indians were not. Indian mythology is full of religious instructions on how to avoid going out to sea and nothing about sailing. We struck one of the reefs on the way. The boat, loaded with supplies, including the electricity generator, was heavy and unwieldy.

It struck a reef and ended up perched on the reef in such a way that it rolled from side to side when struck by the waves. The tide was going out rapidly and soon the boat sat there like the proverbial 'shag on a rock', leaning heavily to one side. I knew it was serious, but the other little children thought it was fun to lean on the side close to the water and play.

As always when nearly drowning, we waved and shouted for help at a few Fijian sailing boats going past at some distance. Perhaps they thought we had stopped to fish because they simply waved back and kept going. The frantic effort to start the engine resulted in a broken fan belt. I think there was no panic because, as usual, my father showed no signs of panic. He seldom did, no matter what was happening. He shouted and ordered everyone to sit at different sections of the boat to keep it stable and set about pleating a tight and almost perfect fan belt from a rope. He was one of the first King's Scouts in Fiji when he was a boy and had a wonderful practical knowledge of machinery and tools for survival. When the tide turned, the boat lurched from side to side with the waves, with water lapping and sometimes smashing into the boat. Some of us had buckets to bail out the water.

The boat was not leaking badly and as soon as the pump commenced working it soon steadied and floated again as the tide rose, and somehow it got on an even keel. As the engine was not damaged, save for the fan belt, it started again and began coughing, pumping and gushing out the water and everything was fine. We were on our way again. When we landed on Vomo Island many hours later I saw the rope fan belt was worn and stripped and had lost almost all the strands or threads that lay near the front of the engine with a fine gossamer-like effect, like thin dust on the floor. I always remembered that sight. It was on Vomo Island that Gautam and I thought it would be a good idea to learn to swim.

The prevailing swimming culture was different then because there were no swimming lessons for children and very few were taught to swim. Indian parents seldom went for a swim. They went into the sea for a 'dip' and that literally meant a dip or a dunk in the water, after which they came out of the water quickly before they could get wet and catch a cold, and they writhed and dried themselves and went home. Those who really could swim had no idea how to teach children to swim. They mostly 'taught' the children by just tossing them in the sea in deep water but close to the beach and then they waited to see what happened next. It was amazing just how quickly little drowning children became drown-proof in such circumstances, but no thanks to the parents.

Learning to swim meant no more than being taught to float and paddle for a while before help arrived. The only technique in safety and survival we were taught was to scream with all our might when in trouble until help arrived. We found great difficulty in screaming for help when we went under in deep water.

In a sinking boat, children were told to paddle like mad and scoop the water with one hand and raise the other hand for help.

The fact was that some of the Indians, mostly in the coastal areas, were very good swimmers, but were self-taught. And parents gave a new meaning to the term 'lend me your ears' because when children were gasping for breath and thought they were sinking in deep water, some giggling adult would appear from nowhere in a relaxed mood and casual gait, and in slow motion would pull the children up from the water by both ears. I know because some family members have long ears!

On Vomo, I quietly noticed many things while standing on the shore—the gentle breeze with swaying coconut trees, the endless white sandy beaches with coral reefs only metres from the shore, the nights full of blazing stars, the pervading stillness until the first murmur of dawn.

Rainy nights on Vomo were different, too, with no pelting patter of rain on the tin roof that drowned all human conversation like those on corrugated iron roofs back at home. Instead, this was soft, silent, weeping rain that trickled and landed like beads of perspiration on the ground or dropped softly on the side of the thatched dwelling as we stood silently in the wide doorway to watch and listen, perforated from time to time with a swish and thud from falling dry coconuts or leaves. We felt sheathed, sheltered, safe and insulated from the noise and storm under the thatched roof and between the sturdy walls. It was like being in a deep bunker with little sound of a raging storm coming inside.

And when sometimes it really poured, as it can only do in the tropics, then the weepiness yielded to bawling and the heavy gushing and drenching rain fell from the side of the thatched roofs like rivulets or numerous leaking taps, all lovely to watch from the dry safety of the doorway, and sometimes we would stretch out our hands to cup and drink it too. These dwellings were heavily thatched, large structures, and the roof was about a foot or more thick; the occupants inside felt coddled and cocooned.

Several years later when attending a night school, which my father had opened for adults, I related what had happened at sea when we nearly drowned to one of my Fijian friends who was learning English and was much older than I was. He could have been the one who later became the President of Fiji. He listened silently and said something that I had heard before from my brother, Vidya Sagar, who taught these Fijians. But my friend gave it a slight twist and in a different language asked: 'Why did the Indians have a whole bloody ocean named after them when they can't swim, can't sail, and can't even play football?'

We never cease to marvel that many famous and intrepid sailors from Europe, including Captain Cook, Columbus, Vasco de Gama, and Magellan, saw Indians on every continent they landed on, including Red Indians in America, when most Indians on the Indian sub-continent had difficulty finding their way around their own little villages and were not fond of sailing out to sea. I have given an account of the religious mythology to explain and support their lack of interest in the ocean. But we had little time to seek solace in mythology when furiously bailing out water.

## *An Indian chief*

It so happened that my father was a great advocate of the urgent need for Indians in Fiji to understand, accept and respect the Fijian native traditions. He wrote and gave speeches to Indians to persuade them to learn to speak the Fijian language. He respected and followed Fijian customs, and he attended many of their formal ceremonial events in the local koro. He spoke Fijian fluently and followed their tradition of deep respect for communal values. He knew that it would be impossible for Indians to adopt fully the Fijian way of life, but he wanted the Indians to acknowledge and show respect for Fijian traditional values; in fact, other Indian leaders had the same view and worked to achieve communal harmony and respect.

The Fijian chiefs responded by treating my father like an Indian 'chief'. And so, on our arrival in Vomo, Tui Vomo gave him the traditional Fijian welcome with the *meke* and *yagona* ceremony and the

## CHAPTER 3

rest; these are joyous but solemn occasions. We children were taught to greet these chiefs as 'Tui'. I had no deep knowledge of their chieftain hierarchy but understood that the title was akin to 'king'. So, we thought we were calling them King of Vomo or King of Waya because the reference was always to Tui Vomo and Tui Waya, and these two chiefs were our favourites when we were little.

I particularly remember a son of one of these two chiefs because my father tutored him when he was studying for entry into a degree course in England. We called him Moses. I had no idea what his surname was or even which of the two chiefs was his father. I never knew or checked his surname. I believe he eventually completed his degree in England and went on to become a senator in the Fijian Parliament. I never met him after these early days, but years later when I wanted to know what had happened to two of my favourite Fijian chiefs, Tui Vomo and Tui Waya, my father mentioned Moses and spoke of his achievements as a member of parliament in Fiji.

My father was very popular with the Fijian people in the Western Districts because of his business and trade union involvement and because he genuinely believed that without some understanding of Fijian customs and traditions there would be continuing friction between the two races. He, in fact, taught in the school he established for adults quite a few Fijians who later became union leaders. But many Indians laughed at the suggestion of trying to understand the Fijians and tended to treat them as inferior. All that contributed to the heavy price the Indians paid after the departure of the British. I recall the President of Fiji under the Bainimarama Administration, Iloilo, was educated in this school by my father and taught by my eldest brother, Vidya Sagar, and these were adult students. There were no schools catering for those who did not or could not attend school when they were children and my father wanted to give them the opportunity to learn as adults, and some local chiefs attended our school.

We were greeted on Vomo Island with the traditional fanfare and a feast. Tui Vomo had two very large bures or residential quarters for the exclusive use of Tui Vomo and his family, and these were right on the beach. He gave the best and the nicest looking bure to my father, and he was in the next bure. These were very large and very beautiful.

## Jean Simmons

At the time I was recalling and writing this about Vomo Island, sometime in February 2010, I read that Jean Simmons, the famous British actress, had died.

It made me think of the time on Vomo Island when Gautam and I saw Jean Simmons. It was 1947 and she was in Fiji for the filming of *The Blue Lagoon*. During the filming, she and the other actors and film crew arrived in a most beautiful and sleek motorboat and stopped right in front of our bure, which was a matter of several hundred metres from the beach. I had no idea at the time where the filming was done.

That fine morning when they landed on Vomo Island, it was just another morning for us. We had been there for two weeks and nothing jades the senses of children more than too much of a good thing. It seemed that it was going to be just another day with nothing to do but swim and eat paw-paws all day. I was sitting on the beach gazing at nothing and suddenly a group of little local children turned up with Gautam in tow, pointing to the horizon out at sea. I saw a sleek, white motorboat nosing and intruding into our space, our beach. It had a sailing mast but was being powered by a motor, and it stopped a few hundred metres in front of our new abode, and there were some very smart-looking Europeans, both men and women, on board.

I walked right up to the beach and sat and watched. Presently, I saw a most beautiful girl with several other women popping in and out of the water near the boat and occasionally diving from the boat. There were six or seven in all and later some swam and others paddled to the beach in a tiny dinghy and spent a long time on the beach. They were laughing, some had a wine glass in hand, and they were mostly acting like most people do when they are immodestly dressed for swimming and running on the beach.

The beautiful girl seemed to be the centre of attention, and she looked small and slender by comparison to the local girls who were generally quite big, but I was no authority on the size or shape of girls at that time. She looked petite and I assumed that she was only sixteen or seventeen (she was actually twenty). In shape and build and in her slender, slight looks she was like some Indian girls of that age in Fiji, and she too had dark hair; the only difference was that she was stunningly beautiful even to the untrained and under-developed eyes of a boy of eleven or twelve.

I had seen that shape and face on the religious statuettes of Indian goddesses. She also reminded me of the beautiful faces I had seen on packets of baby soap; it could have been on Lux soap, but I am not sure. At the age of eleven, most beautiful women looked alike and perhaps she was like someone on packets of talcum powder for babies. There were very few women's magazines in our house in those days; otherwise, I would have made more comparisons at that time.

This landing on the island remained a memorable occasion because this was a party that was filming a movie in Fiji. I marvelled later that there we were just sitting and staring at Jean Simmons.

We learned later that *The Blue Lagoon* was filmed in the surrounding islands in the Yasawa group of islands in Fiji. We never saw any movie cameras with them. Perhaps they were on Vomo Island having a break from work. I once saw a photograph of Jean Simmons taken on one of the islands during the filming of *The Blue Lagoon,* and what struck me was that it was exactly as she looked when she was on Vomo Island. The photograph looked like it was taken on the western end of Vomo Island. She was even dressed like she was on the island.

The men on the boat went to see Tui Vomo, who told my father later that the people on the boat wanted to rent one of the bures and were prepared to pay anything for the one we occupied. They wanted us to shift to a smaller one and make way for them. He told my father that he declined because my father was a guest, and he could never do that. Jean Simmons and her group remained on the island for many hours, swimming, laughing and chatting and then they went away. In some ways, it is a sad story because how could anyone only eleven or twelve, no matter how precocious, be expected to appreciate Jean Simmons. What a waste!

## *Symphony on the ocean blue: how the ocean sang and danced*

We did watch and listen to the ocean sing and dance and here is a description pouring out of me in my late age as I sit and write about our island life in the distant Pacific, now so far away from Brisbane where I have lived for the last sixty-five years. I will now describe to you how the ocean sang and danced as we listened and watched and waited on the beach.

It was a feature common to most islands we stayed on. We would experience it at dawn on quiet early mornings when not a blade of grass stirred. An eerie silence, save for a few snores coming from the neighbouring little bures, would greet us. Gautam and I would steal out to the beach barely a hundred paces from our bure to watch the glassy sea and to hear the occasional 'plonk' of fish that momentarily popped out of the water and remained suspended for a split second with a 'come and get me if you can' look before vanishing, leaving a large circle on the silent and silky-smooth surface of the water.

There was no motion on the breast of the sea and no waves to speak of on these early dawns save sighing heaves from time to time as if the mighty ocean were toying with the idea of waking up and then deciding to slumber on, all in silence and empathy. We knew and understood how the ocean felt because we too had experienced the same reluctance to get up on some early mornings … thus, we sat, and watched, and waited. And as we watched and listened, we noticed that the heaving and sighing in such silence created a murmur of tiny waves like a series of horizontal pleats that gently landed on the beach, licking and lapping the sandy shoreline and all in relative silence. Thus, with our little imaginations, we plundered the beauty of the early morning sea as we again watched in silence, not daring to wake the ocean still at rest and seemingly fast asleep.

There were dawn variations on this symphony on the sea, some changes in the theme. Sometimes on the flat smooth and silky sea, there were intermittent waves, no more than 30 cm high (a foot), which broke on the shore in a most amazing way. Again, these little waves came to the beach in horizontal gentle pleats except that, before breaking, each wave seemed suspended in mid-air for a moment, and then would collapse almost where it stood with a heavy thud that shook the whole length of the beach with so much power and with so little effort and with such dramatic impact!

We would hear the big 'thump' and feel the tremor under our feet. Sometimes this wave orchestra played another tune when little waves came landing in quick succession like someone punching a piano keyboard. It was as if the hidden hand of the silent sea were engaged in thoughtful tap-dancing with its fingers.

So it was that in the absence of other activity, we sat on the beach at dawn before breakfast, watching and listening. No doubt all this is a commonplace experience for people who wander through the vastness of the Australian coastline, but it was still fresh and new in my time.

It produced sublime conditions for existence and reflection. I'm sure many would agree that deep communion with nature, entirely free of human distraction, is only possible on a deserted beach or in the desert air. I have never crossed the desert and would be inclined to leave it to those with grander aspirations. I would stay with the sea, which is more pleasant and even sensual and was our original home, the birthplace of humanity.

The morning gentleness then reluctantly and teasingly yielded to the peeping tom on the horizon (the sun); as soon as this intruder joined us in the watching game, a strong breeze would spring from nowhere, waking the coconut and paw-paw trees in the little koro on the beach. The ocean would then churn and burst into motion as if engaged in a morning ablution of its own, gargling and spitting as the humans did back in our little town. I used to see the old men in the early morning brushing their teeth and spitting on our main street in Lautoka. The Indians took every bit of their culture with them to Fiji, including gargling and spitting, which became more spectacular when they chewed their betel nuts.

Then, once awake, the ocean suddenly coughed and thundered on full throttle and shouted and carried on with a powerful voice for the rest of the day, and the countless coconut trees, in turn, joined the daily parade with the ceaseless 'hula' and 'meke' dances. As in most human processions and parades, suddenly everything was alive. The rest of the day in this paradise was greeted with the usual cacophony of chirping birds, hungry children, and muttering adults all clamouring for food and attention, and the sound of pots and pans could be heard all over the place in the village. Then, at least to our eyes, the whole place erupted in turmoil, with even the sea turning angry and starting its daily routine of merciless and ceaseless pounding of the beaches, all without respite and seemingly forever and ever. That was our island in the seas.

The enjoyment of beauty before breakfast is not everybody's cup of tea. Even with us, it came a close second. Intellectual rigour may come with fasting, but beauty is best appreciated on a full stomach. How else may one explain the bacchanalias and feasts accompanied by music in many societies? So, on most mornings when on the beach, Gautam and I foraged for food first, which was easy on the island. No one looked for coconuts because mostly we tripped and fell over coconuts everywhere. Those familiar with the Fijian communal life would need no introduction.

At the back of the little koro on Vomo Island, there was a plantation of all kinds of tubers, including tapioca, dalo and ubi, and in addition a whole large plantation of paw-paws of many kinds and bananas. The local people could always be seen either working on the plantation and growing things or digging up the taro and dalo or picking large, rich and very sweet paw-paws. We, too, were allowed by Tui Vomo to pick whatever we wanted and whenever we wanted it. Tui Vomo was a great admirer of my father. They enjoyed each other's company and mostly talked in Fijian, and as we did not understand the Fijian language at that age, we had no idea what they were talking about. Those who have never lived in the tropics or the sub-tropics such as Fiji would have no idea how rich and sweet tropical fruits can be. Certainly not the children in the cities today, those forced to eat fruit that has been kept frozen for some time. We on the island were so spoilt that Gautam would pick several large paw-paws and only eat the ripest part of them, as one could see by the rich orange colour of the outer skin, and he would then throw the rest away.

There were so many paw-paws and ripe bananas around that no one ever said to us that we were wasting the lovely fruit. Now when paying for paw-paws in shops, I feel like bursting into tears. Paw-paws sold in shops are lousy, pathetic imitations of this noble fruit; they are sometimes limp and tasteless things that look more like sagging mammary glands. These large corporations that have a monopoly on fruit and vegetables charge by the grams and swindle us as if providing an extra service. Truly scandalous. A good case can be made for a charitable society for the protection and preservation of paw-paws. It is difficult not to feel emotional when thinking about the sweet paw-paws in the sub-tropics!

## A REFLECTION

At this point in my writing, I am amazed that I can remember so much and wonder how this is possible when one is getting old. I suppose that with age the human mind sometimes recoils and avoids glancing back, but at other times relishes and marvels at the daring and the cheekiness of it all. The half-forgotten memories of certain doings take on a special glow and significance, all burnished by time. This is when what was ordinary with the act of recollection becomes extraordinary and the human mind, thus enlivened, senses that there is still a lot of sugar in the residual molasses!

So now this is a phase when memories materialise and cascade, all cured in the brine of time and we relish the past like we relish some cured morsels. We as children loved rancid butter on toast; this was when we had no refrigeration. When we came to Brisbane, we found that the butter was not rancid but very bland with no taste at all.

These then are the sweet, aged, and brine-brained recollections of our many islands in the sun. The idyllic paradise seen on travel brochures was seldom idyllic to the elders born and immersed in daily toil in any island paradise because the burden of living made things very ordinary in the Pacific paradise. I do have recollections as a child of doting on the paradise around me or being deeply taken by the blueness of the ocean or the stunning sunsets that now seem dazzling with the distance of time.

In my town, for the adults, these were just boring daily events because the sun rose and set every bloody day without respite. I can imagine that those who are born to eat caviar from an early age complain about the ordinariness of their experience; too much can make anything feel ordinary. There were times when I too found that living in the sub-tropics did not make me aware that we were living in paradise; sometimes those soaked in rich experience or sensations see much but experience little. Sometimes we do not notice much because paradise is always where one wants to be and not where one is.

However, there is no denying that the remembrance of the many islands we visited or stayed on during holidays as children were perhaps as close as one can get to the never-never of the past.

This then is a glimpse of the past, the residue which remained in the silence of my maturity; somewhat tarnished but deeply ingrained. A remembrance of a time when we lived in blissful ignorance; a time before we were sent to Australia to be educated and civilized, so we could return and make some progress in life back in the colony. When we left home to study abroad, we were still in the quest for adventures, and we were still seeking and finding fun in the sun. However, our idea of a golden age was now coming to an end.

# Photo Gallery

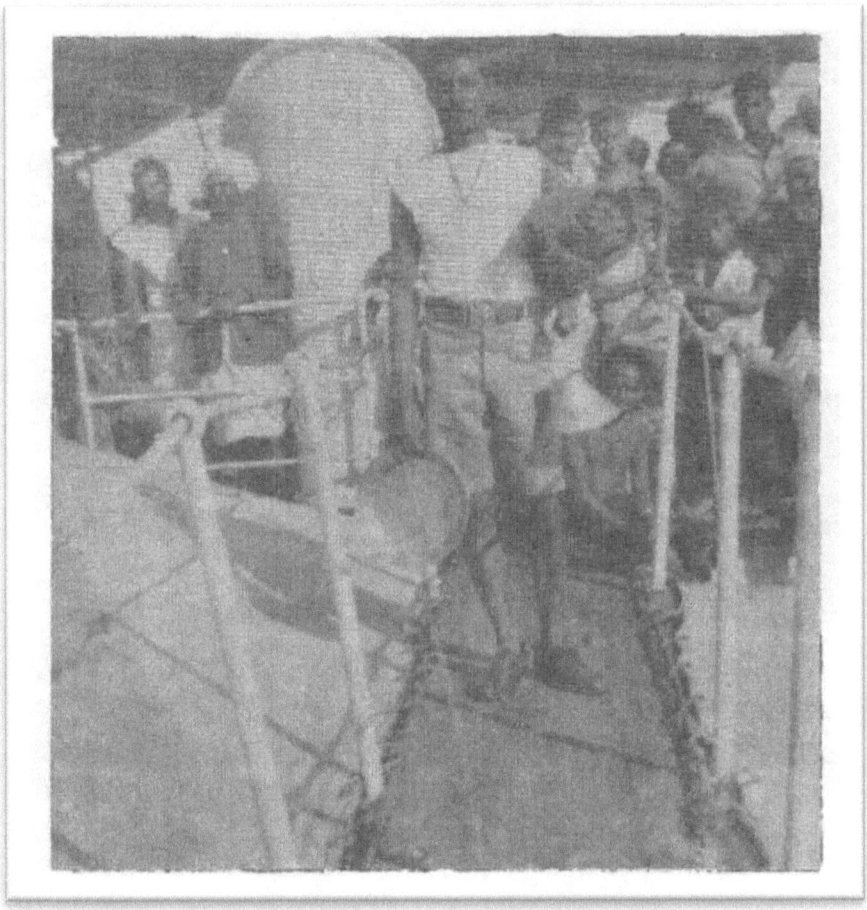

*Above*: My father boarding the *SS Ganges* garbed as an indentured labourer. Taken in in 1927.

*Above*: My father walking behind Pundit Nehru, at a meeting of the Indian National Congress in India in 1933.

# PHOTO GALLERY

Lord and Lady Atlee with my father on a visit to Fiji after World War II.

My father in Hyde Park, London, pleading for the Indians in Fiji. Taken in 1972.

Family photo taken in June 1956 when Gautam and I left Fiji.
(I am fifth from the left and Gautam is sixth from the left.)

My Kodak camera, a gift for my 14th birthday. We were
told that the Kodak brand would last for decades to come.

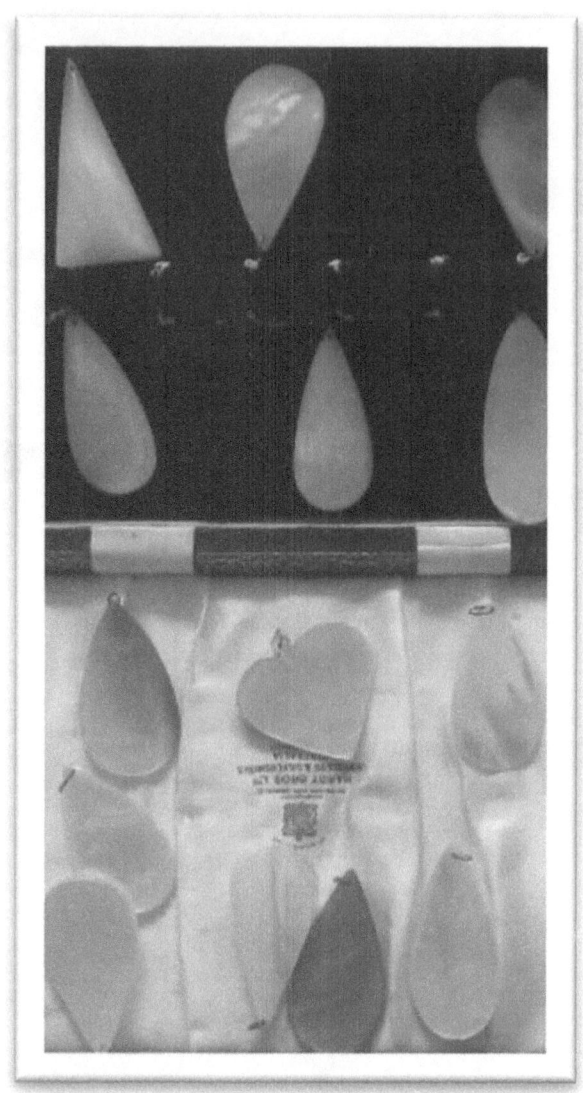

I kept these pendants as souvenirs of our pearl-shell button factory, one of the earliest industries in Fiji.

# PHOTO GALLERY

Mahatma Gandhi Memorial College for Adults, 1948
Gautam and I are sitting in the front row. See close-up below.

Same photo. Gautam is second from the left and
I am second from the right. You can see how little
we were compared to the Fijian students.

Taken with my parents when I graduated with degrees in Arts and Law in 1961.

Taken on my admission to the Bar in 1963.

With my brother Gautam whilst at the University of Queensland. Most of the childhood stories centre around him. He died when I was in England on leave.

# PHOTO GALLERY

*Left*: In 1975, I had just finished a multiple rape trial when I had to go to Fiji to see my mother. Mum wanted me to see the tribute paid to my father by Mrs Gandhi. She wanted me to pretend to sit on her lap like I did when I was little. I am holding the special award to my father from Mrs Indira Gandhi.

*Right*: Mum praying in her sacred space at home in Fiji. When I showed her a painting of Christ, given to students by the nuns, she took it and reverently put it with her other sacred objects on the board. I looked hard, but Gautam and I were not on the board.

Left: My younger brothers receiving the award and medallion from Mrs Indira Gandhi in 1982. No elders were present.

Family photo taken in our home in Brisbane in 1972.

# PHOTO GALLERY

My mum with my son, Neal Rohan (left) and my son, David Sagar (right).
Taken in Brisbane in 1985.

My mum with two of my daughters, Catherine Devi (left) and Lalita Lakshmi (right).

These are two of my sisters, Suman Kumari and Princess Sadan Devi, with Mum in 1982.

प्रधान मंत्री भवन
PRIME MINISTER'S HOUSE
NEW DELHI

Camp: Melbourne,
October 7, 1981

Dear Prince Vyas Lakshman,

    I was sorry to hear from your cable of your father's passing away.

    You and your family have my sincere sympathy and condolences.

Yours sincerely,

*(Indira Gandhi)*

Prince Vyas Lakshman,
C/o Deuba Freehold Private Mail Bag,
Suva (Fiji)

Letter from Mrs Indira Gandhi conveying her sincere sympathy and condolences on the passing of my dad, a freedom fighter from a remote British colony.

# PHOTO GALLERY

*Left*: This was taken in 1953 by a relative who had a photo studio in Fiji. I also took one on my Kodak camera, but lost that photo. The Queen drove past our home and we were only three metres away from her majesty. I thought about it when I was invited to the garden party in London in July 1991.

*The Lord Chamberlain is
commanded by Her Majesty to invite*

*Mr. and Mrs. Atray Vishal Lakshman*

*to a Garden Party at Buckingham Palace
on Tuesday, 9th July, 1991, from 4 to 6 p.m.*

*Morning Dress, Uniform or Lounge Suit*

This invitation was printed on some very hard cardboard. Buckingham Palace was swarming with lords and knights of every description. There were bishops and Commonwealth representatives too. We were told that this was a relatively small party of only five thousand guests. Normally, there were seven or eight thousand guests. Princess Di was there, only 20 metres away from Rose and me. I always liked small parties.

because it is in a city. The Trustees have their own principles but I thought I owed it to you all to tell you that your decisions are not always accepted as the best or most in keeping with Gandhiji's ideas by others. As I have said above, I have purposely refrained from writing and making suggestions and requests so far and I do not wish this to be treated as a request for reconsideration of your decision. It is only intended to give you my reaction.

Yours sincerely,
Rajendra Prasad

Shri G.V. Mavalankar
'Sewakutir'
16 Maharashtra Society
Ellis Bridge
Ahmedabad.

## 158. From Vishal Lakshman

P.O. Box 92
Lautoka, Fiji
26th January 1955

Dear Sir,

From a distant and small island of Fiji I greet you. I do feel unworthy of your notice, but the urge to write to you on India's Independence Day has made me bold—please pardon me.

I am 19, and a British citizen; a loyal subject of Her Gracious and beloved Majesty Queen Elizabeth II. Here we enjoy freedom of speech, action, and thought. And are, comparatively, in a better condition than the Indians in other Colonies. This we owe partly to India's powerful voice in the mighty world organisation, the United Nations.

We celebrate India's Day every year with all pomp and splendour fit for the occasion. Our love for Mahatma Gandhi, his courage, and his indomitable will, is unfathomed, and we now turn to you for inspiration.

Sir, I enclose some Fiji stamps as token of my deep regards to you and hope you would accept them.

Yours sincerely,
Vishal Lakshman

Dr. Rajendra Prasad
President of India
New Delhi.

I discovered this recently in a book published about the first president of India. I had written to him about a year before I came to Australia. He acknowledged it. You will see that I write glowingly about our queen. I had no idea that someone dealing with millions in India would keep my letter for his book. He wrote back personally to me. He told me that he was going to give the stamps to his grandchildren.

# CHAPTER 4: COMING TO AUSTRALIA

Many of the students from Fiji who came to Brisbane and stayed on and eventually settled here doubted whether their Australian friends and acquaintances ever knew or cared much about their beginnings and personal backgrounds. The Australians did not seem to be interested in our origins. They were struggling with the question of their own identity and destiny with the arrival of Greeks, Italians, and many others.

The Australians were mostly nice to overseas students, and these students rarely felt the sense of exclusion or blatant discrimination experienced by migrants from other parts of the world. Overseas students were seen and accepted as guests. They generally had good communication skills and mixed well with Australian students. The Australian students tended to be more cosmopolitan and broadminded than the rest of the population. We were somewhat surprised to learn that many Australian students had no time for colonial empires and wanted change. When the overseas students complained, it was mostly about the government of the day, not the people. The main area of complaint was the acute shortage of accommodation and housing after the war, which persisted into the fifties; we were competing with the migrants, the locals and everyone else for suitable accommodation.

Many of us from overseas would not have been successful in completing our university degrees without the help and kindness of the Australian people.

## MY EXPERIENCE

I was twenty when my brother Gautam and I landed in Australia in June1956; this was barely a decade after the war. It was our first flight on a plane too; we had never even been on tiny local planes in Fiji. I still remember rows of electric lights forming large squares and semicircles on the ground as the aircraft descended to land in Brisbane.

It was bitterly cold. Our hands and feet felt frozen, and we shivered all the way to Berry Street, Wickham Terrace, in Brisbane, where we lived whilst attending Brisbane Grammar School. This cold reception by the country was the harbinger of things to come later in life.

Some would dismiss the idea that Brisbane is ever bitterly cold, but when it comes to the weather, it is all relative and is in the eye of the sufferer. When Gautam and I first arrived in Brisbane it felt so bitterly cold that after several weeks we contacted our parents and told them that we wanted to return to Fiji and were prepared to work in our father's printing press rather than put up with the severe cold.

To the denizens of the tropics and the sub-tropics, even spring, the month of September, in Brisbane is still cold. By the middle of September, people are generally up and about in the early mornings in short-sleeved shirts and shorts, greeting and nodding to blushing spring. It is the time of the year described as pleasant, and the signs of emergence from a severe winter are everywhere.

Even today, after decades in Australia, the friends who visit us at home have never ceased to be amazed that in October I am still to be found huddled around the fireplace in our old colonial home seeking warmth and comfort. Our relatives and friends who live in Melbourne and Sydney take photographs of me huddled with a beanie, as tourists do when they see some peculiar sights whilst on tour. I remember when we were at university, Gautam and I missed most of the lectures on winter mornings because we could not bear to get out of bed before ten o'clock, and the poor landlady used to check to see whether we were sick.

I had never heard of Brisbane until some students from Fiji went to study at the Brisbane Grammar School in 1953, some three years before our arrival. We were determined to go to England to study, but our chequered educational background and lack of suitable qualifications made it impossible for us to get into any university in England or

## CHAPTER 4

New Zealand. In the end, the climate was the main determinant of our location for further education. Melbourne and Sydney were completely out of the picture because they were thought to be too cold. I recall us all huddling around my father as he studied a world map and drew a line on the same latitude as Fiji, pointing to Cairns as the place that he was going to send us. We had never heard of Cairns. Just imagine the dismay if a student in Queensland was told that he was to be sent to the Solomon Islands for higher education.

As it happened, there were no universities in Cairns. As his ruler slid south, we knew that we were bound for Brisbane and not Botany Bay. Decades later, and after appearing in the Circuit Court in Cairns on many occasions, I often thought that if given the same choice today, I would choose to go to Cairns, and it would not have bothered me one bit whether there were any schools in Cairns. At least Cairns is right on the beach and has coconut trees, banana plantations, cane farms and paw-paws, and it has rain and lightning. Cairns is so wet, so slushy and sloshy, so muddy and so happy, and people sweat there without putting in any effort. It is, in many ways, a place exactly like Lautoka.

I remember feeling so embarrassed about attending a school where the students in my class were so much younger than I was. I also felt uncomfortable wearing shoes and long trousers and a school tie. School prefects pulled up any student who wore his tie, shirt or coat in a sloppy way.

When we left Nadi, our mother was distressed because she feared we would be mistreated by the people. Australia was thought to be like South Africa, and she knew all about Gandhi's struggles in South Africa. The fact that she had received no education when young meant that she could not read English newspapers and Australia had a bad reputation with the Indians. It did not help that my father thought that both Menzies and Arthur Caldwell were classic examples of racists. I still remember a quote attributed to Caldwell. I do not remember the exact phrase he used, but it ran like: 'Two Wongs don't make a White'.

But my father did read a lot about Australia and liked the climate in Queensland. He reasoned that, geographically, Australia was closer than

London—in case we needed to be rescued! The experience of many overseas students showed that, to the contrary, the Australians were very supportive, and many of us would have never completed our courses but for the moral and other support we received from the local people. No wonder few wanted to go back home after completing their studies.

However, we arrived combat-ready and willing to confront prejudice and fight for our rights with our father as our role model. It was in this state of mind that we discovered the people of Irish descent had sympathy for our views and understood the seething undercurrent of resentful sentiments we harboured. We had often heard of the black Irish but had no idea what it meant; some beleaguered students thought that it was a good idea to join them!

When Gautam and I attended university, most of our friends were of Irish descent or Jewish background, and when doing Political Science, we, in a manner of speaking, kept a copy of *Das Capital* under our bed. I mean Karl Marx did look like some Indian holy man or guru; he looked unkempt and probably unwashed. I still have *Das Capital,* and it sits next to the Bible. It was just a fact that the poor and the oppressed liked the theory behind socialism.

Modern capitalism is nothing but a hybrid or fusion of capitalist and socialist principles; by any definition, capitalism is now deeply infused with socialist principles. We no longer send children to work and die in coal mines or let women and children starve. We all now believe in social justice, an unfamiliar concept to the early capitalists, who essentially believed in the winner taking it all.

In 1956 Australia, Gandhi was a pariah and a caricature for some, and sections of the Australian community may still have that view. The Australian commitment to King and Empire was echoed repeatedly by Menzies and Caldwell, the 'unsung heroes' of the so-called White Australia policy. The opponents of this racist policy were regarded with suspicion. Of course, there was no actual 'White Australia policy'; rather, Australia had a collection of laws and policies starting from the *Immigration Restriction Act 1901* that sought to keep out non-Europeans—effectively, keep Australia white. By the time we arrived in

# CHAPTER 4

Australia, these laws and policies were being gradually challenged and dismantled. But there was still a way to go.

The people in the Pacific thought that Australia was getting an easy piggyback ride on England. For Australia, the spectre of the Common Market was yet to come. Many Indians in Fiji thought that there was nothing wrong with the British Empire and that the only problem was that they had no share in it!

This was a time when Australia, with its small population, felt threatened by the yellow hordes. So, anyone of white extraction could settle here, including the Nazis and fascists, provided they claimed that they were escaping the tyranny of communism. Some two million Indians had fought for the British Empire but could not live here.

Even little children were being deported because they were not white. I recall that a decade or so after our arrival, a little girl of five, Nancy Prasad, who was an Indian Fijian whose father had not been allowed settle in Australia, was deported to Fiji (despite having family in Australia who wanted to take her). It was in August 1965. There was a public outcry, but the Immigration Minster signed the deportation order. Then, at the airport, Aboriginal leader Charles Perkins appeared from nowhere, grabbed the child and took her away.

The Menzies Government wanted Perkins charged with abduction and kidnapping. The child was eventually deported, going home to her parents in Fiji. Fifty policemen, some armed, made sure that this little martyr offered no resistance. That is why I have said that Menzies was the real 'hero' of racist policies, even if he did soften some of the harsher elements of the White Australia policy. It should not be forgotten that this man allowed atomic tests to take place in the Australian desert with scant regard for the tribal Aboriginal people. (As an aside, in 1973, the then Whitlam Government allowed a teenage Nancy Prasad to immigrate to Australia.)

Things were different in Fiji when it came to fighting for the Empire. My father, who was in the Legislative Council in Fiji, and other Indian leaders, refused to fight for the British Empire unless the Indians that were recruited to the army were paid the same as the white soldiers.

The descendants of the indentured labourers did not propose to die for the empire without an adequate share in the benefits that came with victory. This was our symbolic equivalent to the 'Boston Tea Party', our idea of no blood (taxation) without representation. The Indians wanted a proper share in the government.

The British were no slouch when it came to retaliation—they would make the Indians pay later when Fiji got independence. They would leave the Indians to the mercy of the Fijians! There is always a price to pay. There is no such thing as a free lunch in life—unless you are a politician.

## LIFE AT GRAMMAR SCHOOL

When we went to Grammar, we did not know how to cook, so we used to drink a large amount of milk in the morning, and during the morning break, we would buy sandwiches at school for our meals.

The overseas students loved the 'Grammar mothers', and I recall that in my final year I was one of the few senior students asked to address parents and teachers after dinner. While the others focused on how life was at school and thanked their teachers (load applause) and dwelt on the school's sporting acumen and so on, I spent the whole of my address extolling the virtues of the Grammar mothers and how unjust it was that, unlike the teachers, they had no common room for their use! Every time I used the term 'Grammar mothers', the place erupted in claps and cheers because most children love their mothers and love people telling them how good their mothers are. I did not have my parents present. After the event, I was surrounded by Grammar mothers who told me how much they loved their task of making cakes and sandwiches for the students

Decades have passed since I went to Grammar. Two of my sons went to my old school, and whilst they were there, my wife provided the students with the same sort of service. All Rosemary's Grammar friends, now mostly in their eighties, still have 'Grammar mother' lunches to this day!

I have good memories of our sojourn at Grammar. But two big differences between Grammar and our life in Fiji stand out in my memory.

## CHAPTER 4

During the school breaks and at lunch, the students would gravitate to their friends while my brother and I would go to the other overseas students. It is a normal thing for students to gravitate to their mates, so this is not meant as a complaint. In any case, there was a complete transformation in their approach to us, and it came about in this way.

Mr Bevan was a rigorous taskmaster in History and one of my early mentors and heroes. When he gave classes in History, the whole class was very quiet, and when he called for questions, it was rare for anyone to raise their hand—except Gautam. For example, supposing there were X number of causes for the French Revolution and Mr Bevan only mentioned one, then Gautam would raise his hand and tell Mr Bevan that he had not mentioned the others and give his view on the subject under discussion.

Sometimes the whole class would swivel around to look at Gautam, expecting the History master to put him in his place. But Mr Bevan loved this type of discussion. He never put down my brother but would mention other History books that were not on our list of books. He would do the same with me. He even invited Gautam and me to his holiday home on Bribie Island. (In those days, there was no bridge linking the island to the mainland, so it really felt like an island.)

Anyway, our popularity with Mr Bevan made us popular with our classmates. There was a complete transformation in their approach to us. Some would appeal to Gautam to keep Mr Bevan engaged in class until they completed their assignments from the previous lesson. We became good friends and in fact some of them did Law with me. Many were very good in their written work. Years later when we met at school reunions, some of them told me that I might not have got the first prize in History but for those class discussions.

The other striking difference between home and Grammar was that at home we were taught to treat all teachers and elders with reverence. So, we were surprised that students referred to their teachers by what we thought at that time to be friendly and perhaps fond nicknames. We took note of these. Mr Bevan was called 'Buster Bevan', another 'Shorty', and our English and form master was called 'Creepy'. Now, 'Shorty' was at least 6 ft 5 inches tall and the Deputy Principal.

One day one of my student friends said something to the effect that if I was going past the Deputy Headmaster's office, he wanted me to drop off something there. I went to the office and the Deputy Principal emerged. He looked at the envelope and said that it was not for him. I insisted that it was, assuring him that I had been given instructions to give it to 'Shorty'. He exploded and wanted to know who it was who had said that. I think I knew that during the war he was a Colonel or something. I had already gone through an interrogation as a child by an American MP, so I named my friend. I have no idea what happened next. I think all teachers knew their nicknames, but no student had called them that when addressing them in person.

At the end of the first year, a dramatic event ruptured my relations with my brother. He told me that, no matter what, he was not going back to school. He had had enough. I mentioned that he was a good problem-solver. So, during the holidays, he went to the University of Queensland and had a discussion with the Dean of the Faculty of Economics and Commerce (one Professor Gifford) and convinced him that, despite not having matriculated, he could easily do a university course. He was exempted from whatever the requirements were and became a university student leaving me to struggle to complete matriculation on my own!

He decided that as I was still at Grammar and he was at university and getting home late, it was my job to clean the flat and cook. I declined. He telephoned my father to complain. I stopped cooking for him and prepared only enough food for myself for a while. There was a compromise, and we went back to sharing domestic chores.

There were some other students from Fiji attending Grammar and we often talked about how on our return home, in some distant future, we would be telling our children and grandchildren about our remarkable journey to study in Australia. We wanted to leave some sign or mark to say that we had been at Grammar. It was a bit like people visiting sacred Aboriginal caves full of ancient paintings and defiling the paintings by scratching near them 'Johnny Brown was here'. Something like that.

# CHAPTER 4

We had noticed that in the Great Hall at Grammar, there were scrolls of names of students who had distinguished themselves, and this included eminent governors and judges of the State. It so happened that the first Chief Justice of the High Court, Sir Samuel Griffith, was mentioned too.

We wanted our names on the list in some small way, even if it was in a neglected corner of the Great Hall. At the end of 1956, after being there for only six months, I won the Albert Murray Smith Memorial Prize for an essay on the Economics of History. So now I had a niche in the Great Hall. You cannot imagine how pleased my father was when I sent him a glowing report of how hard the competition had been and how valiantly I had struggled to win the prize! I really went on and on until I ran out of superlatives.

In the following final year, I won a prize for the 'best English essay on a selected subject for the Empire Essay Competition'. Now I had two scratches on the Board in the Great Hall. I also won the prize for the best student in Senior History. Now I was ready to accept the challenges that awaited me at university.

But the university course was so very hard for me, and I must tell you now that all I got there, and with some difficulty, were pass degrees in Arts and Law. University examinations were tough. The only comfort I have is that some of my friends who did Law and went on to be appointed as judges also only had pass degrees.

## LOVE OF HISTORY

I have always loved history and have read almost everything written about the rise and fall of Hitler. Hardly a month goes by without there being something new about Hitler on YouTube. I also have read and re-read the following books and would like to take them with me as part of my reading list in eternity:
1. *The Lessons of History* by Will and Ariel Durant.
2. *The Historians' History of the World* by Henry Smith Williams (1903), which was in my father's library before being swept out into the ocean.

3. *The Decline and Fall of the Roman Empire* by Edward Gibbon.
4. *History of the Peloponnesian War* by Thucydides (431–404 BC) I have endless commentaries on this work. Thucydides is a historian like no other.

## YOUNG BACHELORS LEARN TO COOK

As a student, I learnt to cook on a student budget, so I shall digress here to share with you some recipes. This is Indian vegetarian cooking for men (or anyone) who would rather not cook. It is Indian cooking for beginners who have patience for only one lesson followed by practice and self-assessment only. The only prior knowledge required is knowing how to boil water. This is how students cooked when attending college, and mostly the food selected suited the student budget.

The idea is to cook three or four vegetarian dishes simultaneously (more or less) and all within 45 minutes. This entails taking shortcuts and does not include the time taken for peeling and cutting garlic and onions, which is the only time-consuming task. That could be done well in advance before the simultaneous or consecutive cooking exercise.

The ingredients used are virtually the same for each dish, so there is very little need for thought or creative thinking. Please buy all the stuff from an Indian shop in 500g packets because you can keep them for many months and even a few years without affecting the quality. In 1956, there were no such shops in Brisbane; now you see one on every corner. The good thing is that insects and other creatures have no stomach for curries.

This cooking advice is for your personal use and not for publication or distribution. It would give the author a very bad name with those who can really cook Indian food. I am mostly dealing with vegetable cooking and not meat curries. Meat curries have an entirely different combination of ingredients, and special skill is required to cook them. I cook mostly meat curries, but this would be a wasted art-form on vegetarians, who essentially are grass and gross feeders.

These observations are simply meant as passing comments on the purpose, method, structure, style, and even the philosophy of Indian cooking. It is a colonial account of what is mingled, mangled and served up and called curry. Indian cooking can best be compared with the art of painting with coloured paint, where the results are entirely the creation of the artist. Like the nearly infinite variations in the individual strokes of painters and artists, curry appears on the canvas we call a plate; we then admire this creation and consume it.

Indian cooking does not lend itself to the exact measurement of ingredients used, any more than brush strokes can be measured. Writing out recipes for Indian cooking presents some problems because printed recipes are somewhat like painting by numbers. The result is rigid, contrived and stultified. Indians do not use written recipes. Cooking is learning at the feet of mothers, grandmothers and old aunties. In European cooking, it is usual to use precise measurements: a spoon of ... half a cup of ... half a pint of ... The Indian method, like a painter with a brush, goes like this: ... take a pinch of ... a little bit of ... just a tiny bit, not too much ... etc. They use spoons but not to determine the exact amount. There are copious demonstrations; little girls cook for adults at the age of six or seven. My elder sister did a lot of cooking for us. This cooking tradition is handed down from generation to generation and is varied and chopped and changed over time.

Different families admired each other's cooking as tasting unique and different despite using the same ingredients. It was the individual colouring technique that made the difference. Take a thousand Indians, and you get a thousand variations in cooking. There are near-religious rituals that go with the preparation of food. Most cultures have a rich variation in cooking, but on magnitude and scale, no other culture is as rich as the Indian culture. The variation is infinite.

In Fiji, we were not familiar with all European cooking but knew something about English cooking, and some Indians thought there was a sharp difference—a bit like playing a game of draughts compared with chess.

Before giving you these four recipes, note these important cooking hints for Indian food:

## *Important hints*

1. The amount of water used in cooking depends on how long it takes to cook the dhal. If not cooked, keep adding a few cups of water from time to time and mash until cooked. To get the consistency of the dhal right to suit *your* taste, either add more water or, if it is too thin, just cook it longer until it is of the thickness you like. If it has been kept in the fridge for a while after cooking, then heat the food well and stir it during the heating, which will bring back all the flavours. Don't hesitate to put in a cup of water if it is dry and sticky from being in the fridge. This applies to all curries. Dhal is really a boiled soup of a sort, after all.
2. Keep tasting tiny morsels of the dhal or curry whilst cooking so you can add more salt or chillies to suit. Salt should be added initially during the cooking process itself. It will have no taste if you cook it without salt or if there is not enough salt to make it taste good. To only sprinkle salt on the food after serving does not work—the salt must permeate the food while it is cooking. Taste it many times whilst cooking.
3. Do not leave the kitchen but stay near the stove and look after and stir the different pots of food that are cooking. You must be at the stove all the time—nothing works with a timer.
4. Remember dhal is made to accentuate the flavour of the lentils and so should have very little curry powder. Some cooks use no curry powder, relying on the other ingredients for making dhal.
5. Turmeric can leave a stain on clothes that is difficult to remove by scrubbing. Just wet and leave the item in the sunlight for a few minutes, and the stain will vanish.
6. There is no need to cook all these four dishes together; two dishes at a time will be easier to handle.
7. Coriander leaves used in cooking is the secret, and when available use them liberally.
8. The other secret weapon is to use either a good bottle of white wine or several cans of beer in a very special way during preparation

and cooking; this is a slight variation to the usual method and was developed to suit the local native customs—generally, no alcohol is used in cooking. The matter is discussed later under the heading 'How to use alcohol in Indian cooking'. It tends to make even ordinary food taste good.

## Dhal

*Ingredients*:

Lentils are required, and there are many varieties. The most popular and obtainable would be mung dhal, split peas (in Hindi called *mattar*), and toor dhal.

Slowly, over time, experiment with different varieties until you find the ones you like. Deal with the dhal first because it takes the longest time to cook.

*Method*:

1. Wash 2 or 3 large cups of dhal/lentils and put them in a large pot in about 2 litres of water. Bring the pot to the boil. Then put in the following, *all at the same time* without even waiting for the water to boil:
    - (i) 1 teaspoon of curry powder *or* 1 dessertspoon of curry paste if that is handier
    - (ii) 1 teaspoon of mustard seeds
    - (iii) 1 teaspoon of cumin seeds
    - (iv) 1 teaspoon of turmeric
    - (v) 1 teaspoon of salt
    - (vi) 1 whole onion chopped
    - (vii) 4 or 5 cloves/knuckles of garlic
    - (viii) 1 teaspoon (or more) of chilli powder or real red chillies
    - (ix) some curry leaves for added flavour (optional)
    - (x) lots of coriander leaves when available—it is the coriander leaves that separate good dhal from ordinary dhal, and they can be added early or kept for the stage mentioned in step 3 below.

The important thing is that you put everything mentioned in the cooking pot as soon as you put the dhal on. That is the key to making dhal, but the next two steps are also important.

2. Whilst the dhal is cooking, grind it frequently with a potato masher to reduce it or break it up—it needs to look like a very thick pea soup. The potato masher is also useful for pushing unwanted people out of the kitchen; it has a flat surface and leaves no mark.
3. Finally, when cooked and of the right consistency, take the dhal off the stove so that it *stops cooking*, and then add the following (or use any other vegetables that you like). Chop up 1 large tomato, a cup or two of fresh or frozen beans and a good amount of coriander leaves, if available, and put in 1 or 2 tablespoons of butter/ghee/ margarine (whichever is available). Let these float on the top and do not mash; no need to cook it further—the dhal is ready.

Two or three cups of lentils would be sufficient for four to eight people. For fewer people, reduce the quantity of each ingredient. However, it is best to cook a good quantity as it will keep in the fridge for several days. It is very good on toast.

It took some time to explain all that for the dhal, but it should take only minutes to 'plonk' in all the ingredients and get the dhal going. Then you can immediately put the next lot on. I will start with salmon curry.

## *Tinned Salmon Curry*

A pot or frying pan is best, and 1 or 2 tins of pink or red salmon should be fine. Use the following quick method:
1. Put several tablespoons of oil in the frying pan and heat.
2. Add the same ingredients as listed above for making dhal in the following order: Put ingredients (i) to (v) in the pan and fry them slightly for two minutes or less, then add (vi) to (ix) and cook for a few minutes or more. No exact time is required—just do it when you are ready.
3. Add the tinned salmon after removing at least some of the skin and draining the liquid. Cook for 10 minutes or so, and it will be ready to eat.

The other previous hints about salt and chillies apply. You can add potatoes. Cut in small pieces and half-boil the potatoes before adding them to the curry.
4. The only important change for salmon curry is that the curry powder should be 1–2 dessertspoons and the turmeric 1 dessertspoon or twice the amount in the dhal.

## Tinned Corned Beef and Potato Curry (a starving student's delight!)

Take one or two tins of 'traditional' corned beef and follow all the steps for tinned salmon curry—i.e., all ingredients and times.

## Hot Easy Tomato Chutney

1. Take 1 large (800 gram) tin of diced tomatoes.
2. Then follow steps 2 and 3 for making salmon curry with the following variations:
   - Add a lot more chilli powder or real red chillies—no chillies, no good chutney.
   - Cook it until it is rendered thick.
   - Mix some powdered cornflower in water, enough to thicken the chutney (or some powdered lentil or just ordinary flour will do) and cook until 'gooey' and thick.

## Hot-Sweet Pumpkin Curry

The method and all ingredients are the same as in the salmon curry, except put in a tablespoon or more of sugar as well and put the lid on tight. Cook on very slow heat. The pumpkin will gradually melt. No water is required for cooking; just stir frequently. Add or subtract salt and chillies as required. The measure for some ingredients is as given in step 4 under salmon curry—this is important.

Whilst all this is going on, cook plain rice, which requires less-than-moderate skill. Plain rice is best for Indian cooking. You can have it with chapattis or even toast.

The whole cooking operation should take only about 45 minutes. There are many side dishes you could prepare, but something bland such as a salad or yoghurt with cucumber is sufficient.

## *General note*

To repeat, Indian cooking has a lot in common with painting as an art form. That is, when given a set of colours, the user has almost infinite possibilities for what he might paint. Even the most accomplished artist can never reproduce exactly what he did earlier. It would always vary in shades and shapes. Similarly, cooks do not measure things by 'spoons' or 'grams' but use expressions like 'a little bit of' or 'only a tiny bit', 'quite a lot of this or that'. Some cultures use exact measurements and use the timer. The difference in the result is like the artist who paints using his imagination and the one who is taught to paint by numbers. The result may look similar, but the man who paints by numbers reproduces and does not create.

It may be fashionable now but in the past, no Indians ever cooked by following written recipes. They never used recipe books. Cooking was purely from oral tradition with the scope to mix, improvise and 'paint' with the ingredients. There is no final authority or master chef in this tradition. You are the ultimate judge of what tastes good. Indians meet and discuss cooking ideas and only rarely prescribe recipes, and all cooking and reference to taste are 'local' and regional and never 'global' or universal.

Indeed, those who do creative things take a perverse delight in making mistakes! The visual image of these cooking artists should be exactly like those of witches at the cauldron we used to see in comics as children, including the witches with their front teeth missing going 'hee, hee, hee' while stirring the pot!

## *How to use alcohol in good Indian cooking*

Cooking gurus in most societies since ancient times have thought it a good idea for beginners in the art of cooking to sip a glass or two of either a good white wine or a few cans of beer whilst cooking. Alcohol is a necessary lubricant used as an accelerant on the conveyor belt of consciousness and, as such, is of some value in the cooking process. In some mysterious and inexplicable way, barely understood by modern science, this lubricant is the driver of the human creative urge; and incidentally adds to the texture, smell and taste of the food. A common experience in most cultures is that most food tastes good after a suitable number of sips of good wine, taking great care not to spill even a drop of wine on the food—waste not, want not.

# CHAPTER 5: MY LEGAL CAREER

At the beginning of 1956, I was working for my father making pearl-shell buttons and working as a compositor in his printing press, helping print newspapers for the farmers and doing small printing jobs. I was also making concrete blocks for his little building projects and bagging copra for sale to the Japanese. I studied hard at his school for adults but never sat for any examinations. The expectation I had was that at some time I would be married and languish in Fiji.

Yet that very year I found myself in Australia, and barely eighteen months later, in 1958, I had enrolled to do degree courses in Arts and Law. This is not unique. This has been true for untold numbers of people who have achieved their goals in various fields—mostly cases of opportunity colliding with ambition.

Some sages and thinkers have pondered for several millennia on such questions under nature or nurture. I think it is inexplicable without the intervention of the divine. 'There's a divinity that shapes our ends; rough hew them how we will' (Hamlet).

We all know what university life is—each generation gives a similar account. It is about trials and tribulations, and how glad we were to escape and join a lucrative field armed with a few pieces of paper to show our accomplishments.

I remember that in my second year there, I gravitated to just one more lunchtime meeting of just one more student society or association to look at the progressive power struggle between different student groups for the control and running of these bodies. I was doing an Arts course, so I went along to a meeting for the election of office bearers, taking my bottle of soft drink and some ham and salad sandwiches.

# CHAPTER 5

I was told that this was a hotly contested election between the Labor and Liberal candidates. It seemed that the votes were likely to be equally divided. So, I was startled and nearly choked on my salad sandwiches when one of my friends, who was backing Labor, nominated me! I got up to object, but he pulled me down and assured me that the idea was to divide the Liberals because I had many student friends in the Liberal camp (some of these friends went on to become members of state and federal parliaments). I wanted to tell him that I had just as many friends on the Labor side of politics, but he would not listen.

To the utter shock of everyone (especially me), I was elected President of the Arts Students Association! I had no idea what this body did. However, I found out quickly why the battle raged for the control of this student body. There were several conferences in Sydney and Melbourne, all expenses paid! So, this clueless President who could barely pay his rent and lodging was now at the head of a delegation. I went. I enjoyed. I came back. I have absolutely no memory of what was discussed but great memories of looking at that little creek that masquerades as a river (the Yarra) in Melbourne. I also had a good look at the Sydney Harbour Bridge.

The most enjoyable part was being at the centre of many functions when luminaries came to have lunch or drinks with us. The most memorable occasion was when Sir Malcolm Sargent (the great British conductor) attended a function that we held in front of the university. I was sitting next to him for over an hour, and many female students, even those who did not know me or had never spoken to me before, came over to say hello to me, no doubt in the hope of meeting our illustrious guest. I introduced them to him, and he lit up! I can tell you that I never discussed music with him.

He was interested in Fiji but spent most of the time looking around. At some point, he turned to me and said something like, 'Don't you think Australian women are striking?' I do not remember my reply. I probably said nothing because I was still in the middle of a learning curve when it came to Australian women! Some years later, my wife Rosemary told me that when she lived in London for a while, she went to several concerts where Sir Malcolm Sargent was performing. Rose recalled that many of her friends described Sir Malcolm as 'very dapper'.

Limelight is addictive and just being with Sir Malcolm was a grand opening for me. We speak about people being 'power drunk'. However, hogging the limelight is more insidious.

I next remember meeting the great British writer and commentator JB Priestly and Nobel Laureate Linus Pauling in Brisbane in 1959. Pauling had won the Nobel Peace Prize in 1952 (later, in 1962, he would also win the Nobel Prize in Chemistry). Priestly and Pauling came to Brisbane together on two separate occasions.

They were in Australia in 1959 to attend the Australian and New Zealand Congress for International Co-operation and Disarmament and Festival of the Arts, held in Melbourne. Pauling did not disguise his contempt for the Menzies Government, which prohibited anyone from a communist country from attending this conference. He spoke very highly of the trade union movement in Australia, which supported change.

In November 1959, I saw them twice. There was a public meeting in the City Hall and some fifteen hundred people gathered there despite the strong disapproval of the Australian Government. They all cheered, clapped and stamped their feet, and the police were there in force to keep the peace. The only disturbance during the three-hour meeting was the cheering and clapping. The audience voted overwhelmingly in favour of a 'declaration of hope' resolution.

When JB Priestly addressed the meeting, he had to stop many times to allow the clapping and shouting to die down. The next day, the *Courier-Mail* reported that Priestly had told the audience that it was the government and not the people that made wars and that no people he ever met wanted nuclear weapons. He wanted nuclear weapons banned. He said: 'I say clear the world of these filthy weapons!' [cheers] and he told the crowd that we now lived in a world of dossiers and telephone tapping.

I then attended a meeting organised exclusively for university students. This international cooperation group received little publicity

## CHAPTER 5

in Australia and so there were only some twenty students present. Both Priestly and Linus Pauling regaled us with stories about their recent encounters with politicians and the press.

I remember telling Mr Priestly that I had read some of his books, including one dealing with the history of literature in Fiji. I blurted out that I had thought he was dead! I knew that Nehru had openly supported this movement to ban nuclear weapons, so I wasted no time in telling him that my father knew both Gandhi and Nehru and that he had spent time in prison with Gandhi. That message went over very well, and both men spent time talking to me about Nehru and Gandhi.

Gandhi was then a figure of ridicule in Australia. I do not believe many people knew that his statue stood in Parliament Square in London. There are statues of others, too, but Gandhi is the only one there who never held political office.

It was during my university days that I met local identity, the Very Reverend Dean Baddeley. He used to visit me at my flat, and I remember cooking Indian meals for us. He did many radical things and earned the nickname 'the Racing Dean' because he went to the races in Brisbane often, sometimes in his church dress. He also raced about a lot and was often in the local news. He officiated at my marriage to Rosemary at St John's Anglican Cathedral in the heart of Brisbane in 1965. I also remember that he presided over one public gathering attended by JB Priestly and Linus Pauling, and so I got to meet them again after the meeting.

The Arts-Law course was a five-year course, and most of my time was spent attending lectures. The early sixties were a time when people in the city were mostly attired in suits, and I do not recall seeing many obese people compared to the large numbers now.

How times have changed! In those days, the pubs closed at 6 pm, and a common sight was sartorially dressed men in suits standing on the footpath finishing their beers before going home. This was a period when Asians and coloured people were not allowed to go inside a pub, and some even had notices to that effect, sometimes in offensive tones.

However, one day my brother and I decided to go into a pub to see what would happen. This was in the Brisbane inner-city suburb of West End. We never drank much at all and hated the taste of beer. We had no idea how people mixed drinks. However, in time and in keeping with the local tradition, we adjusted and embraced alcohol. We later told friends that we too wanted to be real Australians!

We walked into the pub and suddenly, as if on cue, the whole crowd stopped shouting and talking and looked at both of us. We walked to the bar and I said to the bartender that I wanted drinks for two. There was absolute silence, and everyone could hear me. The bemused bartender said: 'What do you want?' and I said: 'Could you please give us two glasses of sherry.' The whole pub exploded in laughter.

I was puzzled because I had said nothing funny and wondered why they were laughing. All we expected was that we would be told to leave. Then a scruffy large man approached us at the bar and said something to the effect: 'Here, mate, you should try the real stuff', and he ordered a beer for both of us. Others gravitated to us to find out what we did for a living and where we came from. I remember drinking that nasty stuff, which we hated in Fiji—the smell of beer was terrible to us. We both suddenly realised that no publican could throw us out with a crowd supporting us. We went back to that pub many times without the locals ever complaining.

## CALLED TO THE BAR AND ALMOST DEPORTED

I think it was in 1960 that I got articled to Owen Fletcher of Morris Fletcher and Cross. This was one of the largest and the most prestigious firm of solicitors in Australia.

Owen Fletcher was my mentor and supporter. I do not believe that I would have completed my course and advanced my career without the support of Owen and Betty Fletcher.

Article-ship involved a lot of running about delivering briefs to counsel and a lot of drafting of court orders and preparing wills and studying the laws of intestacy. However, just a year or so before completing my articles I decided to enrol and get admitted as a barrister.

# CHAPTER 5

I wanted to appear in court instead of doing the useful but tiresome work of a solicitor. Owen Fletcher helped me secure a clerical position with the Public Trustees Office, which had a section called the Public Defender's Office, which was engaged in defending cases in our criminal courts. I thought that I would have an opening in that direction. As soon as I was called to the Bar, I was put in charge of a huge conveyancing section because of my background at Owen Fletcher—and this work involved checking hundreds of wills and transfer documents!

I noticed over time that the Public Defender always made excuses for not granting me work that would take me to court and allow me to perform as a barrister. He always used the services of two other Australian barristers who worked in our office. On one occasion he worked alone for a whole month when these barristers were away and made excuses for not allowing me to go to court. He was evasive and I heard oblique remarks from others that he had no intention of giving me work that required an appearance in court as counsel. I decided to confront him, and he told me: 'You should stick to some solicitor's type of work because you will not go well with a jury.'

As he sat on the appointment committee for the office, this news was ominous. The next thing that happened was that he appointed a recently qualified solicitor who had done the Solicitors Board course to a relatively senior position, in preference to me. I appealed and all the details came out in the public arena and there was wide public criticism. Nonetheless, I lost the appeal, which was disappointing enough. But then I was dismissed from the public service. I heard talk that although I was a British citizen, because of the White Australia policy I was not eligible to work. All this despite the fact I had filled out all my details when I had applied to work in the public service. This was conveyed to me in the official language of the first order:

> I am directed to you that His Excellency the Administrator of the Government ... on the recommendation of the Public Service Commissioner has terminated your appointment ... and further advise you that you are now appointed Temporary Legal Assistant ...

And it went on to say:

> Except in the case of the termination of your services for misconduct, this appointment is terminable at any time by giving of one week's notice ...

The reason given was that under their rules I was only on a temporary visa. However, the only requirement was that the applicant had to be a British subject, and there were other British subjects from other parts of the world including racist South Africa who were white and were given employment in the government. I was entitled to vote in elections and did so as soon as I became eligible.

This was shattering news for someone who had obtained his legal qualifications under rigorous Australian standards, wanted to practise in the profession, and who had come from a little Pacific Island colony. Now I could be dismissed with one week's notice. I then found out that the government, unknown to me, had communicated with the Immigration Department to ensure that my visa was not renewed.

I wrote to the Speaker of the House (Mr Nicholson), who was a friend of Dean Baddeley, and he agreed to fight for me by asking the Premier of Queensland, Mr Nicklin, for his intervention. I pointed out that the reduction of my status to Temporary Legal Assistant would of necessity deprive me of numerous advantages, including the right of appeal against arbitrary and unjust dismissal and a right to promotion, but to no avail. There was no precedent for such arbitrary action that was taken against me. I pointed out that there were other white British subjects working for the government, and no action was being taken against them. I appealed to Jim Killen, a prominent and colourful Member of Parliament, for support and advice. He and I had studied Law at the University of Queensland. Jim Killen approached the Minister for Immigration, Hubert Opperman, who was then busy getting ready to deport a little girl of five who was from Fiji (little Nancy Prasad). Opperman replied that I had come under a Student Plan and must return home or face deportation at the end of 1964.

# CHAPTER 5

I wrote back to Jim Killen in September of 1964. I pointed out that I had a visa until the end of 1965, yet the Minister now wanted to make me leave at the end of 1964. I told him that I came under no student programme like the Colombo Plan, and so this was simply a racist act. I have this letter before me, written close to sixty years ago.

I am now bemused with what I said to Jim Killen in the last paragraph of my letter to him: 'No doubt I will see you before the annual examinations. I wonder whether you have written some of the cases for the Bar Board' [this was necessary for admission as a barrister] and went on to comment that some students had written 20-page reports, which could hardly be described as 'concise' as per the requirement.

So here I was, struggling to write the cases required for admission as a barrister and not a solicitor while being threatened with deportation. I had no idea what to do next, but my growing resolve to go down fighting can be summed up in a Western movie I saw years later where some character said: 'When the going gets tough, the tough get going.'

I decided to take the fight directly to the Minister of Immigration and to go down fighting as my father and others had done. I pointed out to the Minister of Immigration that I had not come to Australia under any Commonwealth Government Scheme but as a private student, my parents had paid for my passage and bought my books, and I worked late at night. Further, the private overseas students paid 50 per cent more fees at the university than the Australian students paid. I told the Minister that the Colombo Plan did not apply to us in Fiji. I complained that he had released his advice to Jim Killen to the State Government to enable the government to terminate my services immediately, which it did.

I have always seen a comic twist to anything that happens to me; it is some form of safety valve in difficult times. I have mentioned that instead of gaining extra time, Jim Killen's intervention meant that my visa was reduced by one year to the end of 1964. I quipped that all this happened after Jim Killen had made representations on my behalf.

It so happened that while I was writing to the Minister, Jim Killen was being admitted to the Bar. I told the Minister for Immigration that, in future, I might never use the services of Jim as an advocate! I thought that Mr Opperman would get on his bike to tell my friend Jim Killen that I was ditching him!

I cannot believe what I wrote next in this communication. This is not the way to gain friends and influence people. I must have had a death wish as far as my pleading to remain here was concerned. Would you write like this if you were pleading for mercy?

At the end of the letter, I wrote:

> Perhaps now I should ask nothing for myself. But I would plead on behalf of four-year-old Nancy Prasad who is presently being harassed by the Department of Immigration and I entreat that she be shown the same consideration that you would expect towards your children from Lakshman if, by some kaleidoscopic tilt of history, I am the Minister for Immigration of some country and they submit a case to me for consideration. I sincerely assure you that I would treat them with compassion and understanding denied to Nancy Prasad.

In the last paragraph, I expressed what I believe to this day about our system of government. I knew at that time that in many countries, I would have been deported first and given spurious reasons later. This was never true in the British system of justice. So, in the very last paragraph, I wrote to the Minister:

> Finally, I do consider it a privilege that I live in a society where you have patiently entertained my case and nothing you do to inflict further penalties on me would affect my deep appreciation of this fact.

In the meantime, I had got married, but I insisted that I would never use that fact to further my case. I had met Rosemary at university, and she had agreed to leave everything behind and follow me to Fiji. Rose was making all preparations for this eventuality. However, Jim Killen found out that we had married recently and spoke to Dean Baddeley, and Jim must have also told the Minister for Immigration. I am not sure.

The department granted me permanent resident status without much of an application. I did not have to beg like most blacks and coloured British subjects did. This development was a shock to those who were gloating over my misfortune and were waiting for me to be deported.

I asked for reinstatement to my old legal status in the public service. I also decided to expose the hypocrisy of the government.

I knew that the overseas students from Australia were seeking freedom to criticise aspects of the immigration policies and needed fodder for their cannons. I thought that in a democratic society, genuine criticism would lead to better understanding and reform.

## ASIAN AND POLYNESIAN WOMEN DEEMED PROSTITUTES

In Queensland, we had the *Vagrants, Gaming and Other Offences Act 1931*. This Act dealt, among other things, with prostitution. Prostitution was regarded as a form of vagrancy, and parts of this Act were directed at landlords who kept premises for the purpose of letting them with the knowledge that they would be used for prostitution. In short, it was an offence for the keepers of lodging houses to allow reputed prostitutes to use these places for meeting clients. Section 55(v) stated:

> Proof that any house or part of a house wherein any female of Asiatic or Polynesian race dwells, or is lodged or is found, is frequented by or is in the resort of male persons apparently not of Asiatic or Polynesian race at any time between the hours of nine o'clock in the evening and six o'clock in the morning shall be prima-facie evidence that such a house or part of the house is a brothel.
>
> The court may decide upon its own view and judgement whether any female charged or produced before it is a female of Asiatic or Polynesian race.

Notice it talks about any female 'produced' before the court, like producing a sack of potatoes. At the time, it was fashionable for white women to get suntanned, making themselves a shade darker than Chinese girls from Malaysia and Singapore. Hence, identification was more problematic!

Prostitution, as we all know, is a universal problem; therefore, one would expect the laws dealing with it to apply regardless of race, creed, or colour. It was an embarrassing blot because it failed to protect the innocent, stigmatising anyone of Asiatic or Polynesian appearance.

In this period, we were living in a new world where late-night parties were frequent, and there were large numbers of Asian and Polynesian females both at these parties and organising them. The parties were boisterous with much loud dancing and singing.

I telephoned the Editor-in-Chief of the *Courier-Mail,* who was a powerful person and, incidentally, a close friend of Owen Fletcher's, and he agreed to put the story on the second page. He was startled that the law was there. I wanted it to be a body blow to the State Government that was giving me such a hard time. It was bad enough that they were refusing to reinstate me to my legal position, but they were grudging and would not restore my seniority, and so I had to start with a loss of seniority of several years.

The *Courier-Mail* article came as a big shock to the matronly landladies who were housing these Asiatic females in their respectable private dwellings. Now they feared that their homes could be declared or deemed brothels.

The news was widely published in other states too. It so happened that there was a Commonwealth Law Conference in Sydney on at the time, and the Australian delegates were preaching to others about equal justice for all and pontificating about the rule of law in Australia. I was told that the relevant State Minister woke one morning in Sydney and, while still munching on his toast, nearly choked when he read all this in the newspaper. Delegates from many countries were attending this conference, and they sneered at the discomfort of the Australian delegates. The Pakistani delegates were emboldened to comment on their own good laws. Women's groups came out in force. I knew from my experience in Fiji that a howling mob of women is a sight to behold!

## CHAPTER 5

I sent a copy of my article to the student newspaper at the university, *Semper Floreat,* but the publishers refused to publish the article without some areas being excised. So, the editors left blank the front page with empty columns marked with the words 'We' and 'They'. I was very surprised, but later I was told that the editors had added material that was wrongly attributed to me. However, I was happy with the empty front page because it had never happened before. Sometimes any press is good for you; the good, the bad and the empty. Hundreds of students wanted to know what it was about.

I have a copy of *Semper Floreat* before me as I write. It is dated 9 September 1965. The paper has a very small article about the Law Conference in Sydney. You recall I said the Pakistanis were emboldened to speak about their good laws in Pakistan. The article read:

> An interesting idea was put forward in a paper by the Chief Justice Cornelius of Pakistan at the Law Conference in Sydney which he called 'punishment by crippling'. The Chief Justice of Pakistan told the Conference that criminals used their limbs for evil, so they should lose them for the greater good of the community. He concluded 'Modern surgery would make this easy'. He relied on statistics in his part of the world and pointed out the low theft rate in Arabia where the punishment for it was cutting off both hands.

I knew that many little shopkeepers who were robbed and bashed with some regularity would have pleaded for this method of punishment for a short trial period.

I knew some women in the community who read the speech of Chief Justice Cornelius of Pakistan, and they wanted to know what the punishment was for sex offences in Arabia. I know that they had some very creative ideas on punishment for sex offenders! I hate to think what will happen in the future when they dominate Parliament.

## THE JUSTICE DEPARTMENT

In the meantime, after my article on Asian women, the Public Curator's Office had just about had enough of me and decided to throw me out of the frying pan into the fire. I was told by my friends that I might be put before a firing squad because I had applied for and was now transferred to the Justice Department in the Solicitor-General's Office. I remained there until I retired in 1992. The standard of performance was very high, and it is no reflection on the Solicitor-General that I had to spend time doing prosecutions in the Magistrates Courts.

I was then told that I was being transferred to the new Public Defender's Office, which was now being run by a highly experienced trial lawyer who had been a skillful Crown counsel. I have no idea what happened to the Public Defender who would not let me go before a jury.

I was immediately given a robbery case, which was a re-trial. These can be messy to deal with, as there are volumes of material from the previous trial. I had my gown, but my wig had not arrived from London. I was worried about this and wanted to buy some time. So, I told the Public Defender that perhaps I might do the next trial and wait for my wig. He smiled and said I could use his wig!

This was the first time I had appeared in the criminal court as counsel. I was confused, and when I walked into the court, my ears were buzzing.

There were some thirty or forty on the jury panel. Also appearing for the Crown was a tenacious and able counsel who later became the Chief Crown Prosecutor and then was appointed a judge of the District Court. We later became good friends, and he wrote a wonderful letter to me when I retired. I still have it with me. The defence feared him. At the Bar, he was known as 'Killer Miller'! Now I had him as counsel for the Crown in my very first case. As if I didn't have enough problems already. The jury was selected mostly by him because before I could think of challenging a candidate, the candidate was being sworn in.

This was a case of armed robbery, and the accused was a Sicilian Italian whose name sounded like 'Jahko Montenio'. He was charged with robbing a jewellery shop in the Valley in Brisbane. When the police raided his home, they found the place dripping with precious jewellery, and this was placed on the bar table by the prosecution.

# CHAPTER 5

In the past, I had frequently interviewed prisoners who told unlikely stories. The accused told me that he had never stolen anything and that the police had planted all the jewellery on him! He was married to an attractive Irish woman, and they had four little children. She wanted to know whether she could come into court with her children because she had no babysitter. I told her that the courts were open to the public and, as far as I was concerned, she and her children could come and sit in the public gallery. I told the accused that if he gave evidence, he had no chance of an acquittal because he would be cross-examined by a highly experienced prosecutor. The accused wanted to give evidence. I thought, *Oh God, why did I have to get this as my first case!* When the Crown case was being opened, I was so busy flipping the pages of the depositions that I did not hear much of the opening. But whilst sitting at the bar table and staring at the jewellery on the bar table, I decided on a possible attack. The accused had told me repeatedly that 'the cops call me Al Capone all the time'. The police evidence was that during the interview he kept telling them that he was known as 'Al Capone of the Valley'.

When the first police investigator gave his evidence, I rose to cross-examine him. I pointed to the accused and put to him that he had lied when he said the accused walked into the interview room and told the police that he was Al Capone of the Valley. I asked him if there were other police officers present, and he said at least three others, perhaps more, had heard the accused say that. I told the prosecutor I wanted all the witnesses who had heard the accused speak those words to be called. So, some six or seven police officers were called, and they all swore that they had heard the accused say that he was known as Al Capone of the Valley.

Meanwhile, the wife of the accused was sitting in the back of the court with her young children. When the children screamed for daddy, she would hush them and take them outside, returning shortly afterwards, and the same problem would recur. This very senior Crown prosecutor told me that I should ask the wife of the accused to leave the courtroom permanently because the jury kept looking at the children. I told him that that was his problem and that, in any case, I would object to any attempt to prevent her from hearing the case. It was an open court.

When the Crown case concluded, I called the accused, and he kept on repeating the unlikely story that he had not stolen anything, and he kept pointing to the police and saying repeatedly that they had called him Al Capone. I had no idea why he was so worked up about this.

Mr Miller gave a very impressive address and canvassed all the evidence that pointed to the guilt of the accused. I could still hear the distracting children in the background.

I then rose to address the jury. I told the jury that fabrication of evidence was endemic. It was being reported frequently in the newspapers and repeatedly the accused had complained of it. I told them even little lies can make a big difference in a case and that if the jury believed the accused that the police had lied, then they must also consider the possibility that one day a member of their own family or a friend could be convicted on lies told by the police. I told the jury that it was better for society to let some guilty go free than to have the police fabricating evidence to seek a conviction and that, unlike hardened criminals, innocent persons were more susceptible to bullying. I said that this case was not only about the accused but about their values. If they found the police were fabricating evidence to link this Sicilian accused to another notorious Sicilian, then they should not reward the police by finding him guilty. I pointed out how easy it was for the police to parade witnesses and asked whether they believed that so many would have heard the accused.

Finally, I pointed to the accused and said that he could not speak much English. I pointed out that he was a Sicilian who was now seeking the type of justice that you would like if you were in a foreign country and you could not understand what the police were saying to you, but they gave evidence that you repeatedly told them you were 'Ned Kelly from Australia'. I told the jury that this was not a case about the accused alone; rather, it was about the betrayal of our system of justice.

There was a fair summing up by the trial judge, and the jury retired to consider its verdict, returning a verdict of not guilty and glaring at the police. I was very surprised. The judge then made the usual order for the return of the stolen property to the rightful owner. The accused tugged the arm of my clerk and wanted to know whether that meant that he could take all the jewellery back home with him!

I then did something that I never did again. In a light vein, I told a shocked Crown prosecutor that the accused wanted his jewellery back. He exploded because he thought I was being serious. After that, I seldom commented on jury verdicts again. The moral of this case is that a sophisticated society would not have police concocting evidence. Frankly, that was the only bit that I believed when the accused gave his account. I often told the investigators that if the jury believed the police were lying, they should not convict even in a murder case.

## ENGLISH OUR MOTHER TONGUE AND SCOTLAND YARD

There was a prevalent perception from my early childhood that the bobbies in England were the best policemen in the world. The British institutions, such as the Parliament and the Judiciary and the nature of the functions performed by these institutions, had a certain appeal to the Indians in most of the British colonies, the world over. The Indians tended to learn the ropes at the feet of the British, whether it was about the way that parliamentary democracy functioned or the importance of an independent judiciary or the need for the English language as the ultimate weapon. Language is the most insidious and the ultimate tool of destruction devised by man.

Language is venerated as the means of communication within and between cultures; so, it happened that in many parts of the world the English language became the lingua franca, and this was true of the Indians. It is one of the official languages recognised in the Indian Constitution. I understand that some 300 million people in India speak English. There was absolutely no point in swearing and cursing in Sanskrit or Hindi when the Indians who had some 300 major regional languages had difficulty in communicating and understanding each other in Hindi and Sanskrit. The new lingua franca had such flexibility that it allowed them to use expletives with creative zeal in their conversations; even the illiterates found that they could speak English when cursing and cussing.

The great Indian thinkers and politicians acquired this new tool for communication, sometimes for the sole purpose of securing the destruction of the British Empire, or at the very least its transformation into a more humane and acceptable empire. Language is the destroyer of cultures and traditions of whole nations and peoples, and this was known in the modern period at least since the Spanish missionaries followed in the wake of Pizarro and other conquistadors to first lull the natives of the Americas with a new language and a new message from the Book, and then to destroy it. Such a fate now awaits the European languages.

Language is also a tool of deceit and deception, and lawyers are accustomed to all this and waste no time discussing and debating it. The tendency is to disguise the simulation under the heading of 'legal precedent'; if that is not pontifical enough, they try 'ratio decidendi'. The ritual of the barristers dressed in white wigs and black gowns and with judges dressed in fancy red gowns with sharp-coloured sashes all add to the solemnity of the proceedings. The Brahmin priestly caste does something similar with great success in the Indian community.

The Indians in the British Empire were knee-deep in adapting the use and practice of this new weapon called English, and one of their main objects was to obliterate or transform the British Empire. And in some colonies, there was much confusion about where the true interests of the Indians lay. There were countless stories of Indians who wanted the transformation and not the destruction of the British Empire. This preoccupation with things British was almost verging on a true 'fetish' because Nehru and Gandhi were the living examples of the infatuation of Indians with British institutions and English as a language.

I have written that my father was imprisoned with Gandhi after the Salt March. The Indians wanted independence for India but were clinging to British ideas and political and judicial institutions. What else could explain that after all the struggle for independence and after launching

## CHAPTER 5

the 'Quit India Movement' and after all the fighting for 'Swaraj', and after inventing and unleashing one of the most destructive secret weapons for social change and reform, namely the Civil Disobedience Movement, they wanted to retain many British traditions.

They dressed like the English and spoke English and even tried to copy their squeaky voices. Gandhi's Civil Disobedience Movement was the precursor of all modern sit-downs. It started a chain-reaction leading to the collapse of many other colonial empires. Indians were now actively engaged in shaping and creating the new 'Commonwealth of Nations'. This was to have all the formal trappings of the British Empire with the Queen of England as the Head of the Commonwealth.

This was a new 'genetically engineered' social club of nation-states, much like Her Majesty's Garden Party. I know because I attended one when I went to London. Just as a camel was designed by a committee, so the new, knackered, heavily castrated eunuch version of the British Empire came into being as the new Commonwealth of Nations.

The Empress of India now appeared in the proverbial 'king's new clothes', and the Indians wanted to belong to this new creation. Indian parents in the colonies were sending their children overseas to study and expecting them to return and become perfect sahibs and memsahibs, and public servants were just as they were in *Yes, Minister*.

Thus, it happened that, in dire need of help in solving our corruption problems, the Minister for Police entreated help from Scotland Yard. Our love of things British made us think of Scotland Yard as a law enforcement agency, a cut above all the rest in the world; and some thought it as peerless. We were disappointed!

I must digress, which is in the nature of ageing, by mentioning how the Civil Disobedience Movement started by Gandhi empowered the unwashed, the greenies, the hippies, the down-trodden and the poverty-stricken. All they now needed was to gird themselves in loincloths and arm themselves with a few meaningful slogans on a placard and shout in unison 'When do we want it?' and after a pregnant pause bellow: 'NOW'. This was enough to unsettle most entrenched law-and-order institutions. The legal profession is generally trained to love law and order because this is essentially a bread-and-butter issue for the members of the legal fraternity. This exclusive guild, like those in the Middle Ages, was designed to resist change and protect its members.

It would be churlish and grossly unfair to leave the women out of this fracas when referring to the peaceful civil disobedience movements spawned by Gandhi. After all, as I said, Gandhi when asked to give an account of how he happened to stumble on this new tool, which can be comprehensively called the sit-down-on-your-bottom movement, made no secret of the fact that he got the idea from the women's suffragette movement in England and the women generally supported these new Gandhi-inspired sit-down-on-your-bottom type of weapons for a change; some even had suitably big bottoms, giving additional weight to their arguments.

It seemed that anything that rattled the men was good enough for the women.

Suddenly, various women's liberation and libation movements sprang up, upstaging Gandhi with his loincloth tricks. Never slow when it came to fashion changes, women the world over simply threw away their bras; some were prepared to disrobe completely for the sake of a good cause.

The men of my generation marvelled at these events, and they ogled and complained in that order. The priestly castes in Australia, of all denominations, including the Anglicans and the Catholics, thought that they were lucky to have survived this experience. As for the new Women's Libation Movement, the last I heard was that now the police drag semi-clad women from the gutters in front of hotels!

This may appear to be a completely unnecessary digression from the very serious topic under discussion, but life is nothing if not one long continuous digression. It may also explain the individual motives and actions of colonial Indians who settled in Australia!

Now back to Scotland Yard. English practices were adopted everywhere, and this may also explain the deep sense of veneration for and admiration of British institutions, such as Scotland Yard. This may also be true for the Australians born before World War II. Scotland

# CHAPTER 5

Yard was an institution shrouded in fact, fiction and myth: a potent combination out of which legends are born.

I had read about Scotland Yard long before coming to Queensland in 1956. That may account for the disappointment and frustration that I felt when dealing with Detective Chief Superintendent O'Connell of Scotland Yard during a corruption trial in 1975 that went for six months (see Southport Betting Case and Herbert's Trial). The Crown felt betrayed and made no bones about it. A decade later, the Fitzgerald Royal Commission recalled the Chief Superintendent and subjected him to a severe grilling over what happened.

I had several instances of contact with Scotland Yard during my career as a Crown prosecutor. Later, I mention the murder trial in Cairns, Queensland, *R v Weissensteiner*. There the accused was charged with the murder of two persons, an Englishwoman and an Austrian adventurer. She had the money, and he had the time, and both fell in love. They had bought a yacht and were going to sail through the Pacific and Indian oceans. They disappeared, and their bodies were never found. The vessel, which was lavishly furnished, was finally located some 5000 kilometres away in the Marshall Islands with most of their personal belongings either still on board or in the possession of the accused. The missing couple and their fate became the subject of a prolonged and extensive investigation stretching over a large part of the Pacific Ocean. Extensive searches lasting several years were conducted in England and Europe. There were numerous communications between the police investigators in Queensland and Interpol and Scotland Yard.

After securing a conviction, I received a plaque from Scotland Yard in appreciation of the effort made by the prosecution in *R v Weissensteiner*.

Plaque received from Scotland Yard for *R v Weissensteiner*

I was unsure how I should regard this 'recognition' because, in modern policing, reformed inmates in prison and drunk informants are also given awards and recognitions. Some of my children think that they give things like that to boy scouts. However, I have kept it with the other trinkets I have collected going back to my childhood, such as the Kodak camera given to me at the age of 14.

The startling disclosures and revelations in the Fitzgerald Inquiry hearings—held a decade after the Southport Betting Case and Herbert's Trial—had a stunning and sobering impact even on those inured to political scandals and other shenanigans. I was now a Senior Consultant Crown Prosecutor in the Office of the Director of Public Prosecutions.

I had spoken to the lead counsel in the Fitzgerald Inquiry at an early stage and had given him copies of memoranda and other communications between me and the Solicitor-General and the Attorney-General. This involved the lack of ethics and some questionable practices used by these Scotland Yard detectives.

The Fitzgerald Report led to a parade of corrupt police officers and corrupt politicians. These were publicly exposed and disgraced and finally tried and sent to prison. I had no reason to be present to witness their deserved discomfort and disgrace. The outcome and the final report were most satisfying to all those who had struggled hard in the Southport Betting Case and Herbert's Trial. There was no conviction in that trial because a member of the jury had been bribed.

It was only when I read the Fitzgerald Report soon after it was released that I realised the extent of misinformation, distortion and deception and especially the lack of candour on the part of these officers from Scotland Yard. At this time, I spoke briefly to Tony Fitzgerald QC on the telephone, mostly to congratulate him and his team on such an outstanding outcome. He wondered how some of us had survived the corruption trial period. It was after this inquiry that a series of prosecutions were launched against the corrupt police and politicians. It was then that I realised that the role played by these corrupt police was much murkier than I had thought.

## CHAPTER 5

Detective Chief Superintendent O'Connell had come to Brisbane in late August 1975 accompanied by another Detective Superintendent at the request of the Police Minister with the consent and approval of the Commissioner of Police at that time. There is no doubt that the Fitzgerald Inquiry, which had access to much more evidence and material, would be more reliable on how and why the investigators came to Brisbane. There is every reason to remember this because at the very heart of the prosecution strategy was the intention to put the corrupt police, against whom there was sufficient evidence, on trial and resist any general inquiry until all the corruption trials were over. That is exactly what happened. The strategy for the other side, led by the Premier of the State, was to have an inquiry first and then in a sea of confusion with allegations and counter-allegations there would have been no way to prosecute anyone because both the guilty and the honest police would be making allegations against each other!

I was aware of this. With the approval of the Solicitor-General and the Attorney-General, we had committal hearings and told the State Government that these matters were now in court, and no one should interfere in such court proceedings.

In Crown Law, we had no idea why these gentlemen from Scotland Yard were invited. We first read about it in the newspapers. It came as a complete surprise to the Crown Law Office. The Solicitor-General had no idea. I spoke to both Assistant Commissioners, Norman Gulbransen and Superintendent William Taylor, and both told me that they had no idea at all why Scotland Yard had been invited before the pending trials were completed.

I understood at the time that the invitation to Scotland Yard was conceived entirely by the Police Minister whilst he was in London and that the Police Commissioner (Mr Whitrod) might have agreed with him out of a sense of loyalty. Mr Whitrod had neither initiated nor encouraged this move, nor did he have much of an idea as to how the services of Scotland Yard would be used.

The two Assistant Commissioners had no idea what was in progress. They phoned me because the Scotland Yard inspectors wanted to see the evidence in the pending corruption matters, and they were aware that I had reservations about that. The committal hearings had been completed by the time they arrived, and I had serious objections to Scotland Yard meddling in these matters.

I had a meeting with Detective Chief Superintendent O'Connell and Detective Chief Superintendent Fothergill at the Crown Law Office. (A case of too many chiefs and only one Indian!). Assistant Commissioner William Taylor met them and was scathing about their purpose and competence, and someone else referred to their method of interviewing other police, making frequent references to these 'keystone cops'. I wanted to know something about the scope of their role and what they intended to do. I gathered that they had no clear idea at this time but wanted to have access to the committal hearing depositions in the corruption matter and the transcript of the proceedings in the Southport Betting Case, which was on appeal to the Full Court.

I interviewed them and told them that they were not to interview any witnesses who gave evidence in the corruption committal proceedings or even prospective witnesses in any other pending corruption matters. They agreed to abide by this direction. I wrote a memorandum to our Solicitor-General, Thomas Parslow QC, outlining this discussion and informing him that both had agreed to abide by this. The importance of this objection by the Crown would be apparent to those in the legal profession. As the story unfolds, those uninitiated in the rituals of the criminal justice system will see why it was important. The meeting lasted approximately one hour, and that was the only time that I saw these two sleuths from Scotland Yard. They never contacted Crown Law in person again.

It appeared from various reports that in their normal quest for information and clues and to do what investigators are required to do, these Scotland Yard inspectors ranged far and wide, including pleading with suspected police to put their hands up if they were involved in graft and corruption! As if they would.

It appeared as things progressed that through accident or design, these two senior detectives had more sustained contact and association

# CHAPTER 5

with police who were thought to be corrupt or with their cronies and associates in the State Government. One of them was a former police officer and at the time a Cabinet Minister with the surname Lane. The honest police called him 'Shady Lane'. This caused concern and alarm, mostly among the police officers in the Crime Intelligence Unit.

The Scotland Yard investigators were feted and entertained at social and public gatherings such as at cricket matches and race meetings. They were also allegedly sought out and cultivated by those bent on undermining the police investigations. Even if that were true, there was nothing wrong with it because police do not get information by going to church gatherings and meeting the local nuns. They talk to madams in brothels and, provided they do not expect to get freebies in the brothels, there is nothing wrong with that. So, socialising with corrupt police is not in itself wrong.

I was acutely aware that attempts could be made to undermine other prosecution witnesses, and I canvassed this in the earlier discussions I had with the Solicitor-General. This was an extremely serious issue. There was the possibility that dishonest police could concoct and dovetail their evidence to somehow fit in with the prosecution evidence and that this could have been done in such a way as to result in an acquittal of all or some of the offenders awaiting trial. Indeed, something like that did happen when some police officers came to the trial to support the corrupt officers.

I had also noticed on several occasions during the early period that copies of some of these urgent memoranda were mislaid or went missing from my room, and I was unable to find them.

The first sign that Scotland Yard was attempting to ignore the undertaking given to the Crown Law Office that no attempt would be made by Scotland Yard to interfere or deal with matters before the courts—which included the Crown appeal to the Full Court in the Southport Betting Case—came when the Commissioner of Police (Mr Whitrod) wrote to the Justice Department seeking copies of the deposition in the Southport Betting Case and transcripts of the proceedings during the committal hearings of the corruption trial of Herbert and others. These were the very matters I had declined to give Scotland Yard. According to the Deputy Police Commissioners, Scotland Yard was prepared to give these new statements to the solicitor for the corrupt police while refusing to give them to the Crown!

The Attorney-General was advised by the Solicitor-General that the evidence being collected by Scotland Yard was not given to the prosecution but made available to the defence! This is part of the communication to the Attorney-General by the Solicitor-General on my advice:

> Mr Lakshman, Crown Prosecutor, who has the conduct of a number of prosecutions against police officers, advises me that he is concerned that his cases may be prejudicially affected by other enquiries proceeding in relation to the Police Department.
>
> You will recall that when I became aware that two officers from Scotland Yard had been given the task of conducting certain enquiries in relation to the Police Force, I was concerned that the activity of this Office in studying material supplied by the Commissioner of Police, evaluating it and advising as to appropriate charges, followed by the actual conduct of prosecutions, should not be prejudiced or affected by such other enquiries.
>
> Subsequently, Mr Lakshman saw Chief Superintendent O'Connell of Scotland Yard and advised me that he had made our attitude clear, pointing out that there should be no conflict or overlapping that would delay or prejudice the pending prosecutions. He advised me he had been quite specific as to the areas involved.
>
> Mr Lakshman now informs me that he became aware subsequently that some members of the Police Force were under the impression that they could talk quite freely to the Scotland Yard officers with some immunity from any subsequent action against them. However, Chief Superintendent O'Connell

## CHAPTER 5

stated that though his enquiries were on a confidential off-the-record basis, no actual promise of immunity had been made.

It now appears that some at least of the prospective witnesses in Mr Lakshman's prosecution matters have been re-interviewed by Scotland Yard officers and in at least one case an officer, X, has resiled from his previous statement. When Mr Lakshman asked the Commissioner of Police for the additional statements resulting from those further inquiries it appeared that this material was being treated as confidential by the Scotland Yard officers and was not available to the Commissioner or, therefore, Mr Lakshman.

I desire to point out that it is the duty of the Crown Prosecutor to assess all relevant material in the preparation of his case and to determine what shall be put before the Court. He is also under a duty to supply certain information, if he does not propose to adduce it himself, to the defence. It is extremely difficult for the Crown Prosecutor to carry out his role properly if he does not have full access to all the material available to the Crown.

Mr Lakshman informs me that each person giving a statement to the Scotland Yard officers is being supplied, as one would expect, with a copy of his statement. Apparently, those persons are being interviewed in the presence of their Solicitors, and a number of Police Officers who have given statements have been accompanied by the same solicitors who are already acting for certain Police Officers already charged with criminal offences. It appears that the defence is thus in the possession of material obtained on behalf of the Crown but not in fact available to the Crown, certainly not to the Crown Prosecutor.

Assuming Mr Lakshman's view of the situation as he has discussed it with me is correct, I am concerned that the Crown might eventually be subject to judicial criticism if the Crown

> Prosecutor can be shown not to have informed the Court of relevant material in the possession of the Crown.
>
> I have no control over this matter as the enquiries by the Scotland Yard officers are quite independent of this Office. I can do no more than ask the Commissioner of Police to supply this Office with all the necessary material and he cannot supply what has not been supplied to him.
>
> In my opinion the Crown should not be put in the position of appearing to be party to any concealment of evidence in relation to a charge against any person but in the present situation my Crown Prosecutor can do no more than act upon the material supplied to him.
>
> Signed: Solicitor-General

The two officers from Scotland Yard suddenly returned to London, and they took all statements and other material with them! Thus, the Commissioner of Police was not able to supply the Crown with any further material. The Crown is not aware of the relevance or otherwise of any other statement that Detective Sergeant X had given to Chief Superintendent O'Connell allegedly withdrawing his earlier statement given to Assistant Commissioner Taylor, which I intended to use in the pending criminal proceeding. I was anxious to know if X had changed his story.

Now before the corruption trial commenced, the Chief Crown Prosecutor was leading the prosecution, with me as his junior, and he had interviewed X who appeared to be a vital witness. X gave us his recollection of his conversation with Chief Superintendent O'Connell on a material aspect. Naturally, we were anxious to learn what he had told the officers from Scotland Yard before deciding to call him as a witness for the prosecution. The Commissioner of Police was kind enough to contact Scotland Yard and the relevant portion of the material was received by telex direct from London. We then discovered some variance between the recollection of Detective X and the material

## CHAPTER 5

supplied by Chief Superintendent O'Connell. The variance seemed insignificant, but as often happens in a criminal trial it is difficult to make such a judgement at an early stage.

I understood that Assistant Commissioner Taylor, with the approval of the Commissioner of Police, then telephoned London and spoke to Chief Superintendent O'Connell, pointing out the disparity that existed. O'Connell could not recollect the conversation and did not have a record of it. In the circumstances, we accepted the variation given by Detective X because at least he was certain. One could only hope that there would be more certainty in other statements that had been taken by Scotland Yard.

I cannot be precise on the words used, but this conversation was taped and the Chief Crown Prosecutor, LG Martin QC, and I have heard it played back to us. Needless to say, the defence counsel seemed to have more opportunity of access to the material in the possession of Scotland Yard than had the Crown, and this aspect received attention in an earlier memorandum to the Solicitor-General:

> Should you consider it necessary to alert the Honourable the Minister for Justice of the fact that the telephone conversation between Assistant Commissioner Taylor and Chief Superintendent O'Connell was taped (and I think we should) then this should be kept very confidential especially as it may alienate the Officers from Scotland Yard who (according to the newspaper reports) are expected back in a few weeks' time. it appears that the officers from Scotland Yard are not accountable to the Commissioner of Police because the Commissioner of Police has indicated in clear terms that he is not able to supply the Crown with material that may prove relevant in the prosecution of the pending matters.
>
> As you would appreciate, the question of relevance is always a matter for the Crown in criminal proceedings and not for investigating police officers. It is patently obvious that these officers are not accountable to the Crown and in the circumstances, nothing can be done to obtain these statements

to assess relevance, if any. It would be an embarrassment should it emerge that some of those statements are relevant and have not been made available to the defence and as I have indicated save and except the X statement of which I had prior knowledge and on the production of which I have repeatedly insisted, nothing has been made available to the Crown. I suppose this is a classic example of a very secret investigation.

I would be pleased if you would bring these matters to the attention of the Honourable the Minister for Justice and Attorney-General and give us whatever direction you consider necessary in the circumstances.

A.V.L. 30-5-1976.

I give all that as a brief illustration of what happens in a political trial. Most of the lawyers in Crown Law do not play politics and let the pieces fall where they will. I did not. I was going to engage with the corrupt police. See more about this in Southport Betting Case and Herbert's Trial in the next chapter.

# CHAPTER 6: LEGAL CASES

The act of mulling over cases from the past is not always productive; perhaps it is meant only for those with a touch of nostalgia for necromancy—or in urgent need of regurgitation, which is onomatopoeically unpleasant right up there with gargling and belching. It may be an invitation to further genuine controversy and confusion.

You will see that most of the cases I deal with here happened in a period of some five or six years before my early retirement in 1992. I had done the same sort of work for some twenty-five years more before my retirement, so I will begin with earlier cases.

## THE SOUTHPORT BETTING CASE AND HERBERT'S TRIAL (1975)

By the 1970s, I must have reached a level of sophistication in my work such that the Attorney-General and the Solicitor-General of the State trusted me with the handling of political trials that led first to the fall of the reforming Police Commissioner (Mr Whitrod) and then to the conviction of corrupt police and politicians who went to prison.

I was entrusted to appear in cases before the High Court in some matters; many more brilliant barristers have gone through life without ever appearing before the High Court. Ironically, I appeared for the Public Service Department in several appeals for promotion of very senior appointees, including one who became Deputy Public Service Commissioner and later was put in charge of Corrective Services. We still meet for lunch from time to time. To think some on the Public Service Board had worked hard to dismiss me from the Service.

This is a case study of corruption in the police force. Corruption can never be wiped out because it is in the human gene. I have briefly given the story of a jury trial that lasted six months. I appeared with the Chief Crown Prosecutor in that case.

This is a brief study of what is now known as the Southport Betting Case. The Fitzgerald Inquiry of the late 1980s regarded this as one of the defining moments in the battle between good and evil.

There is no point in conducting a re-hearing the Southport Betting Case after some 45 years, nor of the corruption trial that followed and lasted for six months. The main purpose here is to show the cynical way in which the corrupt police used the tools of a democratic system to subvert the outcome of a criminal trial.

This was a case in which the corrupt police used the sanctuary of the magistrates court as a public forum to destroy the character of honest police because anything said in open court, unless prohibited by the court, can be used by the news media. No trial is conducted in secrecy and in the past there were some examples of convictions that were set aside because the doors of the court were closed, and the public had no access. The courts are open and here the corrupt used the forum of the court to mount a vicious campaign against the honest police officers who were determined to clean the stable and the stench that was the Licensing Branch; this Branch also controlled brothels in Queensland.

The real purpose of the corrupt police was to smear and vilify these honest police under the privilege and protection that is available in a court. Anything said in court may be published by the press, and it was impossible to sue anyone for defamation for merely giving evidence under oath in court. The intention of the corrupt police officers in this case was to manoeuvre to seek some vague inquiry and to stop the prosecution case that was about to start; the one that eventually went for six months. In most such inquiries, both sides blame each other and recommendations for reform are made but no one is prosecuted. It was fashionable for the corrupt in society at the time, when under pressure, to seek a government inquiry with vague terms of reference.

# CHAPTER 6

There was a view shared by many practising lawyers that generally the outcome was unsatisfactory and did not address any of the underlining issues that had led to the setting up of the inquiry in the first place. It was essentially an issue of design failure of such inquiries. This problem still persists and is true of some recent public inquiries.

So, it was the design failure of the process itself that was at the heart of the complaint and was not meant as a reflection on the good motives or intentions of those who participated. The main grievance was that it failed to address or deliver a satisfactory solutions to endemic corruption in the police force.

However, a matter of more immediate concern was that some members of this corrupt police had good public relations with the media and had a habit of suing people when attempts were made by critics, journalists and other commentators to expose them thorough articles and media statements.

The Crown was fortunate that there were articulate and impressive journalists and writers who made the difference. I believe that the most dedicated and formidable amongst them were Quentin Dempster and Evan Whitton. Quentin Dempster in his book *Honest Cops* and other writings, and Evan Whitton in his books *The Hillbilly Dictator* and *Can of Worms II,* attacked the endemic police corruption and I really believe, with the benefit of the passage of time, that Quentin and Evan made a difference to the reforms that came after the Fitzgerald Inquiry. I retain a memory of them as good advocates in the pursuit of justice. I remember that one of the books Evan published was launched by a High Court judge. I had kept in touch with Evan until his wife became very ill. He used to teach History and we discussed and argued more about History than Law.

I often told Desmond Sturgess QC, who had appeared for the other side in these cases, that he won a few early battles but that the Solicitor-General, Thomas Parslow, and I eventually won the war. The corrupt Police Commissioner and many politicians were finally convicted and sent to prison. None of the police officers who were attacked by them were tried and convicted. I fought for the honest police to the end and had the satisfaction of seeing them vindicated in the Fitzgerald Inquiry Report.

The proceedings in the Southport Betting case lasted some three weeks and the depositions consisted of some 2500 pages. A good portion of this material consisted of legal submissions and sustained exchanges between competing counsels. There were two counsel for the defence and I appeared for the Crown. All this happened in 1975.

The legendary Des Sturgess appeared for at least one of the accused. I knew Mr Sturgess because I had appeared as Crown prosecutor in several criminal trials in which Sturgess had appeared for the defence. Subsequently, I also appeared for the Crown with Lloyd Martin QC in that long corruption trial in which Sturgess appeared as counsel for one or two accused. Sturgess was a respected senior barrister with extensive criminal experience, and we enjoyed cordial and friendly relations during our respective careers. This continued until my retirement when I lost contact with him. Some years after the corruption trial, Sturgess was appointed Director of Public Prosecutions and I was still there as a Senior Consultant Crown Prosecutor.

In the years that followed the 1975 trial, Sturgess referred to the 'infamous' Southport Case and when the Fitzgerald Inquiry commenced in earnest I often reminded him of the now famous Southport Case. This was a reference to the events unfolding during the hearing before the Fitzgerald Inquiry. I was told by some of the police who had been involved in the earlier corruption matters that the Fitzgerald Inquiry led to the trial, conviction and imprisonment of various Government Ministers and even the Premier of the State, Joh Bjelke-Petersen, was tried in our criminal courts.

In the decades that followed, these retired honest police officers who had been vilified felt vindicated; they found some satisfaction knowing their efforts were not in vain. Respected commentators and writers who have written on some aspects of the case have praised them for their contribution to fighting endemic corruption. These critics did not denigrate these police officers but acknowledged that society owed a debt to them. They referred to these cases as 'famous' cases and not

# CHAPTER 6

'infamous'. There was some recognition that the 'honest cops' had fought in a good cause under very difficult political and legal circumstances. Quentin Dempster and Evan Whitten mention them in their books.

It certainly was a famous case, given the hostile and difficult terrain in which the prosecution was being invited to do battle. The Southport saga developed with a massive attack on the honest police; then there was massive media coverage, which was to be expected. But the media was agitated to a high degree and gave a fragmented and sensational picture; and some of the corrupt politicians who were later paraded before the Fitzgerald Inquiry and then marched off to jail were braying for the Police Commissioner Whitrod's blood, who suddenly resigned and left Queensland.

Critics who were more objective and could be referred to as 'those with good intentions and motives' were now aroused and sought some action too; but again, the claims and counter claims made it difficult to distinguish between the good and the corrupt. Inspector Arthur Pitts, who was the main witness for the prosecution, was the central target. Many of the honest police involved recall this event with bitterness even after more than three decades.

I was in the middle of preparing a criminal trial when I was contacted by Norman Gulbransen, Acting Commissioner. I was being urged to intervene personally because the defence alleged that the police prosecutor was a party to an attempt to concoct and conceal evidence. This case now was known as the Southport Betting Case. These allegations were false and were intended to sully the names of investigators who were going to give evidence in the pending long corruption trials of Herbert and others.

This was a police prosecution and the Crown only intervened in cases perceived to be difficult or in the public interest. The starting-price betting case of a few bookmakers could hardly be described as of great public interest.

It so happened that the Crime Intelligence Unit had advised me that in the process of their information gathering they had found that the corrupt police were about to mount a serious assault on the key prosecution witnesses in the pending corruption cases.

I then submitted a highly confidential memorandum predicting an impending disaster but was taken totally by surprise when it happened in a magistrates court in Southport. I had thought that any such attack would come in the actual corruption trials. It was the most unlikely venue and the most unlikely theatre for mounting such an assault on the honest police officers. The choice of the venue and the ferocity of the attack on some of the police took the prosecution almost completely by surprise.

It soon became clear that what on the face of it was just a minor prosecution of several starting-price bookmakers was turning into a nasty and very serious matter that was likely to contaminate a series of pending corruption trials, which included charges against some serving police officers. I had the conduct of the prosecution of this pending series of matters and was expecting a possible disaster such as the one now developing, but not here. The Solicitor-General decided to intervene immediately and have the conduct of this minor case. It was not a matter of choice. I got the guernsey!

The Acting Commissioner of Police (Gulbransen) made an urgent request to our Solicitor-General, Thomas Parslow, QC, and said:

> Mr V Lakshman of your office has been appointed by you to act as prosecutor in the committal proceedings against Jack Reginald Herbert, Patrick McIntyre and Reginald Neal Freier, on charges of official corruption.
>
> Mr Lakshman is presently on leave and conferences have been held with him regarding the matters he has in hand, which are associated with the proposed committal proceedings. This Department is in possession of further material, which will have to be assessed in the light of the matters now before the Court.
>
> The person most likely to comprehend and appreciate the implications and ramifications of this material, which is allied with the matters now before the Court, would be Mr Lakshman, who I understand will be resuming duty.

# CHAPTER 6

It would be appreciated if you would make Mr Lakshman available to assess this material, which is essential and which will be helpful to him in the forthcoming committal proceedings and his opinion as to whether any further charges should be laid would be appreciated.

There is definitely some connection between these matters, and it would seem appropriate that Mr Lakshman should now prosecute the charges against Sieber and Saunders, as he is fully conversant with the material associated with the corruption charges.

I had never heard of the Racing and Betting Act, which is not unusual as many Acts and amendments to them come and go with regularity. The Solicitor-General had given me no particular direction as to whether I should continue with the prosecution or simply offer no further evidence and withdraw the charges because the allegations against the police prosecutor and the other material witnesses in the pending corruption trials were serious. He left the matter entirely in my hands because of my familiarity with the pending corruption trials.

It appeared from the media reports that it was probable that the magistrate was unlikely to convict because, when there were some serious conflicts in the evidence for the prosecution, the magistrate did not have to give elaborate reasons or make any special finding of facts. He could just dismiss the case.

The general practice was that once the Solicitor-General was asked to intervene in any matter that was primarily a matter for some other department any advice given by the Solicitor-General prevailed. The pending corruption matters were already in the domain of the Crown Law Office and the Police Commissioner was never in a position to instruct or advise the Solicitor-General on how the matter should be handled in court.

This was to become of critical importance in the events that followed because what was happening here dealt with corruption matters that had not reached committal hearings, and this was an attempt to stop even the committal hearings. Normally, it was a police function to collect, assess and charge offenders with a crime and if the police laid no charges then there was no particular reason for the Crown to play a part. In any ordinary investigation (say murder) the police are not required to consult the Crown and could either charge or not charge a person or simply drop an investigation for lack of evidence.

The Crown intended to keep the matter in the court system and not allow the Police Minister under political pressure to withdraw any prosecution. In fact, the Police Minister was under considerable pressure from the Queensland Premier to withdraw the case. The Crown happened to have a powerful Attorney-General in William Knox who was also the Deputy Premier, and on the advice of our Solicitor-General, Thomas Parslow QC, he refused to withdraw the case. I had argued that the matter should remain in our courts where all allegations could be tested, and police had to swear on the Bible—not that it made much difference! The Police Department was vulnerable to pressure. The Crown Law was not. So, in a sense, when it came to the power ratio, I was in the box seat!

I might have mentioned earlier that in an earlier life our Solicitor-General had been an army colonel, and he had a very distinguished academic record too. He had a habit of smoking and puffing on a pipe. When we came out of the Attorney-General's Office I expressed the view that we had no choice but to fight this case in such a hostile terrain when one of the witnesses on the tape had called the presiding magistrate 'a weak bastard'. The Solicitor-General told me that he intended to fight this case to the last Indian. That was me!

I had not even read the transcript of the proceedings in the lower court at that stage. This happened on a late Friday afternoon when the courts were just closing. I had no transcript of proceedings and had no idea of what had actually happened in Southport. I had read the sensational media reports about the forging of warrants and fabrication of some evidence, but there was nothing to help me evaluate the true position.

The general allegation against the police I intended calling later in the corruption trial was that they raided the starting-price betting

## CHAPTER 6

operators without a warrant. All the police had given statements that they had a valid warrant, and this was not true. The defence lawyers had statements saying that the police had a valid warrant. This was the centrepiece of their attack on my police witnesses.

The corrupt police had planted their own corrupt police officer in the betting case, and he had tape-recorded all police witnesses discussing the evidence and saying that there was no warrant, but they would, if called, say that they had a warrant. Now, instead of taking the tape-recording to the senior police officers, ranking from superintendents to the Deputy Commissioner of Police, this constable (Davey) took it to one Sergeant Murphy and others who were known to be linked to the corruption and prostitution rackets. It so happened that Murphy was never charged with any criminal offence.

Constable Davey took the tapes yet to be played in court to the police union, which was opposing the reforms introduced by Police Commissioner Whitrod. What happened next was startling and unknown to me at the time when I gathered my wits to appear in Southport. The fact that the tapes were played at the police union Executive meeting on that very Friday night even before it was played in court came as another surprise.

It was difficult to understand the purpose and the significance of this new and very unusual move in which the tapes that had not yet been played in the magistrates court in a criminal proceedings were played for the police union Executive.

The case was still in progress and had been adjourned with Constable Davey still under cross-examination by the police prosecutor. I was startled to learn that the defence team consisting of Sturgess, Macgroarty and the solicitor for the defence, Nolan, were all there at the meeting. Constable Davey, their stooge, who was still being cross-examined was present, but the other police who were under attack and were also members of the police union were not invited.

The presence of Sergeant Murphy, who had received considerable publicity over a long period for his activities and exploits in the police force too, came as a surprise. The activities of Murphy were revisited a decade later, and Murphy was the subject of some attention in the Fitzgerald Report. I soon gathered that Murphy was well-known to the police administration and Acting Commissioner Gulbransen had had some earlier dealings with him. The Fitzgerald Report gave Murphy a fair treatment, and the report should be read by those interested in the details.

Gulbransen was under enormous pressure because he was the Acting Police Commissioner in the absence of Mr Whitrod, and he urgently needed advice and support from the Crown Law Office. He telephoned me at home early in the morning the next day, Saturday, to tell me that he had been summoned at short notice to appear before the Acting Minister for Police (Mr Camm) at the Minister's Office at 10 am for a meeting with the Executive of the police union and the solicitor, Mr Nolan.

He said that he hardly knew the Acting Police Minister and had no idea who had organised the meeting or the purpose of the meeting. He wanted me to attend the meeting with him and suspected that, in the absence of Whitrod, an attempt would be made to cajole or bully him into withdrawing the prosecution.

I thought at the time that I had a very good idea what the purpose of the meeting was. I had some understanding and some political grounding in Fiji from my father's experience. I had even enjoyed the political science component of the Arts degree course I had completed at the University of Queensland. My father's original plan for me was that, once I had completed my degree course, I would return to Fiji and enter politics. He had fought in the struggle for freedom in India when he had gone to India as a student and was imprisoned with Gandhi after the celebrated Salt March of 1930.

The one cardinal rule in politics is survival, which is enshrined in the actions and writings of all the good practitioners of this art throughout history. It is much better to be in the kitchen near the smouldering cauldron of power with a spoon or ladle in hand than to be just looking in from outside. I was in the kitchen and participating in the decision-making.

# CHAPTER 6

This rule, like many other manufactured laws of success, has many fathers and can be gleaned from even a cursory study of the actions of the grandmasters in the field of politics, either those who have written about politics or played some role in it. The mingling of Law and Politics is a dangerous exercise for most and is almost fatal for a public servant. Reflecting on it after close to forty years since those events, it is possible that what I did severely affected my career, even if it did not prove fatal. I was never promoted or considered for any further senior position until my early retirement in 1992.

It appeared that the Deputy Commissioner of Police had no option but to attend the meeting as directed but he wanted me to accompany him, and I agreed. There was no time to consult the Solicitor-General or the Attorney-General early on that Saturday morning. I had never spoken to the Solicitor-General while he was having breakfast, and it is common knowledge that powerful creatures should be left alone while feeding.

I was collected in a police car, and Gulbransen and I went to the meeting. The police union executive members—the president of the police union (Sergeant Eddington), the secretary (MJ Callaghan) and Sergeant R Redmond—were there with Pat Nolan, the solicitor for the police union. I had the impression that some of them were stunned to see a Crown Law officer there with Mr Gulbransen. Nolan spoke for the police union and said that they wanted the Acting Minister for Police to hear the tape, but that they were not prepared to play the tape in the presence of a Crown Law officer. They did not want to discuss any matter in my presence. They wanted a meeting with Mr Camm (Acting Minister for Police) without a Crown Law Officer being present. Mr Nolan spoke for the union and said that it was prepared to play the tape that had not yet been played in court but not in my presence. Good move! I certainly wanted to hear what was on the tape before deciding what was to be done next.

Mr Camm agreed to see the police union first and then the Assistant Commissioner and me. Mr Gulbransen remained very quiet out of deference to the Acting Minister for Police. He was his political master.

Legal officers, too, were generally quiet when meeting the Attorney-General on the rare occasions when they were required to be present with the Solicitor-General. However, Mr Camm was not my political master. He genuinely felt awkward in this situation.

Mr Camm was recognised as a quiet but very shrewd politician. I told him that it would be dangerous to interfere in matters that were already in court and that he should reject any offer to hold any inquiry or to listen to any tapes, and that if he got embroiled in matters actually unfolding in the magistrates court it was possible that the Crown might be compelled to call evidence to show who handled the tape and whether the tapes had been tampered with.

He seemed surprised to hear that the Crown had no knowledge of what was on the tapes, or so he said. It was not bluntly spelt out to him, but I could see he had no intention of being embroiled in any criminal proceedings. He told us that he would give his decision after he had considered the matter further, and we left. He seemed to think that the proceedings in the magistrates court would conclude in a few days' time. It appeared that someone had told him that the case was all over bar the shouting. We left.

On the way back from the meeting, the Deputy Commissioner of Police and I spent some time speculating on what might happen next in the unlikely event that Gulbransen was directed by the Acting Police Minister to offer no further evidence or to withdraw the charges. Mr Camm was only acting in his position, and he had given us no indication as to what he might do. There was intense media speculation following this meeting, which was reported on the front page of the *Courier-Mail*. Given the intense media speculation, it was thought that the Crown had no option but to withdraw the charges.

There was no further contact with Mr Camm, but next morning the *Sunday Mail* headlines gave an inkling of what had happened at the meeting. The article on the front page read: 'Police Seek Full Inquiry by a Judge' and the inquiry was to be restricted to 'a policeman's allegations of police malpractice in a Gold Coast investigation'. Mr Eddington was reported as saying: 'We did not ask for a Royal Commission. We ask that a

## CHAPTER 6

member of the Judiciary be appointed to investigate the allegations'. Mr Eddington was reported to say that: 'The Minister assured us that after Monday when the case is expected to be decided ... every consideration will be given to having a searching Inquiry into the matter.' There was much speculation as to the judge who might head this inquiry, and some cynics in the legal fraternity for some reason suggested that perhaps Judge Broad of the District Court would be a good choice.

Inspector Pitts and his men saw this as nothing more than an attempt to parade Davey as a witness of truth and were terrified that some attempt would be made to concoct evidence to frame them so that the honest police would be charged and the dishonest police, like Herbert and others, would be the prosecution witnesses. It appeared to them that the Crown would just throw in the towel and leave them to their fate. Most of them did not know me and had no idea that I had been briefed intensely by Inspector Basil Hicks of the Crime Intelligence Unit for several months before this episode.

Inspector Pitts and his men felt a sense of betrayal. It may have looked worse because no undertakings and no assurances were given to Inspector Pitts and his men. The fact was that if there was evidence of criminal conduct, then the Crown would have recommended that Inspector Pitts and his men be charged. I was counsel for the Crown, not the police. I had never met Inspector Pitts and spoke to him for the first time in my office some days before he gave evidence.

I thought the taped material was a red herring and a sham; otherwise, it would have been played in court and not hawked about in that way or kept from scrutiny by the Crown Law Office.

There were some 200 pages of transcript up to the end of the proceedings on 19 June in Southport, and I was impressed with the deliberate and methodical way the defence set about doing a good demolition job on both Inspector Arthur Pitts and the police prosecutor, Sergeant Jeppesen, and the other investigating officers. It was clear that this was an effort to derail the pending corruption trial. There were no further discussions or instructions from the Solicitor-General on how to respond. That had already been decided some three weeks earlier in the confidential memorandum in which I had anticipated this attack; and part of this earlier memorandum is quoted in the Fitzgerald Report.

The connection between the Southport Betting Case and the Herbert, Frier and McIntyre corruption case and the other similar pending matters needs some explanation, but first one must look at what actually happened on the first day of that case in Southport. I was not present for this part. Pitts and his men had noticed a massive media presence, some from interstate. Who or what was 'feeding the chooks'? A detailed description of what happened on the morning of the hearing is given in Quentin Dempster's book.

Constable Davey told the court that he had obtained a tape recorder from Herbert, the corrupt bagman who had already been charged with corruption and was awaiting committal proceedings along with others, and that he had taped some of the conversations, which also somehow implicated the Police prosecutor (who, incidentally, had nothing to do with the actual investigation). Sergeant Jeppesen's tragedy was that he just happened to be the police prosecutor who had the conduct of a police prosecution in that case.

## The repeated attempt to denigrate and humiliate the police prosecutor

Once serious allegations were made against Sergeant Jeppesen as being part of a police plot to concoct evidence, the police prosecutor pleaded in vain many times with the magistrate for an adjournment. Both Macgroarty and Sturgess objected strenuously and would not allow the magistrate to give Jeppesen any adjournment.

> JEPPESEN: ... At this stage I'm seeking a short adjournment in this matter.
>
> STURGESS: I object. He's [Davey] the prosecution's witness ... is giving evidence which the prosecution is not enjoying and there's no reason why he should be interrupted. He should be given the opportunity to tell his story, if your lordship pleases. [page 103 of depositions]

# CHAPTER 6

It was certainly true that Sergeant Jeppesen was not enjoying it, and that was a perceptive observation from two very experienced counsel. Both the guilty and the innocent do not 'enjoy it' when allegations are made, especially if they think they are false. Now, this is some of what happened on the first day of the hearing in Southport:

> MR MACGROARTY: I agree with Mr Sturgess. May it please your worship, no reason has been advanced by my friend, the prosecutor, [referring to the police prosecutor, Sergeant Jeppesen] to substantiate an adjournment, and it is obvious as Mr Sturgess says, that the prosecution is not enjoying it but there is no reason why the court should refrain from continuing straight on with the witness's evidence.
>
> MR STURGESS: ... I would be prepared to consent to a short adjournment provided it was a short adjournment and did not run on for more than, say, 5 minutes. And provided the witness is not approached in the meanwhile by anybody. [page 104 of depositions]

The magistrate who obliged the defence whenever required granted an adjournment for just five minutes to the police prosecutor, who had many matters to consider including that he might later be required to give sworn evidence in what he claimed was a completely false allegation. He did not return in exactly five minutes. Perhaps he was busy frantically seeking advice from his superiors,

In the meantime, in the absence of the prosecutor who had not returned within five minutes, Mr Sturgess and Mr Macgroarty, together with Mr Nolan, (the solicitor who was acting for Mr Saunders in the matter and who was also the solicitor acting in the pending corruption trials, and who also happened to be Davey's legal advisor and was the solicitor to the police union) went to see the magistrate in his chambers in the absence of the police prosecutor. The magistrate gave no account of what transpired in his chambers or for how long the consultation proceeded, but Mr Sturgess quite appropriately put this on record when the court resumed:

> MR STURGESS: Your worship, before we continue, I think I should put on it on the record that I saw your worship in chambers in company of my learned friend Mr Macgroarty and my instructing solicitor about five or six minutes ago. The reason why I saw you and my friend Mr Jeppesen was not present was that he hadn't returned, and the period of five minutes of the adjournment had long since expired. I told your worship that I undertook that I'd repeat this openly that I would object to any further adjournment. That I had every reason to expect this witness was prepared to speak of a conspiracy in existence between various police officers and connected with the charging of these two men. I also said that I understood that the evidence that would be given in this direction would be supported by real evidence. [pages 104–105]

The matter proceeded for some time and the police prosecutor again pleaded for an adjournment. He told the magistrate that now that such serious allegations were being made against him as police prosecutor: 'I'm seeking leave to withdraw and asking for an adjournment to another date.' It was a legitimate and reasonable request.

Sturgess repeatedly objected and asked for 'a ruling which would permit this matter to go ahead'. It was the 'interest of justice' that concerned him. He said:

> Here we have a man who's prepared to provide very vital information to the court which would profoundly affect the outcome of this determination ... I'm asking your worship to allow the proceedings to continue so that the man can speak, so that this man can place before this court the evidence that he has claimed he possesses ... It cannot be denied, your worship, that information and evidence is of high relevance so far as these proceedings are concerned.

# CHAPTER 6

Mr Macgroarty, who was patiently waiting in the queue, joined in opposing an adjournment and completely concurred with everything Sturgess had said. He went on:

> But I would add this that the interest of justice in this case will most certainly not be served by an adjournment at this stage ... Your worship, to deny him [Davey] this opportunity to proceed with his evidence ... would deny the interest of justice in this case. [page 134]

Macgroarty went on to say that Davey was 'a courageous man' who might be in some danger. The magistrate refused to give an adjournment, as requested by the police prosecutor.

Davey was suspected of being a stooge that had been planted in the prosecution case by Herbert, and the defence was painting him as some sort of saviour of the community. He was going to claim that the warrant was not properly executed and that some evidence was fabricated. During the hearing of the Fitzgerald Inquiry, Herbert identified Davey as his corrupt cohort involved in graft. This is exactly what the magistrate was told a decade earlier by Inspector Pitts and other senior police who gave evidence in Southport.

> JEPESSEN: This is the allegation of a warrant involved ... I feel it's the duty of the court to grant such an adjournment in these circumstances and these are the instructions I have received ... it could be necessary, your worship, for certain persons to get advice and still appear before this court. I do take exception to the fact that the person Davey is in danger. There's no danger to him ... I consider it no more than a reasonable request in asking for an adjournment to another date. [page135]

> MACGROARTY: I said to take a realistic view one could appreciate that he [Davey] might be or may be in danger.

Macgroarty went on to say that he had no objection to another prosecutor but that he should be found during the luncheon adjournment!

When I read the transcript, I was impressed with this haste. There was no apparent reason for such haste. Macgroarty went on:

> The interest of justice in this case could not possibly be served if this man were to be stopped from continuing with his evidence today.
> [page 136]

There was no reason given for such haste. There was no evidence that Davey was terminally ill and wanted to make a dying declaration. Why could it not wait for a day or so?

> STURGESS: ... But all I'm asking at this stage is that the evidence that this man says he now has be made in the possession of the court, not be retained in his possession, your worship, let it be made in the possession of the court, and then we can go our own separate ways and consider the matter.

The magistrate was about to adjourn for lunch, Mr Macgroarty having already alerted the magistrate that somehow mysteriously Davey might be in some danger. So now Sturgess, in keeping with the spirit, I suppose, made his contribution:

> STURGESS: ... In the very strange circumstances that have arisen here, I'd ask your worship to request this witness to remain in the court, during the luncheon adjournment, if it suits his convenience. ... I don't think either side should be discussing this matter with him at this particular stage, and the best way of achieving that if it suits his convenience is to ask him to remain in the court or the immediate vicinity of the court.
> [page 136]

This was a bit too much even for the obliging magistrate:

> MAGISTRATE: Well, I won't order him to stay in the court. If he wishes to remain in court he may do so of course.

What was this about 'either side' not discussing it? Davey was already discussing it with Herbert and Nolan, the solicitor for Herbert.

# CHAPTER 6

Why this feigned drama of danger or that Davey needed to be kept in the courtroom? The magistrate was not told that that very night Davey, in the company of Sturgess, Macgroarty, the solicitor Nolan and others, played the tape-recorded conversation to the police union executive before it was played in court. It was difficult to imagine how Davey could be in any danger with Sturgess and Macgroarty riding shotgun on the stagecoach trundling all the way to the police union executive meeting where they were met by Sergeant Murphy and other members of the police union who could provide protection. The police could have carried firearms too just in case there was some threat from Inspector Pitts and his men

Surely there was safety in numbers! The taped conversation and the tape recorder were not left in some vault in the magistrates court for safety but travelled with them!

There is a need for a more accurate and detailed account of what was said to demonstrate the true nature of the exercise in the proceedings in Southport and no need to demonstrate that it had a lot to do with the pending corruption trials. There is no suggestion that counsel acted in any dishonourable way. Counsel acted on instructions. That is an important point to make.

> JEPPESEN: If your worship pleases, at this stage there's been certain evidence given with insinuations against myself, and once those allegations are made I feel that I must bring them to your worship's notice. It's my duty to seek leave of the court to withdraw ... and once those allegations are made, I feel that just bringing them to your worship's notice, it's my duty to seek leave of the court to withdraw from the prosecution, as prosecutor, and on instructions received, I'm seeking leave to withdraw and asking for an adjournment to another date, your worship. I respectfully submit that on that basis your worship is duty bound, I don't say is duty bound, but nearly duty bound to grant such an adjournment in the circumstances ... [pages 132–133]
>
> MR STURGESS: Your worship, I object to the adjournment, and I ask your worship to make a ruling which would permit

this matter to go ahead, in any decision of the court the interest of justice is ... Here we have a man who's prepared to provide very vital information to the court which will profoundly affect the outcome of this determination. He's come to court, and he says he has the evidence here in court with him. I'm asking your worship to enable this man to place that evidence before the court, and that's all I'm asking. I'm not seeking to contrive a situation whereby he can't be later cross-examined upon it, or examined upon it, or anything like that. But I'm asking your workshop to allow the proceedings to continue so that this man can speak, so that this man can place before this court the evidence that he has claimed he possesses. Your workshop understands how things have been conducted up to this stage. He's been circumscribed in many of the things. He has attempted to say. He's been subjected to cross-examination. No attempt has been made to bring out this material so that we can have it in court, and I submit that the proceedings should continue until that stage has been reached whereby we have in the court ... in the courtroom the information, the evidence that this man says he possesses. It cannot be denied, your worship, that information and evidence is of high relevance so far as these proceedings are concerned. [pages 133–134)

MACGROARTHY: Your worship, I join with my learned friend, Mr Sturgess, in opposing this adjournment, and the only thing I feel I can add to what he has said ... I completely concur with everything he's said, but I would add this that the interests of justice in this case will most certainly not be served by an adjournment at this stage. As Mr Sturgess has pointed out, this witness, Mr Davey, is here. He has given evidence of these matters to some degree. He says he has real and direct evidence to prove the allegations he makes. Your worship to deny him this opportunity to proceed with his evidence, and place this full evidence before the court, would deny the interests of justice in this case, and the mere fact that some allegations have been made concerning my

## CHAPTER 6

friend the prosecutor [Mr Jeppesen], in these circumstances, do not amount to a sufficient basis for the court to grant that adjournment ... Your worship may well appreciate that to adopt a realistic view, this man, Mr Davey, has adopted what could only be described as a courageous course, and that this man, Mr Davey, might, from a realistic point of view well be in some form of danger until such time as this evidence, this real evidence of which he has spoken, has been placed before this court, and becomes public material ...

There was no attempt to release the secret weapon so that it could be made public before something nasty happened to the 'courageous man' who was in some danger. Please, get it on court record before something terrible happened!

BENCH: Well, is there any objection to substitute the prosecutor?

STURGESS: No, your worship, that couldn't be done so that the information comes out today, and not, say, days later or weeks later or months even.

BENCH: Well, it's ten to one at this stage. I could suggest perhaps we take the lunch adjournment at this stage. Perhaps the prosecution can arrange for a prosecutor in the meantime. [page 134]

JEPPESEN: Well, the situation might arise, your worship, that I cannot get a prosecutor. I feel that at this stage there's sufficient evidence that's been alleged by the witness, Davey, in relation to the prosecutor, that the court is nearly duty bound to grant such an adjournment, your worship. This is the allegation of a warrant involved, your worship. I feel it's the duty of the court to grant such an adjournment in those circumstances, and these are the instructions that I have received, your worship ... It could be necessary, your worship, for certain persons to get certain advice, and still appear before this court. I do take exception to the fact that the person Davey is in danger. There's no danger to him at all at this ... I feel that your worship is duty bound to grant an adjournment ... And will make every effort to secure another prosecutor, but, as your worship would appreciate, there's been a full day's evidence already given, and another prosecutor would have to take time to peruse the brief and catch up on the evidence already given. I consider it no more than a reasonable request in asking for an adjournment to another date. [page 135]

MACGRAOARTY: Your worship, I make it clear that I did not state that the witness Davey was in danger. I said to take a realistic view one could appreciate that he might be, or may be, in danger. I also wish to place on the record on behalf of the defendant Siebers, your worship, that I have no objection to another prosecutor being bound, but I would add, your worship, that if another prosecutor is to be found, he should be found during the luncheon adjournment, so that this man ... this witness Davey be not denied the opportunity he seeks of putting his further and real evidence before this court in relation to this matter, whereas Mr Sturgess said the interests of justice are paramount and could not possibly in the context of this case as it has taken place today, the interests of justice in this case could not possibly be served if this man were to be stopped from continuing with his evidence today, but I don't object to some different prosecutor after lunch. [pages 135–136]

STURGESS: Your worship, excuse me, if I could be given the opportunity of speaking twice on this matter. What I've endeavoured to place before your worship is a compromised proposal, whereby this man is given the opportunity to place all his evidence before the court and the prosecution is then given the opportunity to explore it, to seek another prosecutor if necessary to explore it, and in fact the prosecution would be given every opportunity to look into the matter.

# CHAPTER 6

...

> But all I am asking at this stage is that the evidence that this man says he now has be made the possession of the court, not be retained in his possession, your worship. Let it be made the possession of the court, and then we can go our own separate ways and consider the matter. The prosecution won't be prejudiced by this. The defence won't be prejudiced, and the interests of justice will be served. Your worship is going to adjourn now, I take it. In the very strange circumstances that have arisen here, I'd ask your worship to request this witness to remain in the court, during the luncheon adjournment, if that suits his convenience.
>
> ....
>
> I don't think that either side should be discussing this matter with him at this particular stage, and the best way of achieving that, if it suits his convenience, is to ask him to remain in the court, or in the immediate vicinity of the court.
>
> BENCH: Yes, well, I won't order him to stay in the court. If he wishes to remain in the court he may do so of course. [page 136]

Again, much later in the proceedings the defence virtually took over the case whilst the witness was still giving evidence and in the middle of the prosecution case (page 164):

> MR STURGESS: Your worship, I've discussed this application for an adjournment with my learned friend, Mr Macgroarty, and our common attitude is this. We have no objection to this matter being adjourned, provided we were given the opportunity of asking some few questions of this witness so as to ensure that his story has been fully told. There'd be no matters that have been left out, and so that certain matters which may appear to be a little unfair to the court at this stage should be made clear. There's been no chronological development, by way of example, of this story.

...

And if we could have that leave, and I'd assure the court I wouldn't be long in asking those questions, and I can assure the court that if this course should follow, that would be without prejudice to the right of the prosecution to return here with another prosecutor or several prosecutors and to resume from where Mr Jeppesen has left off. I'm very anxious that the story be told before we go.

...

Very well. Well, I promise I will be quite brief in this matter. Mr Davey, you've heard what I said to his worship. I'm anxious that your story be told completely and in the order of the events as they occurred. Is this the situation that by the 13th of November of ...

BENCH: Yes, well, I'll adjourn at this stage. The matter is listed for hearing next Monday 23rd June.
[page 178]

Davey was still giving evidence and was being cross-examined by the police prosecutor, and the tapes that was supposed to be the silver-bullet to demolish Pitts and his men had not yet been played in court. I concluded that the tapes were played at the police union meeting and the extensive press coverage was intended to force the prosecution to withdraw the charges. I had bad news for the defence.

Then, much later in the proceedings, the police prosecutor again pleads for an adjournment:

PROSECUTOR: (JEPPESEN): Your worship, in the circumstances I'm asking that be a date for mention. It's a matter of whether that matter is referred by our department ... to Crown Law for further prosecution. I realise today is Thursday and it's next Monday. In the circumstances I'm asking for a longer adjournment.
[page 178]

## CHAPTER 6

STURGESS: Your worship, we're anxious for the matter to proceed to a conclusion as quickly as possible. There may be difficulties on the part of the prosecution. I quite see this, but could we leave it on this basis that the matter whether there'll be an adjournment or whether the matter will proceed on Monday can be decided on Monday? There's enough time for the prosecution to look into these matters to be ready to proceed on Monday. I know I've been in court on much heavier briefs than this.

The repeated pleas by the police prosecutor were ignored, and the sole purpose of taking over the prosecution case was to discredit inspector Pitts as much as possible on the pretext that there was some urgency about it. The media, as to be expected, was waiting for all these little morsels.

It did not go unnoticed when the transcript of the proceedings was read for the first time by me that the defence was not entirely unmindful of the interest of the prosecution because Sturgess did urge at the end of the day's proceedings that the prosecution could return with not one but several Crown prosecutors. There were always light moments in criminal trials, and it so happened that I was seeking a clerk to assist me in the case.

I told the Solicitor-General that the suggestion was that the Crown could turn up with several prosecutors. Mr Parslow, the Solicitor-General, just puffed on his pipe, smiled and said to me that it would be 'grossly unfair to the defence to have to cope with two or three of my Crown prosecutors, all at the same time'. I asked for a clerk, but there was not one available, so I went to Southport in a police car every morning and returned late at night. This went on for three weeks.

The courtroom was packed with both the media and other solicitors who happened to have some spare time from other chores in court and during the course of the hearings that went on for some three weeks. Even some magistrates, who were perhaps bored with the usual parade of 'drunk and disorderly' or the tedious grind of dealing with traffic offences of all kinds, found themselves gravitating to the courtroom out of interest and perhaps for light entertainment.

Some solicitors I knew and who seemed to know a lot about Herbert and his cohorts were curious to know the possible outcome; some, unaware of the extent of the corruption matters, thought that I was merely sent there to 'fill in the gap' and withdraw the charges.

I remember that there were senior counsels of all political persuasions, including Collin Bennett who happened to be a member of parliament during the National Hotel Royal Commission and who had appeared in a number of criminal trials I had prosecuted. He had warned me in the very first week of the case to 'avoid falling for the three-card trick' of the defence seeking some form of inquiry.

On Monday 23rd of June 1975, I appeared for the prosecution for the first time. Macgroarty of counsel appeared for both the defendants. Mr Sturgess of counsel was not there.

I feared that once the nature and purpose of the prosecution response became clear there would be an attempt to curtail or shorten the proceedings before the magistrate, and this too happened.

Herbert had cynically used the magistrates court as the theatre of engagement for the destruction of the principal witnesses in the pending corruption trials. I decided to use the same theatre to give these police officers the opportunity to give their account and to use the same forum Herbert and his gang was using to speak about the penetration of the police force by organised crime syndicates. I would show that these honest police were making an effort to clean the stable and give the honest police the opportunity to show that well-organised corrupt police like Herbert posed a very real danger to the administration of criminal justice.

I gave the honest police the same sanctuary of legal privilege that witnesses have to speak in open court under oath and to be reported in the newspapers. The same forum that Herbert and his cynical gang had used to discredit Inspector Pitts and his men who were engaged in fighting what really was a criminal gang. These honest police could not be threatened and sued for giving evidence because in the past at

## CHAPTER 6

least some dishonest corrupt police had developed the practice of suing anyone who made any effort to expose corruption.

The objective was not to give or offer any protection to any police including Inspector Pitts and his men. It would not have mattered to the Crown if they were all later charged with some offence if there was any evidence. The other objective was to protect the evidence that could lead to the prosecution of Herbert and other corrupt police. This necessarily meant giving Pitts and his men the opportunity to tell the court what really happened; to frustrate any attempt to frame those police who were not taking bribes and were not corrupt; to ensure that Herbert and his corrupt gang would actually stand trial; that they should be in the dock; to lean in favour of the police who were struggling to expose the dishonest police.

The prosecution considered seeking the disqualification of the magistrate because he had been called names, but there were simply insufficient grounds for that; any such application had the possibility of further alienating the magistrate, and any delay might have suited the defence but not the prosecution. The very first matter I raised was the position of the magistrate:

> LAKSHMAN: Your worship, there are perhaps several matters that I ought to mention before proceedings continue. There have been some slightly unusual circumstances in which during the course of the cross-examination of a hostile witness the counsel for the defence were given the opportunity to interpose questions which they considered necessary and desirable at that stage of the proceedings. Your worship, the prosecution does not quibble with that because your worship of course would have been guided by frequent suggestions that were made that it was in the interests of justice that the evidence that emanated from Constable Davey should be placed on record before the proceedings concluded for that day.
> [pages 181–182]

…

Again, your worship, there is one other aspect that I mention at this stage and it is this, that during the course of the evidence of Davey, who had been declared a hostile witness, there is evidence before the court that allegedly one of the prospective witness for the prosecution had made remarks about your worship which may be regarded as uncomplimentary. I understand, your worship, reading of the transcript that the reference was that Mr O'Connell was a weak bastard. Your worship I have not had the benefit of reading the whole of the transcript of the matter, but having read what I could, I have also come to the conclusion, your worship, that indeed it is in the interests of justice that the matters should continue as your worship had indicated.

...

It is not the intention of the prosecution at all, your worship, to seek any adjournments, and I might mention, your worship, that at no stage during the course of this trial would it be the intention of the prosecution to seek to have your worship disqualified merely because those remarks were made. Your worship, of course, would note that would be an aspect which was not within the knowledge of the prosecution as the evidence had unfolded. I would of course take it that my learned friend here would perhaps agree with that, and at no stage would the defence make any such applications at a later stage that your worship should disqualify yourself merely on that aspect. I think it is important, your worship, at this stage of the proceedings when such serious allegations have been made, when it has been suggested that witnesses have concocted evidence, that there is evidence of conspiracy to pervert the course of justice, then of course it is essential that the matters should proceed as speedily as possible so that there is no suggestion that any evidence has been suppressed. [pages 182–183]

...

## CHAPTER 6

Well, your worship, having mentioned those matters, I would take it that my learned friend clearly concedes that no question of interest would be raised at any later stage of the trial and, your worship, again, I might mention that as I understand the present position in these matters the witness was under cross-examination by the prosecutor, (Jeppesen) and ... [something missing in transcript] ... except for those few matters that for some reason the defence mentioned ought to be placed on record, so it is my intention, your worship, at this stage to continue with the cross-examination of Davey, and of course, your worship, that is the stage where the trial has reached. [page 183]

MACGROARTY: May it please your worship, the defence here today makes no application to your worship by way of adjourning the matter or in relation to your worship's capacity to continue hearing this case. We make no application at all. We, the defence, made our attitude quite clear on Thursday last that in the interests of justice this matter should proceed and proceed with all due expedition, so in relation to remarks that have just fallen from my learned friend, we, the defence, completely agree and can state that anything my learned friend has said was clearly our attitude on Thursday last and is clearly our attitude today. [pages 183–184).

LAKSHMAN: Your worship, the only reason I mention the question of interest is that it will be my function to cross-examine the witness on those areas on his bias and so on and I did not wish in any way it to be taken that there was a reflection of any kind on the magistrate. [page 184]

BENCH: Yes, thank you, Mr Lakshman.

The broad objective was to disabuse the public of the notion that Constable Davey was an honest police officer trying to clean out the dishonest police virtually single-handed or that he was under some threat or was targeted by the police. The purpose was to show that Davey was planted in the prosecution case by Herbert and his corrupt gang of police officers, which was entrenched in the Licensing Branch, and Davey was part of a plot to destroy the prosecution evidence, and all this was done at the instigation of Herbert, who was at the heart of the corruption.

I had some recollection that when I entered the court, Davey was smiling and even winked a few times to someone in the court, but later as the cross-examination continued, he started fidgeting and twitching; he was no longer nursed and protected. It was clear that an honest police officer would have taken his complaints to other senior police officers and not to Herbert or to the solicitor Nolan, who was in court. It is important to emphasise that the target of this cross-examination was Herbert and his cohort Davey and not Nolan, the solicitor; solicitors sometimes do not have the luxury of choosing and acting for clients and are obliged to act on instructions. The motive, purpose and actions of Davey were the subject of the cross-examination, no matter how the questions were couched.

In this cross-examination, Davey agreed that the Commissioner of Police was honest and trustworthy.

> LAKSHMAN: Mention another senior officer that you trusted.
>
> DAVEY: At that stage I had the greatest admiration for our commissioner, Mr Whitrod.
>
> LAKSHMAN: Yes, did you mention it to him?
>
> DAVEY: No, I didn't.

He told the court that he still had great admiration for the police commissioner but made no attempt to complain to him.

> LAKSHMAN: Name another senior police officer who was trustworthy according to you.

## CHAPTER 6

> DAVEY: Well, Mr Gulbransen. I've never had any doubt to suggest that I couldn't trust him. [He was the Assistant Commissioner of Police.]
>
> LAKSHMAN: Yes, in fact he has a reputation of being a very honest policeman.
>
> DAVEY: That is correct too, yes.
>
> LAKSHMAN: Yes. And it is a reputation which is enjoyed by him in relation to all the police officers, is that right? All police officers virtually think that Mr Gulbransen is a very capable and honest police officer?

Davey agreed that he had never heard anything against Gulbransen (deps. page 196).

> Lakshman: And is it not a fact that you were out to trap Pitts and collect information for Herbert?
>
> DAVEY: No, that's completely incorrect.
> [page 208, 23 June 1975]

It emerged clearly that Davey was deep in the camp of the corrupt gang, taking instructions from Herbert and the solicitor Nolan. He never took the tapes to the Commissioner of Police (Mr Whitrod) or to the Assistant Commissioner of Police (Mr Gulbransen or any other senior police officer (deps. page 235).

Davey said that he was shocked and surprised to hear that honest police like Herbert were charged with corruption!

> LAKSHMAN: Well, I suppose you were really surprised to hear an allegation of that nature made against Herbert, who was such a nice police officer.
>
> DAVEY: I was surprised, yes.
>
> LAKSHMAN: Did you mention this to Assistant Commissioner, Gulbransen?

DAVEY: No, I didn't, no.

LAKSHMAN: Did you mention this to the Superintendent, that you trusted McMahon?

DAVEY: No, I didn't.

LAKSHMAN: Did you mention it to Commissioner Whitrod, whom you say you trusted?

DAVEY: No, I didn't.

It also emerged in the cross-examination that Davey had taken a statement that was prepared for Inspector Pitts had he been required to give evidence for the prosecution. He said that he was acting under the advice of Mr Nolan at all times. So, Davey had taken a police witness's statement and given it to the defence solicitor Nolan because the defence wanted to have a sneak preview of what Pitts might say in court. Davey said: 'there was some panic about what evidence he [Pitts] would give …'. Davey had stolen police property for the sole purpose of giving the defence as much material as possible to discredit Pitts and there was 'some panic about what evidence he would give' (page 364).

The story of this 'courageous' witness began to crumble the deeper the questioning went; repeatedly, Macgroarty objected both on relevance and admissibility and questioned the real motive and the true purpose of the cross-examination. He told the court that Davey was a Crown witness and the prosecution was attempting to discredit its own witness. Indeed, that was true, and Davey had been declared hostile for this very purpose.

The two sides swayed and heaved and the issues that were canvassed in the proceedings as being either important or not took a long time. The incessant trawling in search of motives and intentions was at the heart of this hearing. All this can be sampled from the following exchanges. There is no need to traverse the whole case captured in some 2500 pages. The first 500 pages should give the texture and context and

## CHAPTER 6

the tensions and are best captured from some samples of the running exchanges between counsel.

> MACGROARTY: ... and I object most strenuously. The ... Crown is endeavouring to turn the trial of my two clients into a royal commission to suit their own purposes. Your worship, what Constable Davey's ... said on oath is a matter that must cause the public of Queensland some considerable concern as to some aspects of the Queensland Police Force, and I would think that it would be most proper and fitting that a royal commission be appointed to look into constable Davey's sworn allegations and real evidence such as tapes and documents produced in this court.
>
> ...
>
> Your worship, why should my two clients have to pay for the government's public enquiry into this matter? Your worship, I've given my friend a degree of latitude in this matter. I've given it to him on the basis that what Constable Davey says is relevant to this case should be tested. But, your worship, we've sat here now, going on a day and a half with my learned friend, and during that time most of what we've heard, your worship, has been my learned friend's attempts to indict Constable Davey and connect him with retired sergeant of police Jack Herbert in some sinister fashion, that is, an attempt to discredit your own witness. We've now sat here this morning and listened to at some length my learned friend trying to indict Constable Davey for his taking of certain documents to his [Davey's] solicitor, Pat Nolan, under some attempt to make it look sinister that he's removed, as if it's a suggestion he's stolen from the police department these very documents – that it was the disclosure of the defence to put into evidence in this case. [page 367, 30 June 1975]
>
> ...
>
> Your worship, these matters do call, in my submission, for a royal commission ... This is the trial of two men charged

with being in possession of instruments of betting on the 20th of November, a very simple offence, and do they have to sit here, and pay for the government's attempts to connect Davey with Herbert, to put some ... and Hallahan, and Tony Murphy, and put some sinister cloak. The Crown's attempt to put some sinister cloak on Davey's going to a solicitor and seeking advice because a senior police officer tried to involve him in an unlawful purpose, and as Constable Davey has said that senior police officer said in his presence more than once, Well, I have the commissioner and others, Gulbransen on side, and anyone who doesn't fall into line with me, well, they'll get transferred. And, your worship, I back my submission, my strenuous objection with the law, and your worship is bound by the law, as my learned friend well knows ...

...

Your worship, I repeat in finality why should my two clients have to bear the cost of this endeavour by the Crown to connect Davey with Herbert, Murphy, Hallahan, the police union and put a sinister cloak on his approaching a solicitor when he's asked by a senior officer to do unlawful things? It's ludicrous and a farce that my clients should have to pay for this. This case, your worship, a simple instruments of betting case, could proceed on the evidence very, very speedily indeed and should proceed on the evidence very speedily indeed. I agree ... that Constable Davey's allegations should be looked into and canvassed and canvassed thoroughly but not at the expense of my client, your worship, and I submit your worship is bound by the law. I submit that my friend has far transgressed the limitations that the law places upon him, as to how far he can cross-examine his own witness. He certainly can't in my submission embark on this attempt to besmirch his own witness, because that's to call into evidence his own witness's bad credit and general bad reputation, tying him up with Herbert, Murphy, Hallahan and trying to put this sinister cloak on his approaching a solicitor. Let's get on with the facts of this case, your worship, and the evidence this witness can give relevant to the facts of this case, and if the government wants to enquire into Davey's allegations sworn on oath, then let them appoint a royal commission where all these matters can be looked into, where they should properly be looked into. If there is something wrong with the Queensland Police Force or a section of it, then let it be enquired into by all means, but not at the expense of my clients, your worship. [pages 368, 370).

The magistrate was not in a position to set up a royal commission for the defence. The government might have, but Herbert had chosen the magistrates court. Now that I was engaged in the serious business of showing the true nature of Davey's involvement after the massive media attack on Pitts and his men, there was this appeal for a royal commission. It is not recorded, but I said to Macgroarty that he should relax, and I would give him a royal commission in the magistrates court, the court of Herbert's choice.

> LAKSHMAN: ... I appear in this court on behalf of the Crown, and I have in my possession material, which is very pertinent to this trial, which would show who the conspirators were, what the conspiracy is about, and who is perverting the course of justice. It's very well for my learned friend at this stage, before any of the other prosecution witnesses have been called, to seek to ask you to consider matters which he thinks should be brought before the royal commission. we should not lose sight of what this trial is all about.
>
> ...
>
> Your worship, in our understanding of criminal justice, when allegations are made, when there are other witnesses who can be called to testify to the relevant issues, it would be improper, and certainly there is no precedent where your worship should accede to what really amounts to some sort of a political submission which may be relevant in another

forum. Let's not lose sight of what is happening in this court. Your worship will recollect that, in your very court when the matter came up, it was within the knowledge of the defence, and not of the prosecution that this man had material, whether it is relevant to the issue is beside the point, on which it was clear that one of the Crown witnesses or the prosecution witnesses who may be called was making a very uncomplimentary remark about your worship. This was known to the defence solicitor before the matter came before you. [pages 371–372]

...

Your worship, during the course of that hearing on that day, you had before you, a police prosecutor who was not aware of any allegations that may have been made against him. The defence was aware of the allegations that were about to be made by this witness, because ... it is clear that they [the defence] had all statements from him [Davey]. And not only did we have a spectacle of a prosecutor who had a right, as it were, to be exempted from conducting the prosecution compelled to continue with the prosecution. Your worship would remember, the transcript is before you, repeatedly it was said by the defence that it was in the interest of justice that some material this witness had ought to be made public. [page 373]

...

Your worship, now, at this stage, [he] is worried about cost. Well, your worship, if his clients need any legal aid and there's justification for it, I understand there's some provision for that. Your worship, I bring this aspect to your attention, that when you look at it, and this is the evidence, that the matter comes before your worship with the defence having all the knowledge of what was about to happen. The matter then is placed before your worship on the basis that there was a great urgency that

## CHAPTER 6

this witness should be allowed to make the matter public.
[page 374]

...

The matter then, your worship, is conducted in a way where that very night, on the day on which your court was sitting this witness, who is under oath, who was a party in this proceeding, is then before a union where the tape is being played. In the whole of the circumstances ... when we talk about justice, we do not talk about one man making allegations and then there being some sort of a conclusion of the matter. In this case, shortly, when I have finished with the cross-examination of this witness I'll be giving a brief opening that would show the nature of the conspiracy that existed to destroy prosecution witnesses who held the key to the investigation of other dishonest police officers ...
[page 374]

...

It must have occurred to your worship, that it is a rather sad spectacle in some ways, where you have a public airing of police matters. On the other hand, it is in the interest of the community, it is in the interest of justice, that these matters ought to be dealt with in the proper way in a court of law. No-one quibbles with my learned friend on the question of relevance, but the Crown says, 'relevance would be shown after the cross-examination of this witness concludes'. your worship is already familiar with the unusual course that has developed in this court and it is not the intention of the prosecution, as I mentioned at the commencement of this case when I took over on behalf of the prosecution, at any stage, to seek any adjournment so that no evidence is suppressed, and it does not matter where that evidence leads to.
[page 374)

Several times in the middle of the betting case the defence mentioned the need for a royal commission, and I returned to the subject to say that the prosecution was not asking for a royal commission in the middle of these proceedings:

> LAKSHMAN: First of all, there is the allegation that was contained in this witness's evidence that received wide publicity that tended to implicate other police officers, and now, having reached a stage where his story is out, my learned friend is endeavouring to restrict ... But your worship it is indeed in the interest of justice that some of the material that is in my possession should be placed before your worship for the same reason that the defence gave when it insisted on that day that it was in the interests of justice that some of the material should be made public, heard in an open court, and now the prosecution seeks the same opportunity for the same reasons, and when your worship hears the opening which I'll give, after the cross-examination of this witness is completed, your worship would have no hesitation in allowing the prosecution to put on record, on public record, in this court matters that go to the issues that are being decided before your worship. [page 381]
>
> BENCH: Well, that's the way I see it. But the event on the 13th has no relevance to the issues before this court, and I won't allow further questions on the matter.
> [page 391]

The Jordan matter was introduced by the defence and having got Davey's version alone, the prosecution was being prevented from exploring it to see what had really happened in the Jordan matter. Davey had said the warrants were forged and evidence fabricated. The magistrate obliged, and the prosecution was prevented from pursuing the matter. When the magistrate ruled that the prosecution could not pursue the Jordan matter, I wanted to be heard on the subject. Before even the magistrate could address the matter Macgroarty objected in these terms.

# CHAPTER 6

LAKSHMAN: Your worship might hear me briefly?

MACGROARTY: If it please your worship, your worship has ruled my learned friend ... can't alter your worship's ruling if he seeks a remedy, he has it in another court and I submit, at this stage, your worship, that my learned friend should comply with your worship's ruling and not try and badger your worship into altering that ruling, a matter which, with respect to your worship, as I'm sure your worship is fully aware, your worship cannot alter it. Your worship made a ruling and that is that, and my learned friend should not endeavour to try and badger your worship into altering it. [page 391]

I could see that the defence was really not enjoying it. It was getting more strident and frustrated. Just when the defence had its hands full protecting Davey, it now needed to protect the magistrate. He was being badgered. It would be interesting to see in due course what the full court had to say about the conduct of the prosecution in the light of all that had happened in Southport. The magistrate was not complaining.

BENCH: I'll hear what you have to say.

LAKSHMAN: Your worship, I think the position is, in looking at the transcript, that this witness was allowed – well, Mr Sturgess's cross-examination – to open up matters pertaining to the 13th of November. It's there on transcript. Perhaps your worship might give me a short opportunity to refer to the portions dealing there. Mr Sturgess brought up the fact that on that day, the evidence was concocted ... Also, the men were falsely charged. It'll be a travesty of justice if those matters, which are pertinent now, to the question of who is concocting evidence, that your worship would (not) allow this witness to be cross-examined ... [page 417, 30 June 1975]

MACGROARTY: We could be here for days and days, indeed perhaps the fortnight that my learned friend mentioned last

week, and why should my two clients have to bear the cost in their defence of this charge of the investigation by the Crown of all these matters?
[page 417]

There are repeated pleas that the cost was an issue, and the length of the proceedings was costing the defendants' money. I thought that perhaps Herbert could help them because they had lent themselves to Herbert's plan to attack Pitts and his men. For good measure, at the conclusion of the matter the magistrate refused to allow costs to Siebers, who was represented by Macgroarty. The prosecution was in no hurry.

> LAKSHMAN: ... Your worship, I think that is the sort of argument that should be rejected completely. We will be here, your worship, as long as it takes for the prosecution to present its case properly and effectively and fully.
>
> ...
>
> Your worship, he [Sturgess] had said he had taken over the cross-examination from the prosecuting police officer, because he wanted to put certain matters before the court. It would be, in my submission, not the proper course to disallow those witnesses to give an explanation and to disallow the opportunity to the prosecution to cross-examine this witness in relation to those matters.
> [pages 419–420]

The defence had virtually taken over from Jeppesen during the cross-examination of Davey to place the Jordan matter, because it was said to be so important for the court to hear what Davey had said, but the magistrate was not allowing the prosecution to examine Davey to test his version in detail. It would be interesting to see what the full court had to say about the obliging magistrate in due course.

> MACGROARTY: ... A royal commission? Certainly, some royal commission or some public inquiry should be

made into Frank Davey's most serious allegations about the Police Force of Queensland, but not at the expense of my two clients. And to stand here and challenge my professional integrity is no answer to my submission of law. [pages 593–594]

This may become boring so I will spare the reader the next 2000 pages of the transcript. The purpose here is to show how hard the prosecution fought and how, in the end, the guilty were acquitted.

It shows how the dishonest forces gained control of the Queensland Police Force for the next decade or so; but, in the end, the dishonest reside in the field of ignominy, whereas those who fought to cleanse the system and who are also dead and buried were vindicated in the Fitzgerald Report.

The report vindicated the efforts of Deputy Commissioner Gulbransen, Inspector Hicks and others. Of Inspector Pitts the report noted that: 'Whitrod had been told Pitts was honest, hard-working and efficient, and so he proved to be ...' That is the epitaph one would like on one's tombstone.

Finally, there is a quote from Winston Churchill when he was dealing with nations, but which is quite apposite for the struggle that I have described. He said: 'Nations which go down fighting rise again, and those that surrender tamely are finished.'

This is a story of those who fought and rose again. It is my hope that the children and descendants of these people will read it too.

## JAPANESE VICTIM (1976)

I had the conduct of a case some 45 years ago against an accused called Day. I now have no detailed recollection of the evidence or even his full name. He was charged with the murder of a Japanese student whose body was found, but there were problems identifying him. To prove his proper identity and get more particulars of what he was doing and his whereabouts at the time of the murder, on my advice, the Crown decided to call as witnesses his parents from Japan to give evidence; also, to call a competent interpreter for a jury trial. The Crown paid all the expenses.

This was still a time when some of the judges on the Supreme Court had fought in the war in which many Australians had lost their lives and had been interred in Japanese war camps, some returning with serious injuries. I am relating this because the head of the Japanese Consulate-General, Mr Seijero Shirahama, told me during several consultations that in Tokyo, Japan, the officials could not believe that the Government of Queensland would spend so much money in the pursuit of justice where a foreigner was killed. It is a unique trait of the Australian people that they did care, and no one would have suggested that a Japanese victim deserved less attention than anyone else. He was only stating the fact that many other nations care for their own but would not go out of their way to do such things.

The prosecution lost this case, and I have been nursing a grievance ever since. The trial judge paid little attention to the evidence. I cynically remarked to my friends that perhaps he, too, had served in the war and was not prepared to forgive and forget. Others have pointed out the obvious—namely, that the prosecution led by me did a poor job!

Mr Shirahama wanted the parents and some Japanese officials to be photographed in court to show what happened in a criminal trial in Australia. I was given a part too. I have photos of some of the ladies dressed in beautiful Japanese clothes standing next to me, all dressed up like a penguin, taken in the court.

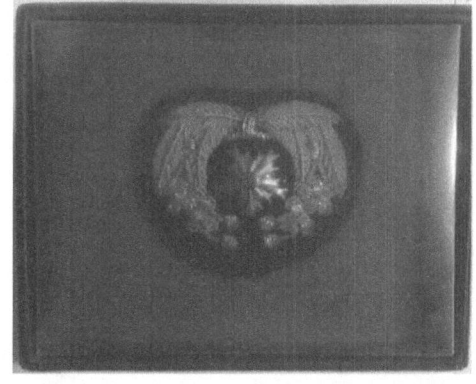

*Plaque presented by the Japanese Consulate.*

I then received an invitation to the residence of the Consulate-General to a function, attended by other guests, for the celebration of the Birthday of His Majesty, the Emperor of Japan. It was at some stage then that I received what you see in the photograph or so I believe. I was also given some beautiful fans. I just happened to be a symbol of their idea of Australian justice.

CHAPTER 6

## *THE QUEEN V JULIE ANNE WRIGHT* (AKA JULIE CASHMAN): ANGEL OF DEATH (1985)

I lost the record of this trial and so, after a lapse of some 35 years, I sought out some of the witnesses in the case to ensure this account is an accurate one.

I do recall that the very first thing I did in this case was to see the Chief Justice of the Supreme Court and tell him that the police were concerned that there was a real possibility of some crime syndicate or some criminals attempting to kill prospective witnesses and free Julie Cashman. The result was that police marksmen were stationed on the top of buildings surrounding the Supreme Court to offer protection. I wondered how I was again handed the poisoned chalice by the Crown Law Office. I have given this dramatic opening simply because this is how it all happened. I know that some of you think that lawyers can be such drama queens. Not so.

Julie Cashman became so dangerous and notorious that she was listed as one of the ten most infamous escapees from Sydney prisons. She is there with Mad Dog Russell who in 1977 escaped from a maximum-security section of the prison that was believed to be completely escape-proof. He was on the run for eleven years before being caught. His escape was some seven years before Julie Cashman was tried in Brisbane on the armed robbery charge.

Now for some details as to why there were armed police protecting witnesses and the court system in Brisbane. Julie Cashman had successfully escaped whilst pregnant when her then partner Bruce Kennedy helped her escape from Silverwater Women's Correctional Centre in 1978. She had been convicted of trying to rob a supermarket. She escaped through a toilet window, shedding all her clothes in the process, and met her partner, who had made a hole in the security fence. The pair were caught in Queensland a few weeks later in a shoot-out that led to the death of her partner, who was shot dead. It seemed that the police were taking no prisoners.

There were extensive searches to find the accused and her new partner Ray Wright, who was a notorious criminal too. They arrived in

Brisbane and on 28 September in broad daylight robbed the Armaguard Security Van at Wolston Park Hospital. The amount stolen, in the vicinity of $250,000, was considered massive in those days. Both the assailants wore large clown masks and could not be clearly identified. The security guard happened to be a very little man who was terrified to see what was happening, but as the assailants were getting in the vehicle he fired his rifle and the male dropped dead in the gutter. Then the second clown jumped out of the vehicle and tried to lift up this large and heavy man while screaming all the time. He identified the scream as that of a woman. The accused then left the scene with this large loot and hitched a ride out of town and just vanished. The photographs of the scene showed a large male, heavily clad in boots, large coat and thick gloves, lying in the gutter.

Some months later the accused, Cashman, was captured by the police in Dandenong, Victoria. She had taken a massive concoction of drugs and was hallucinating. The police made no attempt to question her. Later in the evening the police called a female doctor, Dr Fakia Jappie, to examine the accused.

I looked at Dr Jappie's statement but needed to interview her before the trial.

I have spoken to Dr Jappie again just recently whilst writing this account, and she told me that from the moment she arrived in Brisbane until she caught a flight back home she had armed security police following her for her protection. She had a vivid recollection of what happened in court during the trial and also what she recorded when she gave her evidence. She told the court that the accused was coherent, cogent and physically fit and in fact told this witness things that could only have been known to the accused at the scene of the crime.

Dr Fakia Jappie was born in South Africa, and because she looked Indian to me, I wanted to know more about her. It turned out that she was of some Indonesian/Turkish/Afghani background. And it turned out that she was not just an ordinary GP. She had studied in London and had completed a specialist diploma course in medical jurisprudence. This was a new course conducted by the Society of Hypothecaries (pharmacology). She had specialised in clinical forensic medicine with living bodies. I was anticipating that the defence would call evidence. But this did not happen. The witness gave minute details of her examination and went on to say that when she examined the pubic area she found the word 'Vince' tattooed there. The accused, who had remained sullen and quiet, suddenly screamed, shouted and had to be pacified. I was told later by the doctor that the accused had told everybody that Ray Wright was her one true love and hated to see another name just pop up! Anyway, the accused was convicted and sentenced to nine years' imprisonment. She appealed and the sentence was increased to twelve years.

Most of the money was never recovered but her mother was found in possession of $25,000 and tried for receiving stolen money. The mother told the police that the money was given to her by her friend for the benefit of Julie Cashman's child, but she had no memory of the friend's name! In that case, the defence argued that there were no serial numbers for the Armaguard Van robbery and so there was no proof that the money came from that robbery. I have no idea what happened in that case before a magistrates court.

Now you know why the 'Angle of Death' struck terror in the hearts of serving police officers.

I must now digress to tell you that this was a period in Brisbane when barristers went to court fully attired in wig and gown. They could be seen trundling along George Street, looking like some monks in the Middle Ages. I belonged to a small group of barristers who robed and disrobed within the court precinct; and for a long time most people had no idea what sort of work I did.

One morning on my way to court I noticed very tight security and additional security staff outside. I did not see any of the bailiffs we knew. As I approached the entry point to the building I noticed that all the barristers who were in their wigs and gowns were quickly processed without any questions. I was stopped because I was in my civilian clothes and one security man wanted to know who I was. In those days, Crown prosecutors carried no identification on them.

However, before I could speak, a barrister I knew, who was behind me, told the security guard that I really looked suspicious and that I had been seen prowling around the courts for several days! I laughed but the security man refused to let me enter the building and other officials had to be called to clear me. This barrister had just made a quip and had no idea that I would be stopped. When I met that barrister again in a criminal trial, I paid him back big-time!

These following cases should give a good picture of the work I did just before retirement in 1992.

## *R V KNIBB*: MURDER ON THE BEACH IN CAIRNS (1987)

In this case, journalists Allen Leslie and John Penlington provided compelling evidence leading to a conviction.

On 3 August 1985, just at dusk on a day described by many as glorious, some visitors were enjoying a sunset at Buchan Point. Miranda Downes was seen on the beach. She appeared to look around and then started jogging along the beach. She had some sort of wrap around her waist. It was now getting dark. When some indeterminate time had elapsed and Miranda had failed to return, her friends who had invited her to stay with them on a property very close to the beach, became alarmed. They went down to the beach to search for her and found the beach was quiet and deserted. No one looked at their watch, but they recalled the light was fading.

Miranda Downes had been savagely attacked. When her body was found, it appeared that the incoming tide had dragged it just near the margin of the ocean. It was not thought that the body had been sucked out to sea. The body had been stripped naked and she had severe injuries including some bruising. The forensic evidence showed that she was struck with a heavy instrument and left to drown. On one medical assessment, she was alive and helpless when she drowned. There were marks on her throat and neck consistent with strangulation, and the body appeared to have been dragged into the sea a short distance only.

# CHAPTER 6

The specialist pathologist, who later went on to become a Professor of Medicine at the University of Queensland, and who had given evidence in numerous murder cases, examined the body the very next day and concluded that she had been struck by a motor vehicle. There was a Y-shaped abrasion on the back of her left shoulder. He gave the following opinion:

> Most of the other superficial injuries on the deceased are consistent with and suggestive of the deceased having been knocked over by a motor vehicle. No major internal injuries were associated with these injuries, but it would be possible for the accused to have been stunned or knocked over by the impact without any positive internal findings at post-mortem.

He continued:

> The Y-shaped abrasion and large abrasion on the left shoulder of the deceased were consistent with having been caused by the driver's rear vision mirror of the four-wheel-drive vehicle examined by me.

The pathologist continued:

> Most of the injuries sustained by the deceased are not typical of injuries sustained by the body being washed around in the surf while still alive.

I remember some cynics in the legal fraternity saying to me that the actual crime scene was a crime writer's dream and went on to describe this case as: 'Murder on a sandy beach with no evidence'. The incoming tide had destroyed all evidence near the body; her underpants were found near the body but were wet and yielded no evidence. The other clothing, including a sloppy joe and something that had been seen wrapped around her waist, was also found wet. All evidence had been washed away and the wet, naked body yielded nothing to connect any suspect to this crime of murder. Police conducted an extensive search for a suspect. At some stage, the accused was identified as Ernest Arthur

Knibb, but there was very little to connect him to this crime. The only evidence was that he, in common with some others, could be placed on the beach at about dusk. That was not enough.

This search for clues continued for two long years and, in that time, some of the prospective witnesses who had come from interstate and even as far as London could not state firmly where exactly, in relation to the crime scene, these witnesses were and what they saw see in a few minutes and what exact particulars they could give. I intended calling some eighty witnesses, approximately twenty of whom were near the beach and not on the beach. Most only accounted for glimpses lasting a minute or two.

I became aware of this unsolved case only in June of 1987 when I was assigned to prosecute and to attend to the committal hearing should it be determined that there was sufficient evidence to show that there was a prima facie case. This is what all prosecutors do in Australia. It is just part of our daily chores. I had access to all the main investigators, and they came to see me in Brisbane to study all the available evidence. This is a phase in the investigation when senior investigators play some sort of hypothetical game dealing with all 'what ifs'.

Two years had passed. I wanted to know who this victim was and why she was in Cairns.

Miranda Downes

# CHAPTER 6

Miranda Downes, at the relevant time, was working in Sydney as a screenwriter and living with her partner, James, who was a self-employed documentary filmmaker. They had met in the seventies when she was working as a receptionist at Spectrum Films. The deceased was aged thirty-three at the time of her death. As you can see from the photographs, she was very fit and looked more like someone in her mid-twenties. She and James were living together mostly in his home. When she arrived in Cairns he phoned her, barely hours before her death, to tell her that he was missing her. He also mentioned that his mother was very ill. He was not to know that that would be the last time he would speak to her. All his emotions were there to see in the open courtroom. At the time of her death, Miranda was a self-employed scriptwriter and was planning to go to Yeppoon to make a movie, and that explained part of the reason that she went north.

I am telling you her background because in a trial of murder very little is permitted to be led in evidence about the victim. In this very trial, the defence raised some objection to the prosecution leading evidence of this nature. So, you know more about Miranda than the jury did. Miranda had a wide circle of friends in the film industry and was a vivacious, happy person, much admired by her friends. Her partner, James, told the court that Miranda had arranged to meet and stay with her very close friends from London who had travelled to Cairns to see the sister of a family who lived and worked in Cape Tribulation. He also told the police that Miranda loved bushwalking and attended regular gym classes in Sydney. Again, he told the police: 'That phone call I made on the Saturday morning was to say that I loved her.' These were his actual words. He said that she said to him: 'Please don't forget to collect the mail and water my plants.' Mostly, all that the jury heard was the deceased's identification. Crown prosecutors are taught to be objective. But this is a human story of the senseless destruction of a life. Cases like this make investigators determined to bring the killer to justice.

The police had kept the accused under general observation for over two years, but nothing happened. It remained just another unsolved murder case. This murder would not have been solved but for the involvement of Ian Craig Leslie, a reporter with *60 Minutes,* and journalist John Penlington. Ian Leslie told the police that the Executive Producer of *60 Minutes*, Gerald Stone, wanted him to explore the possibility of dealing with this murder in which nothing had happened for several years. It so happened that the accused had approached *60 Minutes* and claimed that he was being harassed by the police and wanted to bring this to public attention and wanted a chance to tell the world that he had not murdered the deceased. He also said that he wanted to assist the police and was prepared to take a lie detector test, or hypnosis or even some truth drug to prove his innocence. Ian Leslie thought this would make excellent material for *60 Minutes*! He was prepared to have all this on tape and make a movie.

I must tell you that I agonised before proceeding further with the case. Crown prosecutors have no masters once they are on their feet in court. You will see in the Graham Stafford case (mentioned later) that I refused to prosecute because I had concluded that he could not have committed the murder, and no one could have directed me to continue with the prosecution. That is how it worked.

What would you think if a suspect says that he is prepared to be hypnotised and that he does not mind taking some sort of truth serum (there is no such thing) to prove his innocence? Do you think a guilty man would be prepared to undergo hypnosis? If you were guilty of murder, would you submit yourself to hypnosis? If you did, you would have no control and could blurt out that you were there and that you raped and strangled the victim and then threw her into the sea. Would you do it if you were guilty? Ordinary people know that once hypnotised, a person has no control and could start admitting his crime. The accused did not admit anything during this session. He was willing to have the whole thing filmed and shown to the public. A simpleton might do this, but the accused was no simpleton. I concluded that without this taped material, no jury would convict.

Australia is not America. Here no hypnosis evidence is admissible in our courts. So why did the court allow the prosecution to call this evidence? Because the Crown wanted the jury to know that guilty people lie and cheat to cover up their crimes; that only a guilty mind would go through this charade and do things so that they can escape detection. I said that the Crown could show that this was not hypnosis because he was faking it and the Crown could use this evidence as a devastating tool to convict the accused on a charge of murder.

The fact that hypnosis evidence is never received in evidence meant that I had very little material to show how the prosecution should proceed. If there are decided cases, then we could read what to do no next. So, I decided to have a long conference with two leading authorities on the subject and told them that neither the jury nor counsel at the bar table would have any. Both had spent their lives lecturing to students and knew how to teach hard subjects. I am sure that the questions I posed must have sounded stupid to them. I knew nothing about how it worked. I was asking questions and quietly listening. I thought that they must think that I was a real dill!

These two professors in psychology were leading authorities not only in Australia but perhaps in the world in this field and had won many prestigious awards for their research on how you can tell when a man is faking and pretending that he is under hypnosis. Professor Sheehan was a professor at the University of Queensland (my university). His qualifications filled a whole sheet of paper. I recall that when he finished giving his evidence the defence counsel said it would be very hard to contradict his evidence. If the defence disagreed, then it should challenge that evidence. What does it mean? It meant the Crown could tell the jury that the accused was faking it and that he was not hypnotised and there was no evidence to contradict the Crown case on faking. His action showed that he knew or was conscious of his guilt.

I will not produce for you the massive amount of material and the evidence Professor Sheehan gave to the court to show that the accused was faking. So, you be the jury now on what he told the court. He recited the indicia of what you will see if a man is faking hypnosis. I will give you only some because no one wants you to suddenly become an armchair expert on hypnosis!

Professor Sheehan said:

> I consider that hypnosis is essentially a phenomenon that reflects genuinely experienced radical distortions of reality in response to suggestions administered by the hypnotist. To identify the phenomenon, one must rely heavily on the subjective testimony of the subject hypnotised ... I consider memory is a constructive process, it changes over time and accommodates alterations in feelings and information about events and what is remembered.

This was his final answer:

> The evidence overall in this case demonstrates to me an accumulation of indications that Knibb is faking being hypnotised ... he was faking or simulating being hypnotised ... This was not truthfully his memory of additional information ... evidence suggests a motivated strategic attempt by Knibb to respond to cues available to him ...

This was powerful evidence that he was not hypnotised and there was no evidence in rebuttal to dispute this evidence.

I know you the reader is a murder sleuth who is going to solve this case. I will tell you the real problems for the prosecution in this case because I was there and had the conduct of the prosecution case. The body was found naked and washed (by the sea) with no clues; the clothes were wet; no actual weapon was found; and there were no footprints on the sand. So, what was the evidence? You might say that the accused lied and said he was not hypnotised; he was not charged with lying but murder. That would be in keeping with common sense and the law. I will tell you why the noose was now slowly tightening.

The prosecution wanted to put the accused close to the murder scene. This filmed session showed that he was saying he was on the beach that night.

So, the Crown could show that there could be no doubt about his presence near the murder scene. Earlier he had told the police that he was

## CHAPTER 6

never on the beach and then later in another interview when confronted with the evidence of witnesses that his vehicle was seen on the beach, he changed his story. He then said he was on the beach but that he had left the beach before she was killed. How do you contradict him?

The prosecution, from the list of some eighty witnesses, had some twenty-five or so witnesses from all over Australia and from England as well to meet this challenge. When there are serious crimes, the Australian States are prepared to spend any amount of money to secure justice. These witnesses had to be flown in and fed and housed in hotels. These were mostly tourists on holiday who had no notebooks to mark the times, and they only had a few minutes to observe any happenings on the beach of interest to the prosecution. Moreover, they had no reason to look at anybody in particular. I found in my experience that when I dealt with what the witnesses might have seen on a beach, then the only time the male witnesses had a vivid recollection was when they were asked to describe a beautiful blonde in a bikini. Then nobody said that they did not recollect the details! Human nature is so fickle and yet so selective!

These witnesses were being called to give evidence about an event that occurred over two years after the crime was committed, and they were being asked to give details. This is when the defence counsel generally has a field day in court because most witnesses would say that they could not be definite about anything. You might say that if the evidence is so flaky, why waste taxpayer money on this type of witness? Yes, you would be right. But there were also even more obstacles for the Crown to support your view. You know, when this type of thing happens, the poor investigators are under enormous pressure as to what they should do next.

The next problem was with the crime scene. The proposition for the defence was that the prosecution could not discount the possibility that the killing took place on the next adjoining beach and the incoming tide carried the body on to Buchan Point. If the deceased was taken and killed on another beach, then the accused had nothing to do with it, no matter who saw him on Buchan Point Beach. This meant that the prosecution had to put before the jury a massive amount of material proving that the high and low tides and other evidence showed that this was impossible, and this also included the fact that the body had only been dragged into the water when the tide went out and placed back again where it was found.

The tyre-pattern marks on the beach near the body were identical to the tyres on the vehicle driven by the accused. Also, the clothing items found could not have travelled from another beach and be so conveniently deposited near the body on this beach. The jury must have rejected that hypothetical theory!

Tyre tracks from the suspect vehicle, *R v Knibb*

Now back to the problem with witnesses who saw something on the beach. This beach, like most beaches (as you will see from the photograph below), looks like it is curved. It looks like it is part of a large circle. Put it another way, it is not straight but curved. You might say yes but what of it? Well, these twenty witnesses were spread over the curve. Now, to follow what this problem is, just draw a curve on a sheet of paper and then imagine that the curve is 1 kilometre or 2 kilometres long (the beach is that long) so you can follow what the witnesses described about twenty times.

Now, just forget what happened in the murder case and deal with a witness we might call X. Suppose you want to know where X was standing and what he saw. If X were standing on the right end of the circle, then X might say that he looked around to the left and saw Y (the accused) standing on his left and would be cross-examined to show, for example, why it was not possible to see anything from there.

If X were standing on the left end of the curve, then X would say everything happened on the right-hand side because he turned and looked to the right. If X were standing in the middle of the circular beach, X would say it all happened right in front of him.

If the jury members were listening to just a few witnesses, they might have found the information easy to grasp, but there were some twenty such witnesses and the trial went on and on for four weeks. During the summing up of the evidence, even the trial judge had difficulty in deciding what to tell the jury as to what these witnesses actually saw. I must confess that at the end of some long trials, I could not even tell the time of day and did not know the difference between left and right either! Why bother writing about all these trivial matters when dealing with a serious murder story? Because most trials are not romantic or easy to follow. Every day, they involve humdrum work.

Complex murder scene on the beach, *R v Knibb*

The accused was convicted and sentenced to life imprisonment. He appealed. I appeared for the Crown before the Court of Criminal Appeal. The court rejected the appeal and affirmed the conviction. The prisoner then appealed to the High Court of Australia. I appeared before the High Court to argue the appeal. The High Court dismissed the appeal. I mention this for another reason, and that is that very few countries in the world have such a severe filtering system to look at the evidence, again and again, to make sure that no innocent person is convicted. Even then, there is never absolute certainty.

## *THE QUEEN V HUIRUA HOANA HARDING*: A CHILD WITNESS (1988)

This is the story of the prosecution of the accused, Huirua Hoana Harding, on two separate charges of murder that occurred at the same incident.

The case for the prosecution was that two women were brutally killed on the outskirts of Brisbane in a remote and deserted area at Logan Reserve on 16 September 1986. The murders were committed in broad daylight. Both the victims were subjected to a frenzied attack with a carving knife, and both had their throats cut and bled to death. One of the victims was found completely naked on a blood-soaked bed, and she had been raped. The severe injuries to the arms of the victims suggested that the victims resisted with their bare hands, and the knife wounds and slashes, together with the blood-splattered walls and carpets, bore testimony to the desperate struggle for survival in a violent and frenzied episode.

The police mounted an extensive search for the killer, which lasted many months, but a lack of evidence and insurmountable evidentiary problems meant no one was charged. A whole year passed, and no action was taken. The public was incensed because of the brutality of the killings, and a reward was offered, but the identity of the killer remained unknown. Adding to the public outrage was the fact that this horrendous crime had been committed in the presence of a five-year-old child, a little girl who was the daughter of one of the slain victims—the one who had been stripped naked and raped. The murderer had either missed the child in the frenzied attack or had spared her.

The little girl was in the house within metres of her mother. She heard the dying screams of her mother and saw her mother's naked body with severe injuries. The child saw many things that happened before the murders and witnessed the two murders. A short time later, motorists found the little girl wandering a long distance away from the property, leading a horse that belonged to one of the victims. She was very distressed and incoherent but told the strangers who stopped to question her that her mother was dead and that she was trying to protect the horse. The child said the man wanted the horse and was going to hurt it.

Harding was a man of Maori extraction, built like a tank, who had come from New Zealand about a year before. He was tried in 1988, close to two years after the murders, and I appeared for the prosecution.

# CHAPTER 6

There were many problems with this case. While there was no question that one victim was both raped and killed and that both murders had happened one after another on that fateful day, the blood tests and other samples taken from the accused showed beyond a doubt that the seminal fluid did not belong to the accused. His blood grouping was distinct from the general population; from the results obtained from the seminal material found in the murder victim, it was impossible to conclude that he had committed the rape. If the accused had not raped the victim, the chance of a conviction on the double-murder charge was slim. Police had ruled out the husband of the rape victim, both because he had told the police that he had not had sexual intercourse with his wife the night before the attack and because his blood group did not match. The seminal fluid belonged to an unknown and unidentified man.

There were no fingerprints or other evidence found at the crime scene that linked Harding to the crimes. He told the police that he did not know the property or the women. He was seen a few hours after the murders were committed but had clean clothes, and no blood was found on him. He even had an alibi, which he gave to the police. He cooperated with the police and was prepared to give a blood sample and to confront the witnesses. When asked to put on similar clothes and to run so that the suspect could be identified by eyewitnesses who had described seeing a man in the vicinity of the property, Harding was prepared to take part in the demonstration. He gave a statement and signed it. He never asked for a lawyer to be present when he gave the first statement. He never went to see a lawyer for help until he was charged with murder a year later.

The main investigation team in the case was led by Sergeant Costello, who was a capable and thorough investigator whom I had known from previous trials. The police did excellent work from the prosecution perspective because it was the evidence of the early investigation that was critical to the case. Harding told the police many significant lies and finally said that he knew something about the real murderers. He said they were drug dealers and that if he told the police who they were, he would be killed and so he would rather plead guilty and go to jail.

There were notorious cases in which drug couriers had been summarily executed, so this story had some resonance, but it was not convincing. Nonetheless, it had to be taken seriously. Harding never identified the killers but gave general descriptions of the possible suspects, which included one of Islander appearance like himself. Extensive searches failed to find any of the suspects described by the accused.

A man answering the description of Harding had been seen in the area and that could be proved, but there was no evidence at that stage to show that he was on the deserted property at the time of the murder. The closest point that a suspect was seen was on the road near the property some 300 metres away from the gate of the property, but the only witness who saw this could not identify the accused from the photographs subsequently shown to him. In murder trials, 300 metres is as good as being five or ten kilometres from the murder scene. The prosecution could not put any suspect on the Tidy property, which was the murder scene.

The prosecution has some discretion as to which witnesses may be called, but when I first looked at the evidence, I decided that we should not and probably could not call a child of such tender age to give evidence. The very idea that a young child who had witnessed such a terrible event should play any part in the trial was rejected. There were legal obstacles, and it was considered unnecessary and undesirable to introduce a little child for any purpose. I was prepared to marshal the Crown case and thought that the murders could be proved and should be proved by recourse to circumstantial evidence and without any need to involve such a young child.

It was also expected that there would be fierce resistance from all quarters to the introduction of a child in a legal game because of the possible traumatic and long-term consequences to the child.

The question to call or not to call the child remained in the background and a much deeper assessment of all evidence was undertaken about a year after the murders were committed. I still considered it was possible to prove the guilt of the accused without the need to involve a little child. As it turned out, we eventually had no choice but to involve the child.

# CHAPTER 6

This is the story of what happened, and the story of a brave child witness prepared to confront in court the murderer of her mother. It is the story of how a case based entirely on circumstantial evidence nearly collapsed and would have collapsed without the child's evidence. It is an account in which the narrator is also part of the narration so there is no possibility of maintaining complete objectivity because of the partisan nature of the contest in criminal trials. The very qualification that this is a 'prosecutorial' account is an admission of some bias, and bias is at the very heart of the adversarial system in which lawyers function. It is an acknowledgement that the story that is about to be told may be biased in favour of the prosecution and this is more a statement about the narrator than the narrative.

I digress to make a general comment to readers that there are some in the general community who do not understand that 'bias' is a necessary tool and is quintessential to the art of advocacy and that without bias no advocate can practise in the criminal courts. These passing comments are directed to those uninitiated in matters legal and are not intended as a criticism of the legal profession; some lawyers are likely to treat this statement as sacrilegious, offensive or irrelevant to the discussion. In my experience, at least in the initial stages of their careers, lawyers are infused with idealism and are all bushy-tailed and naïve. They think that the legal profession is all about the pursuit of Truth and Justice, as discussed by philosophers. The fact is that those who are not biased or prejudiced, in the sense I mean to convey, would never know what justice is.

The most common trait or feature about criminal justice and advocacy is illustrated in the actions of a marksman at target practice who never fires a shot with both eyes open. The experienced, practised and effective advocate must be cock-eyed; otherwise, he is destined to fail. This is too harsh a judgement, so we must resort to the usual euphemism and merely say that an advocate must be focused, single-minded, and dedicated to the cause he or she represents. That is a nice way of saying the same thing, and no decent lawyer would take exception to that.

And if all this is not confusing enough, then outside the Supreme Court in Brisbane stands a tall statue of Themis, the Greek Goddess of Justice. To save her from bias, she is blindfolded. Lawyers with no stomach for bias in the sense described have no business practising law, certainly not in our criminal courts. In the distant past, such lovely unbiased souls with a passion for pure justice and truth would have been encouraged by the wise to enrol in a seminary and women with any such sentiments would have been simply sent to a nunnery. The sentiments expressed so far on inbuilt bias in criminal trials, without some further qualifications, would be dismissed as misguided, incomplete or a mere quibble.

A recital of the facts in a case based entirely on circumstantial evidence is a tedious exercise. Many hours are devoted to deciding which pieces of evidence are relevant and admissible. There is no precise way of assessing and evaluating which pieces of evidence may assume some significance and have weight beyond expectations, nor to identify pieces of evidence that may buckle, fizzle and vanish when subjected to rigorous cross-examination. There is much trampling and kicking done to destroy both the weight and substance of these frail, tender and isolated threads of evidence.

However, experienced trial lawyers have always acknowledged that these isolated, frail, tender tendrils of evidence, through a simple process of accumulation in a meaningful way and especially when piled layer upon layer, can form a rope and a noose from which there is no escape. It is easier to destroy the credibility of an eyewitness or to attack a confessional statement as a police fabrication than it is to destroy the evidentiary value of mute pieces of evidence pointing to the guilt of an accused. These pieces of evidence bounce about when kicked around but keep popping up without blinking, never showing human frailty or emotion. It must be heartbreaking for those poor lawyers who have a hard-earned reputation for bullying, cajoling and threatening witnesses to have to deal with cases based solely on circumstantial evidence.

I have sat and watched with glee some of the cross-examinations of expert Crown witnesses by the defence counsel in lengthy criminal trials.

# CHAPTER 6

It is an extremely difficult assignment as most of the evidence in these types of cases is spread over different areas of the police investigation and appears to lack cogency and cohesion unless given proper context and explanation.

I recall in one such lengthy case a very experienced defence counsel walked into court one morning to be confronted with a large volume of such tiny and tenuous pieces of evidence, which he described as being 'all over the place'. He said to me, probably in jest: 'Vish, what is the bloody prosecution up to now?' and continued: '... looks like this case is glued together with spit and shit.' I thought that I was being complimented because in villages in India and even in Fiji cow dung was used as a binding agent like a sort of cement and was used in the construction of dwellings and thatched sheds. When working with pathologists and forensic scientists, there was often a real sense that we were knee-deep in 'spit and shit'. Such cryptic one-line comments at the bar table during serious criminal trials made some judges lean forward to see what was so entertaining and why counsel was nodding and grinning in the middle of a serious episode in the trial.

It is the jigsaw elements in circumstantial evidence cases that are baffling. The accumulation in a meaningful way of little pieces of evidence lies at the very heart of such cases. The more threads there are, the more entwined the tendrils, and the more these threads cumulatively point to the accused as the perpetrator of a crime, the stronger and firmer the noose. To the uninitiated, the presentation of such evidence may give a false impression. It is the frail gossamer effect that is misleading, and sometimes it gives the impression to the casual observer that the case is resting on thin ice or on a delicate gauze that could be rendered with a stroke of the cross-examiner's pencil-sharp mind.

To the uninitiated, the reliance on such pieces of evidence gives the appearance of desperation as if the prosecution is scrounging around for something no matter how tenuous to connect the accused to the crime. The prosecution may appear to be clutching at straws, but the right number of such clutches at straws result in threads that make a strong rope, a noose from which there is no escape. The more such clutches of straws there are, the more dangerous the prosecution case.

It is a very ordinary experience in our courts for the jury to be told that circumstantial evidence is a powerful tool used in the legal process for the discovery of other reliable and relevant facts and circumstances going to the guilt of the accused. In its true nature, circumstantial evidence is not tenuous and fragile but more like tensile steel, which may bend and buckle with the weight of cross-examination but not yield or break; and once the trap shuts, there is no escape.

A popular misconception is revealed in such statements as: 'Oh, it's just all circumstantial and nothing more!' Lawyers who read these comments may find all this trite because they have heard it all before, but the bored lawyers are not the audience in the mind of the prosecution. The almost unassailable quality and property of circumstantial evidence when properly adduced and properly tested have never been doubted as the strongest and best form of evidence in criminal trials.

This was a classic case based on circumstantial evidence. It also was a remarkable case, which required a rescue operation for its very survival at every turn. In the beginning, the prosecution team was buckling under the enormous strains imposed by the absence of reliable evidence. The investigators did not doubt the involvement of the accused and wanted the Crown to take the matter seriously. The Crown always took such matters seriously, but it was considered best to proceed only when there was evidence to support the deeply held conviction by the police that they had the right man. The facts should be given in more detail than so far recited.

On 16 September 1986, Donna Beverley Tidy, aged 41, and Kathryn Mary Payne, aged 36, were murdered on a relatively secluded, seemingly deserted property at Logan Reserve, which was on the outer edge of Brisbane. The murder was committed in the presence of a little child, Kirsty Payne, the daughter of Kathryn Payne. She was barely five years old. The police were baffled as to why the murderer had overlooked the child. He had either not noticed her or, for some unknown reason, had decided to spare her.

# CHAPTER 6

The child had witnessed the murder and rape of her mother from several metres away, and the murderer ran the risk that she might point a finger at him if he were caught. The victims were subjected to a frenzied and vicious knife attack, and the scene was like a slaughterhouse. The throats of the victims had been slit open. In the case of Tidy, there was what the pathologist described as 'severing of the carotid arteries on both sides' and a 'complete severing of the windpipe'. In the case of Payne, 'the windpipe and the left carotid artery and jugular vein were completely severed'. Death would have occurred within a matter of minutes after the infliction of these severe injuries.

The attack happened inside the house, and some of the walls were splattered with blood, indicating a frenzied attack. The smears on the walls were silent witnesses to the victim's desperate attempts to fend off this monster. The body of Tidy was found some metres away from the house, clutching a fistful of grass and showing signs of her attempts to get away despite her horrible injuries. The medical evidence was that the death would have occurred within minutes after the injuries. Tidy had eight stab wounds to the right side of the neck and on the armpit and some glancing blows to the right shoulder.

The deceased Payne was subjected to a sexual attack and raped and possibly sodomised. Her body was found naked on the blood-soaked bed apart from a gold watch and a gold chain around her neck. Payne had severe wounds and many cuts to the front of her neck and chest.

There was evidence of many cuts and bruises on the victims, suggesting a desperate struggle for survival. Defensive slashes and cuts on arms, armpits and other parts of the body were attempts to shield themselves and avoid the infliction of more severe injuries with a sharp instrument such as a knife. The assailant, if alone, must have been very strong to kill two females in quick succession and then leave swiftly, vanishing mysteriously into thin air in broad daylight.

The murders were committed on the property occupied by the Tidy family in a sparsely populated locality at Rossmore Road, Logan Reserve on the very fringe of Brisbane where a stranger would be expected to stand out.

The Tidy family had lived in Queensland for some 15 years, having moved there from South Australia, and had occupied a 150-acre property at Rossmore Road, Logan, in Queensland. The property had been leased some three years before the murders and was used for running horses and agisting other people's horses to help pay for the lease. The husband was a building contractor. Their small side business dealing with horses and known as 'Arabian Stud' was the love of Donna Tidy's life, and she ran the business. The Tidys had known Kathryn Payne and her family for some years and were close friends. The women saw each other often because they shared a common interest in horses and often went riding together. The Tidys had a stallion called 'Simi', which was one of Kirsty's favourite horses.

The husband of the deceased Payne was an area manager of a small company and the president of the 'Arabian Horse Association'. In addition to running her horse stud, Donna Tidy was the treasurer of the Association. The Paynes lived on a three-acre property at MacLeans Bridge, which was not far from the Tidy property as distances go in the vastness of Queensland. The Payne family, too, kept horses, and Kathryn Paine was a competent rider. Horses were a family hobby that all shared and enjoyed. They had two children, Kirsty aged five and a son about two years older than Kirsty.

The little girl who was present during the frenzied attack and saw the murderer was found incoherent, dazed and traumatised wandering in this isolated area a long distance from the house where the murders were committed. It first appeared that the murderer had missed the child whilst she was in the house. The little girl was seen by a man who had an appointment to meet Kathryn Payne at Tidy's property for a dressage lesson at about noon. He found Kirsty on foot on the side of the road leading the stallion, Simi. This witness knew the family and saw that the child was distressed. He asked her what she was doing alone so far away from the property and was shocked when she said: 'Mummy is dead. The phone is not working.' The little girl of five had tried to get help, but the phone was not working. The phone lines had been cut or ripped from the wall, and she told this man that she was running away from the place

# CHAPTER 6

so that no one would hurt Simi, the horse. He left the child on the road and rushed to investigate and discovered the carnage already described. He then hurried to call a local doctor.

A short time later, three women in a car who were passing by noticed the little girl alone leading a horse on this deserted road, and they stopped to find a dazed girl with a shocking story. One of them was a nursing sister. These women took the horse from the child and tied it to a tree. They had to keep reassuring the child that the horse would be alright because the child became agitated at Simi being left alone. The women took charge of the little girl and comforted her and got her in the car, but she was still worried about Simi being hurt by the man. They hurried back to the horse farm to investigate.

One harassed and tired policeman who was told to report for duty and get to the murder scene said much later that all the police needed in an investigation of a brutal murder was to have a group of Miss Marples swarming over the area before the police arrived and trampling all the clues. There was some risk of that happening, but police from Criminal Investigation arrived soon, and the scene was cordoned and not disturbed.

The police officers who rushed to the house to take control of the murder scene and stop these people from trampling over the place were horrified both with the ferocity of the attack and the fact that one of the victims had been raped and murdered within a few metres of her little girl. To describe the police operation as a manhunt is too American and perhaps too dramatic a description, but over the next several months, wave after wave of police from Brisbane Homicide and the Gold Coast and other adjoining districts joined the search for clues.

The police officers included those who had no direct involvement with the investigation, but they too were converging on the whole of the district seeking clues. In those days, many did not seek overtime or any rewards. They simply wanted this monster caught. The problem with most monsters is that they look like the rest of the community and so are difficult to detect. The police are generally methodical and systematic in their approach to serious crimes and are objective and dispassionate.

Contrary to popular belief, they are not given to rash statements and emotional outbursts. The fact that a child could have been killed also did not prevent them from proceeding dispassionately and methodically with the investigation. The only thing remotely showing bias was that some of them would say: 'Wait till we get our hands on this bloody bastard.'

The search for the killer continued and there was hardly anyone with the remotest connection to the area who was not questioned. One of the chief investigators told me much later that if the police had missed checking the background of someone within a radius of 20 kilometres, it was the result of an oversight and not because of want of will or effort. It was thought that the clues as to the identity of the murderer would be found at the scene.

The pathologist, Dr Anthony Ansford, who had given evidence in many notable murder trials and who went on to become a Professor of Medicine at the University of Queensland, entered the widening intensive murder inquiry. A whole battery of scientific officers and photographers also descended onto the murder scene; it was baffling to the police that a murder could be committed in broad daylight in a sparsely populated area and go unnoticed. In a busy place such as a railway station with people milling around, a suspect could vanish in a crowd of people, but in a sparsely populated area someone should have seen something.

There were news flashes and massive coverage in the media, and slowly people who were in the vicinity of the murder scene that day, either travelling in their cars or working within a radius of 20 kilometres, began to respond. The husband of one of the deceased was in a car driving home when he heard the details. He stopped the car and broke down, and someone stopped to help him. He thought that both his wife and child were dead. The other husband was found combing properties looking for the lost horse, and confusion reigned.

The police wanted to establish the movement of the two women. How and at what time did both women come together that morning? At what time did they meet at the Tidy property that morning and what were the movements that morning of both the victims and the child? That was the focus of one team of investigators bent on establishing precise times. The killer or killers could have been known to one or both victims or could have been total strangers. Precise times can be critical to identifying a suspect because they can be used to track and trace the suspect's movements to the murder scene.

The investigation heaved and lurched with the inclusion and exclusion of clues and sightings of possible suspects; the passage of time is one of the important bugbears and the destroyer of circumstantial evidence cases. A suspect may give a false alibi or be shown not to be in the neighbourhood at the time for many reasons. In the early stage of the investigation, suspects came and went with rapidity. There were many possibilities and much room for error, and the police had to guess and explore them all and record most of them.

Many things that sound exciting and rewarding in murder mysteries in the hands of a fiction writer can be depressing and bad in real life for the investigators and the prosecution. A fiction writer may find his work rewarded even in a botched murder mystery but there were no candidates in the police force awaiting special recognition in a botched investigation. There were no satisfactory clues or answers in this case. Both male spouses were able to give an account of their movements. The victims were at home early in the morning, and Payne was excited about going to the Tidy property with her little daughter. The husbands had left to go to work early in the morning. They were contacted by the police or found out for themselves the horrible way in which their wives were killed.

The murder scene now became the centre of intense police activity. In the end, the prosecution would call seventy witnesses to try to find, identify and convict the murderer, relying heavily on circumstantial evidence in critical areas. Were there several assailants or just one, and was it the accused Harding or someone else?

It may be debatable in the minds of the ordinary reasonable man whether there is such a creature as a purely circumstantial evidence case. Most cases rely both on direct and circumstantial evidence. Some facts do not require much evidence and are almost self-evident, but in contested criminal matters in our courts everything is put in issue, including the fact that the deceased is truly dead. In the more primitive colonies, a deceased person with six spears poking through the body found hanging upside down motionless for days does not require too many inferences to be gleaned from the facts and circumstances to prove beyond a reasonable doubt that the victim is both dead and murdered.

In our courts, the ordinary man may be puzzled that in similar cases the prosecution spends an inordinate amount of time and energy producing a medical witness to swear solemnly that he examined the cadaver carefully and found the remains to be dead and that, as proof, he issued a death certificate accordingly. The uninitiated mind may wonder whether the trial judge has a macabre sense of humour when in the summing up he solemnly tells the jury that death is a question of fact and it is for the jury to be satisfied beyond a reasonable doubt of the guilt of the accused, which includes proof that the victim is dead and that the six spears have not landed on him accidentally; it is common for the defence to put the onus on the prosecution.

Lawyers have no difficulty in understanding all this because of their familiarity with the evidentiary requirements dealing with the elements of the offence, and because they are aware that the same evidence may be relevant in the disputed facts in issue. The defence is entitled to make admissions of facts that are in issue, but in some circumstantial evidence cases, it is found safer to make no admissions and compel the prosecution to prove every element of the offence. The prosecution also prefers to lead all the evidence on some pretext or other. In some cases, the defence counsel will offer vigorous objections to the Crown tendering photographs of the scene, including photographs of the mutilated bodies of the murder victims.

The general rule of survival for the prosecution and a good rule of thumb in a circumstantial evidence case is to put in evidence everything, bar the kitchen sink, although in one case I did put in the kitchen sink because it was relevant (see De Jackson Case). This approach avoids any suggestion that for some hidden motive the prosecution has not put

## CHAPTER 6

in evidence that might appear to be irrelevant and innocuous only to find after the trial that a combination of such excluded pieces of evidence might have led to a different result. There are some cases in which after conviction the defence seeks to have a retrial because of fresh evidence that was not available during the trial and many more cases in which the evidence was either available or easily obtainable, but the prosecution had not bothered to introduce the material in the trial.

So, the practical rule of thumb is to put in everything unless there is some objection by the defence. When there is an objection to the reception of evidence for tactical or other reasons, then the defence would be precluded from claiming later that there should be a retrial on the basis that the evidence was somehow fresh; or that the prosecution had some hidden motives to conceal evidence; or that the prosecution was negligent or shoddy or both. Judges have always given great latitude to the Crown in circumstantial evidence cases and have not placed many restrictions on what bits and pieces of evidence the prosecution may lead, save in matters that are extremely prejudicial to an accused.

The medical, and particularly the scientific, evidence in the Harding case was detailed and extensive, and there was no option but to present all this. Dr Ansford, the pathologist, dealt with each knife injury and each bruise on each body and in detail. He dealt with the usual items in the menu of a pathologist and covered the dimensions, trajectory, and angles and gave comparisons of injuries and defined the difference between a slash and a cut and a bruise and a wound to see whether one or several knives were used. The scientific evidence led to an endless discussion on the possible murder weapons with comparisons of blade marks and impressions on the bedsheets and on articles of clothing and the dimensions of blades to see the possible type of knife or knives used, because no murder weapons were ever found.

The presentation of scientific evidence overlapped the medical evidence and took several days and dealt with many items of clothing and furniture, carpets, bedsheets and the description of bloodstains on the walls. The results of the examination of every inch of the rooms and of the motor vehicle, which belonged to Payne and which was found abandoned days later, were covered and this is the staple in such cases. The motor vehicle was stripped bare, and panels were removed to find clues and traces of blood. After the Chamberlain case, to which I make passing reference elsewhere, some police investigators were in the habit of telling the prosecutor that they particularly looked on the dashboard and found no blood or other evidentiary goodies for the prosecution. The jury heard detail after detail because the jury must hear it all.

There were traces of blood on the front seat, which were more consistent with the blood grouping of the deceased but not the accused. So that was no help. There were no fingerprints found in the car. That appeared strange because there was no evidence that the accused wore gloves. Nothing seemed to give many clues until the vaginal sample taken from the deceased showed that there was seminal material, which was obviously left by the murderer. If a suspect were found, his blood grouping could be compared for identification purposes. This appeared to be a vital clue, but it then collapsed because the blood grouping did not match the accused's. With that, the prosecution case crumbled and withered.

The police investigation came to a grinding halt. There was mounting public pressure with a murderer on the loose and a substantial reward was offered, but no one was charged and a whole year passed when in September of the following year, 1987, Sergeant Dennis Chapman and Sergeant Robert Pease started a fresh investigation, and a more intense police search began. Harding, who was the prime suspect almost from the beginning, was interviewed again and was later charged in September of 1987.

Crown prosecutors do not sit around waiting for the next unsolved crime. That is not their role. I was busy prosecuting other matters, and it was common from time to time to be assigned to look at some of the problem cases. This was the period when some of us sensed the decline in the number of experienced Crown prosecutors who were leaving for various reasons. The working conditions were atrocious, and there were better opportunities at the Criminal Bar.

I was first approached by Sergeant Robert Pease, who was one of several good police investigators who had appeared as a witness

## CHAPTER 6

in the complex murder trials I had prosecuted. Over several decades I had discovered that when it came to police investigations, there were no more severe critics of police methods and practices than the police themselves. Most were quite prepared to expose the weaknesses in police investigations and police methods—provided always that it was not their own case that they were being asked to tear apart.

The need to expose any weakness in a case and tear it apart is always important, as well as common practice. And some of these police officers in senior positions simply enjoyed getting away from their desk jobs and subjecting a police investigation to some critical tests of their own and to strip the prosecution case bare. I had a level of seniority that enabled me to ask the Police Department to release a few of the senior police officers to assist in the marshalling and evaluation of evidence in a trial. The roles were interchangeable, and sometimes it was easy to demonstrate how poor the evidence was. At other times, the police pointed out how the evidence would not stand up to any serious test from their extensive experience in criminal investigation. This case was a good example of what happens when the police arrive to discuss matters at the Office of the Director of Prosecutions in the Attorney-General's Office. Often, the poor typists would look alarmed when the police arrived in our congested office with murder weapons and large charts and photographs.

I was assigned to look at this case one year after the murders. There was nothing new in method and style except the review was more thorough and the evidence was subjected to much more severe stress tests. The discussions were sometimes meaningless and speculative and full of 'what ifs'. Some 100-odd statements were reviewed again, and witnesses were re-interviewed. A new approach was taken to see whether the murderer could be identified and whether distances identified from the sightings of the accused to the scene of the crime gave him the time to commit the murders. The evidence collected in the first 12 months dealing with description and identity was detailed but riddled with apparent inconsistencies and conflicts.

The role of Crown prosecutors in serious criminal investigations in Queensland is quite different from that of the district attorneys in

America who seem to participate in the investigations much earlier and who, at least in fiction, get to wine and dine beautiful women even before they do anything. No such incentives for solving crimes were available to the prosecution team in Queensland—more's the pity.

The normal Crown involvement was after an accused was committed for trial unless, as noted earlier, such intervention was necessary. It is important not to overstate the role of Crown prosecutors in criminal investigations. The prosecution case is only as good as the police investigation. In most criminal trials it is the strength of the case and the work of the police investigators that have some bearing on the outcome. The police are the ones who go through the ordeal of sleepless nights and thankless tasks.

In this case, the sparsely populated terrain and the sightings of the suspect over a large area led to the production of maps of the area, which were given to each member of the jury. The prosecution took hours to explain what could or could not happen, but this is common in many trials. It was not clear whether the witnesses were describing the accused or someone else. Harding had denied ever being near the Tidy property.

The boring details on the laundry list mentioned earlier suddenly become alive in a circumstantial evidence case as juries begin to pay attention and even ask questions. On the basis that the murderer raped one of the victims, it was baffling that the semen found in the body did not belong to the accused. He had returned home a short time after the murders were committed and had put all his clothes in the washing machine, telling his de facto that she was not to touch his washing. When he walked in, she said he had no signs of blood on his clothes.

The de facto said that she had picked up and smelt his shirt in the laundry because he had a habit of picking up other women; so, she said that she used to smell his clothes, including his underpants. What women do to keep their men!

When questioned and on being asked by the police to give an account of his movements, he had told the police that he had gone to a hotel to see if he could pick up 'a stray'. He had also hired a car after the

## CHAPTER 6

murders and with his de facto had gone to the casino on the Gold Coast for the rest of the day and the evening. The de facto did not notice any behaviour out of the normal, apart from the fact that when he returned to the flat, he looked 'nervous'; but that was not much good because a man looking for 'a stray' might have looked nervous with his de facto present.

He had some money, which could have come from the money stolen from the dead victims, but he said that he was involved in drug deals and was given money by drug dealers. He gave many accounts, which all proved to be false. This was important but lies alone are never sufficient to prove anything. He was not charged with being an inveterate liar, and his conduct after the murders did not seem to fit the conduct of someone who had left a murder scene. He did not go into hiding but was seen in the afternoon and had hired a car. Would a murderer go to a casino and look normal after such a horrendous and grisly attack? The identity of the murderer was the central issue. The layman may feel mesmerised by the term 'circumstantial evidence', but it is the staple diet in the ordinary daily communication between humans. In daily life, there is hardly a judgement without some reliance on circumstantial evidence; it is full of inferences, and instinctive judgements.

Take the issue of identifying the man seen at various places. Was the person seen the accused or somebody else? Did the accused have the time to commit the crimes in the timeframe required by the prosecution? What was he doing in these places, and why was he seen covering relatively long distances after the murders? There were at least twenty-five different points on the map at which either the accused was seen or something relevant to the case was noticed, and these were spread over relatively long distances.

The prosecution had to show that it was the accused and no one else who was seen at the very gates of the Tidy property. The problem was that the prosecution could not put the accused near or in the house on any individual reliable account. It had a composite picture up to the gate but no single reliable witness and no reliable evidence to show that he ever went into the house. It would have been different if some of the blood of the deceased had been found on his clothes or some fingerprints or even the murder weapons, and the foreign seminal fluid was no help.

The emphasis here is on a 'reliable' witness. The prosecution had to rely on various sightings and prove beyond a reasonable doubt that it was the accused seen near the gate of the Tidy property. The only witness who saw a suspect near the Tidy property when shown a photo line-up with the accused in it could not pick anyone answering the description of the man he saw. The suspect was seen, sometimes running, sometimes walking, but always moving towards the property. People did not keep exact times and could only give an estimate. The identity of the suspect was the central issue in the trial.

The jury must have found the individual descriptions given by witnesses confusing, but when that was combined with the identification of the accused from the photo line-up, the identity was established. It must be difficult for the uninitiated and those who have never sat on a jury to understand the problems of identifying a suspect. It would be a mistake to think that every shade of evidence that was presented in the case is recited here. This is not a re-run of the actual trial but is meant as a brief glimpse into the complexity of such trials.

Those individuals seeking neat solutions and exciting reading should stick to fiction. These examples are meant to show that without a painstaking sifting through of the circumstantial evidence, many people guilty of horrible crimes would escape punishment. Murders and other serious crimes are rarely committed in front of witnesses. Very often, the only evidence pointing to the accused is mute evidence of a circumstantial nature.

Circumstantial evidence is a reliable and powerful tool in the search for truth. However, while the search for truth may be important to the jury, lawyers know that it is not the primary objective in criminal trials. Criminal trials are all about the consequences that flow from the reception of admissible evidence. Truth and facts found by the jury based on admissible evidence are not necessarily the same as the truth based on hearsay evidence; historians simply recite hearsay stuff.

# CHAPTER 6

I think that this would sometimes come as a shock to readers. The search for truth is not the primary purpose of the criminal justice system. Truth and justice are not synonymous. In law, it is the evidence that counts, and the jury must go where the evidence leads. If a statute defines white as meaning black, then our courts would act according to the definition in the statute. There are many statutes in which, for practical reasons, white is defined as black, and we rely on some 'deeming provisions'. In fact, the Japanese were defined as white under the Apartheid regime in South Africa.

So, the real question was whether it was the accused who was seen at various times before and after the murders, and this is a good example of the confusion that prevails in such cases. There were seventy witnesses in the trial, and what did they hear or see?

First, take the distances covering the radius of many kilometres from the murder scene. No good storyteller would descend into such boring particulars. I must. I want you to experience what I had to do in this and other similar cases. It will be like reading an old shopping list.

The distances were:
1) Palm World Nursery to Tidy's gate – 6.4 km
2) Tidy's gate to Rudduck St via Logan View Rd, Logan Reserve Derby Rd and Chambers Flat Rd./Kingston Rd./etc./ Jacaranda Ave/etc./Bardon Rd – 16.3 km
3) Palm World to intersection of School Rd and Logan View Rd – 2 km
4) Palm World to intersection of Logan View Rd and Henderson Rd – 4.6 km
5) Palm World to point on Rossmore Rd – 5.5 km
6) From Tidy's gate to intersection of Logan View Rd and Rossmore Rd – 1.2 km
7) From intersection of Rossmore Rd and Logan View Rd to intersection of Logan View and Logan Reserve Rds – 1.9 km
8) Tidy's gate to intersection of Derby Rd and Chambers Flat Rd – 4.8 km

9) From intersection of Derby Rd and Chambers Flat Rd to intersection of Koplick Rd – 300 metres
10) Where car left in Rudduck St to Council Chambers – 700 metres (approx.)
11) Council Chambers at point where Rudduck Street can be seen to Stubbs Rd (Harding's residence) – 1.1 km
12) Stubbs Rd (Harding's residence on 16.9.86) to railway subway, which leads to the Chicken Hut – 300 metres
13) Cab rank Jacaranda Avenue to Marsden Park Shopping Centre – 3 km
14) Cab rank Jacaranda Ave to Palm World – 7.4 km 15) Palm World to Marsden Park Shopping Centre – 4.4.km 16) Club Hotel Waterford to Palm World – 7 km.

This list was used to prove that the accused had the time to commit the murders. The problem of identity looms large, and an accurate description of a suspect is important, but this never happens in most criminal cases, and this one was no exception. The movements of the suspect and how he was identified are part of the story, and he was seen and identified before the murders and after the murders.

- *Witness 1*: Taxi driver – knew accused. Before 9.46 am, he was in his cab on Kingston cab rank. He knew Harding, who was also a taxi driver at the time. Harding got into the cab and wanted to go to the Waterford Hotel. When near the Chambers Flat Road turnoff, he asked to go to Palm World. The taxi left Harding outside the Palm World Nursery and returned to the Marsden cab rank, where he got his next fare at 9.46 am. He had a definite time. Harding's movements in the morning began to emerge. He repeatedly told police that he could account for his morning because he was at the Palm World Nursery and some other places. This was found to be false. He never went there. The rest of the witnesses were merely describing a suspect observed for a short time, and some of the descriptions appeared wild.

- *Witness 2*: He had travelled to School Road and saw a male person walking along School Road at approximately 9.40 am, in his 30s, possibly late 30s, 6', dark-skinned, not black but copper (part-Aboriginal), large across the shoulders, thick neck, dark hair, neat style, with large curls just below collar length. He was shown a photo line-up of many faces. He selected two (both very similar in appearance and build), and one of these was the accused.
- *Witness 3*: He had left St Bernadine's School at Browns Plains at 9.40 am and drove to School Road, where he saw a male person walking along School Road between 9.55 and 10.00 am. He described him as probably a half-caste Aborigine, 5'8" to 6', medium build, black curly hair. He thought that the man was clean-shaven, wearing a pale blue tank top, possibly with white edging. He wore well-worked blue jeans. He later returned along School Road, but the road was deserted, and he saw no one again. Could not identify anyone in a series of photographs shown to him.
- *Witness 4:* About 9.30 am, the witness was driving down Logan View Road. Saw a male person walking from Logan Reserve Road. Returned on the same road at 10 am and no sight of anyone. He described the male as late 30s/early 40s, close to 6' tall or slightly less, athletic-style build, looked fit, very muscular arms, broad shoulders with a V-shaped waistline, no pot belly, Maori or South Sea Islander appearance, slightly chubby face, short black greasy or very shiny hair, possibly wavy, neatly combed, square clean cut at neckline at back, brushed back, normal-length sideburns, wearing a T-shirt with collar—sky-blue or possibly navy-blue trim, sleeves short, light-coloured dress slacks, footwear. Shown photo line-up, and selected photo of Harding to be the one most like the man he saw.
- *Witness 5:* Between 10.00 and 10.15 am, the witness was walking from his home to Logan View Road (home set back 500 feet from the roadway) when he saw a stranger walking

through the property, 35–40 years, 5'10" – 5'11", medium build, muscular arms, very dark hair, short and curly, heavily waved, brushed back and well-trimmed, short-trim type beard on the outline of his chin, moustache, sideburns nearly to bottom of the ears, dark complexion, not Caucasian, possibly Indian or Middle Eastern extraction, light-coloured singlet, pale-blue or light-coloured trousers. Shown photo line-up and clearly picked Harding.

- *Witness 6:* Working on his property in Logan View Road and at about 11.00 am, the witness saw male, Island extraction, not Aboriginal, about 30 years, medium build, olive complexion, 6', close-cropped curly black hair, sky-blue singlet top and blue jeans or trousers. Behaviour was suspicious. Shown the photo line-up and identified Harding—'certainly looked like him' and was 'almost certain' he was the man.
- *Witness 7*: At approximately 11.10 am, the witness saw a male in Henderson Road who then turned left into Logan View Road. Late 20s, about 6', medium build, dark curly hair, not tight curls, dark complexion like an Islander, dark brown Tongan complexion, dark blue singlet and dark blue trousers. He was unable to identify anyone from the photo line-up but described the peculiar way in which the man was running. The police asked the accused to show how he ran. Unknown to the accused, the witness saw the accused running in police company on 30 September 1986, almost a year before the accused was charged, and the witness described his 'shuffle dancing run' like a boxer as what he had seen on 16 September 1986. When the witness saw the accused in court, he identified him as the man he saw. Dock identification is frowned on, but permissible, and he was positive.
- *Witness 8:* Lived in Logan View Road. At about 11.30 am, he heard his dog bark and saw a male no older than 28 years, 5'10" – 5'11", slim build, three-quarter caste Aboriginal, dark hair, messy not brushed, collar length, appeared scruffy hair,

CHAPTER 6

wearing blue jeans and navy-blue singlet. Unable to identify anyone.
- *Witness 9:* Lived with the previous witness in Logan View Road. At about 11.30 am, the witness heard a dog barking. Saw a male walking along the road near a dam. 20–25 years, 5'10" – 5'11", dark complexion, black wavy hair, wearing blue jeans, thinks he had a blue singlet on, medium build. Unable to pick anyone.
- *Witness 10:* Lived in Logan View Road. At around 11.00 am, the witness saw a stranger walking along the road. About 30 years, about 5'9", dark-skinned, appeared Pakistani or Indian origin, thick black collar-length hair, possibly wearing a moustache, light-coloured singlet and blue trousers. He did not pick anyone from the photo line-up.

When this witness gave evidence and mentioned that the suspect was 5'9" and of Pakistani or Indian origin, some of the jury members gave a furtive glance at me because I am Indian and exactly 5' 9" tall. I took no chances and did not ask the witness whether the suspect resembled anyone he saw in court! This had not escaped the attention of the defence counsel. He had worked in the Crown Law Office as a clerk and had appeared to instruct me in several criminal cases when he was a student. Now he had a flourishing practice at the Criminal Bar and was later appointed a District Court Judge.

He told me later that but for his respect for me, and in recognition of my reputation for verbal retaliation in previous cases in court, he was sorely tempted to ask the witness whether the man resembled the Crown prosecutor. He said: 'Just imagine the sensational scene of a Crown prosecutor being dragged away for further questioning.'
- *Witness 11*: Between 10.30 am and 10.45 am, the witness was riding a horse in Rossmore Road. Rode to Tidy's gate. As he rode away from the gate, the witness saw Tidy travelling home in her motor vehicle. Stopped and spoke to her and got money from her. As he rode up Rossmore Road, the witness saw a male person walking towards Tidy's property, 30–33 years, broad

shoulders and starting to thicken at the waist, good physique, good olive complexion, dark hair, golliwog type at top and front, hair straighter at back, slight kinks in it, collar length, neatly cut, moustache bushy but not covering his bottom lip, Islander descent, 6', definite cheekbones, light-blue singlet, arms a lighter colour than the face, 'gym-type boot' sneaker shoes, lace-ups possibly white on side of shoes. He could not recognise anyone in the photos.

The evidence became compelling because many witnesses gave either a good description or, failing to do that, they instantly recognised and pointed to the photograph of the accused. Some did not. They saw a man at least of similar description or recognised the man and pointed to the accused in the series of photographs in which there were other people of a similar build, shape and size.

The man was walking in Logan View Road and then Rossmore Road in the same timeframe relied on by the prosecution at the time of the killings and he was walking in the same direction and on a road that led to Tidy's gate, which was in a dead-end and isolated area.

Of note, all witnesses saw only one male person of dark complexion, not a number. In this case, the Crown needed to eliminate the possibility of several assailants. It was not possible that all were wrong, and even if it was not the accused there was only one coloured man of the same height and build at the very gate of the property. The prosecution case was that, according to the little child, there was only one perpetrator of this crime.

## What the witnesses saw of the suspect after the murders

This body of evidence on identity immediately after the murders was weak in one sense in that all the witnesses were traveling in their own vehicles and had less time to observe. Also, the person they were describing was moving because he was driving a car.

They had only a passing glimpse of the man, but they recognised the car. It was a white Cortina sedan like the missing car, and some

## CHAPTER 6

recognised the car from the photos they saw later and were positive that it was the actual car.

The witnesses who had only a passing view of the suspect gave similar accounts in which there were variations and conflicts on detail, but they were describing the same man. The descriptions were similar, but something more telling happened. This time the suspect was not seen walking or running, but he was in a car which some witnesses described and then identified as the car that belonged to the deceased woman Payne. Surely this must be the murderer. The descriptions after the murders do not have as full a description as one would expect from the previous witnesses who saw the man walking or running. The suspect was in the car so the descriptions of facial features and of height and size were less reliable. But it is a black man or a part-Aboriginal or a Maori or Pakistani that is being described and he is in a car taken from the murder scene. Who was this man?

- *Two witnesses travelling in the same vehicle described what they saw*: Approaching the intersection of Chambers Flat Road, they saw a white car travelling inbound on Chambers Flat Road. It was a Cortina sedan. Only one person was in the vehicle: 35 years, dark complexion, black curly hair brushed back from forehead – not black but dark complexion, with what appeared to be a beard. The witness was positive that the vehicle was the Cortina sedan and recognised the car both from photographs and when shown the vehicle.
- *Witness living in Rudduck Street*: Sometime just after 12 noon, he saw white Cortina stop beside fence of home with only one person in the vehicle. He had wavy hair thick was taller than roof of the car 5'8" – 5'11", athletic type, muscular, well proportioned, broad back, wearing a singlet, pale blue or pink, long trousers faded blue, dark complexion colouring between Maori and Aboriginal, 25–30 years. Had a white object tucked up under left arm possibly a towel. He walked across the park and removed his singlet. He wiped himself with a white object. Two white towels were missing from the Tidy residence.

- *Hertz Rent-a-Car*: Between 1.15 pm and 1.30 pm, X received a telephone call from Harding who booked a motor vehicle. Picked him up at 2.00 pm and he dropped her back to her office. Paid $110 in cash. (When the accused left home in the morning he only had $5.) Next day, Wednesday 17 September 1986, obtained cab and requested to travel to Koplick Road. Taxi was being driven by Harding who spoke about the murders. Saw marks on joggers he was wearing. He recognised Harding as being the driver of that cab. The marks on the joggers turned out to be human blood but had only weak traces.
- *De facto at the time*: Harding left unit about 9.00 am – medium grey trousers, dark-blue shirt, long sleeved, Trax brand shoes. Arrived home about 1.30 pm wearing same clothes. Appeared nervous and agitated. Stated he was going to the casino. Stated he had $100. Had a shower and put clothes he was wearing into the washing machine.

## The mystery of the unidentified seminal fluid in the body

The unidentified and unexplained spermatozoa or the seminal fluid found in the dead rape victim stuck in the throat of the prosecution case and was hard to swallow. It was a classic case of unpleasant and unwanted evidence. Investigators are not miracle workers, but they were now searching for clues or compelling evidence to dispel any doubts about the seminal material.

There was no evidence of two assailants. The child saw only one man and the other evidence supported that, but the prosecution at this stage had no intention of calling a child of such tender age to give evidence. The psychologists and social workers (including my wife, who had graduated in Social Sciences) thought it would be shocking to put a little child into the witness box. I had no intention of doing that. There was overwhelming medical and scientific evidence that one of the victims was both raped and murdered at the same time. The state of the evidence on rape thus far did not look like a story with a market in the jury room. The seminal fluid was not her husband's, and nobody

# CHAPTER 6

knew anything about her having an extramarital affair. This would have been great for fiction writers because they can wriggle out of anything and get paid for wriggling.

The investigators did not have any such luxury. Fiction writers can contrive a good tidy plot, but there is no such thing as a good plot in real life. Things happen randomly. Life itself is a random thing. As one American with an uncanny knack for stuffing things up once said: 'Stuff happens'. The problem defied a solution.

There was the possibility that the victim had had an extramarital relationship, but there was no evidence of that in the police investigation. The husband had told the police that he had had no sexual relations with the deceased on the night before the murder. The police were still searching for answers. I was in the middle of all these discussions and expressing some scepticism about the state of the evidence dealing with rape, pointing out that the evidence was unsatisfactory.

One frustrated investigator said, 'What do you want us to do? Get seminal fluid from the whole bloody district for comparison purposes?' I reminded him that as the area was sparsely populated, that possibility should be on the table. I believed in desperate measures in desperate cases. This may have been too much for one of them because in response he said:

> We don't know all your customs in the Pacific Islands, but here it is not quite like milking a snake for venom where all you have to do is grab hold of a snake by the throat and ram its jaws into a jar and get the sample. It's not easy ... We have to persuade people and stroke their egos and may have to go even further to get a sample like that ...

I thought that a good Crown prosecutor should always leave all good options on the table. I did notice that after this short exchange the police did not consult me for fresh new ideas for some time. As if I cared. I had to grapple with the fact that the Crown could not place the accused near or in the house where the victims were murdered.

The presence of the foreign seminal fluid and the possibility of several assailants (because several knives were used in the attack and the claim by Harding that he knew something about the murders but was not involved in any way) threw the case into utter confusion and the evidence needed to be re-examined. The seminal material excluded Harding. He had a relatively rare blood grouping and could not have raped the deceased woman, and the overwhelming evidence from the way the victim was found was that she had been raped before being murdered.

As a result of the new clues as to what could have happened, the search for other possible clues continued. The de facto of the accused had returned to New Zealand and the investigators either went to New Zealand or persuaded her to return to Brisbane and this time their interest was only in Harding's social and sexual contacts. The de facto told the police that in her long relationship with the accused, which included numerous sexual encounters, the accused never used contraceptives and that she had wanted a child but could not have one. The accused was not able to ejaculate for some reason and had, in fact, sought medical advice regarding this problem.

The de facto was sure that during their long relationship the accused had never ejaculated during intercourse, and they had unprotected sex. The police found several other women the accused was seeing and with whom he had sexual liaisons. He had numerous sexual contacts with each of them and had refused to use any protective measures. He had told these partners that it was safe and that he could have vigorous sex without ejaculating, and some were mature women who said they could tell that he had not ejaculated during intercourse.

The prosecution called all these poor helpless witnesses who were shocked to learn that they had to give evidence to show that the victim was raped and that if the accused were the assailant, then one would not expect to find any evidence of his AB blood grouping in the seminal material. The prosecution now found a suspect who could be the rapist who left no trace of a seminal fingerprint at the murder scene. The prosecution could now argue that the absence of seminal fluid from the

## CHAPTER 6

accused was no evidence of the absence of sexual intercourse with the deceased.

It was now thought that if there was strong evidence that the accused, for medical or other reasons, could not ejaculate, then he remained a good suspect. The way the body was found, and other evidence, clearly showed that the victim was sexually molested and probably raped and sodomised. The accused was charged with murder and not rape, but sexual molestation was at the heart of the case. It was the central plank in the circumstantial evidence case and could not be brushed aside as irrelevant to the identity of the killer.

This evidence removed part of the obstacle but did not deal with the question of the foreign seminal fluid, which did not belong to the accused and did not come from the husband who had sworn that he had not had recent intercourse with the deceased. The medical and scientific evidence was now subjected to more rigorous review and analysis, and further experts were called in to examine other possibilities.

The following then is the story of the evidence called by the prosecution to explain and eliminate the presence of the foreign seminal fluid as a decisive critical factor in the question of the identity of the murderer to show that it had no bearing or relevance to the outcome of the trial. The prosecution would show that, wherever and whenever seminal fluid came from, its case was slowly getting stronger and stronger. The task was to establish beyond reasonable a doubt that it was the accused who had murdered both women regardless of the presence of seminal fluid that belonged neither to the husband nor the accused. The next piece of evidence, too, can only be described as seminal to the prosecution case.

The prosecution needed evidence to explain the presence of seminal material that was not deposited by the accused. It was probably consistent with a large section of the community but from the blood grouping data available, it was inconsistent with that of the accused. The husband did not have sexual relations with his wife the night before the murder and was not sure whether he'd had intercourse for several days. In fiction writing, there are stories of men who tenderly remember when last they had sexual relations with a mistress but have no memory when it comes to their spouses—another universal truth. I went home that night and slept and slept for a long time; at last, there was some light at the end of the tunnel.

I must now deal with an important witness for the prosecution. Sergeant Pease and I discussed another murder case in which a professor at the university, Professor Glover—who was an acknowledged authority on all matters seminal—had given vital evidence on an entirely different subject. He gave evidence on the life cycle of a special kind of moth, which was critical to the time of death. In the absence of that evidence, it would have been impossible to place the accused in that case at the scene or in the area where the murder was committed.

In that case, two murderers had to be in the district at the relevant time, and both claimed to have alibis. The murderer had to be in that district at least. One of the accused in that case denied being anywhere near the place. Professor Glover was a renowned authority on the life cycle of moths. Sergeant Pease was the Chief Investigator, and I happened to be the Crown prosecutor. The alibi evidence did not hold, and some weeds and grass seeds found only in that district determined the fate of the prisoner

It was agreed that he should be contacted again. I spoke to the good professor several times and concluded that his evidence was vital to the resolution of the dilemma. I was surrounded by specialist forensic scientists who told me that his evidence would be critical to the case. He could give evidence that would eliminate the presence of some other stranger at the murder scene and explain the absence of any seminal fluid from the accused in the rape of the victim before her death.

Professor Glover was at the University of Queensland for some years but by the time the Harding trial came on in September of 1988, he had returned to England on the understanding that should he be required as a Crown witness, he would be prepared to return to give evidence. He told me that he would be delighted to return to give evidence and renew acquaintance with his friends in Brisbane, and I had the impression from my interview with him during the previous murder trial that when not

## CHAPTER 6

preoccupied with the sex life of moths and other insects he, in common with other travellers and visitors to Queensland, loved visiting places and loved the warm climate and the people.

The evidence he gave at the trial is also a small illustration of what an ordinary jury in such cases (there was nothing too complex in this case) is expected to grasp. It is not easy to lead an expert witness when there is little understanding or clue about the nature and complexity of the evidence to be given.

I usually followed the Socratic method and so told the experts in advance that I had no clue what they were talking about, apart from the conclusions, and expected them to address the jury more like a class in a lecture theatre. If I could not follow the evidence, then the jury would have difficulties too. Expert witnesses can be led, but only if the examiner knows what he is talking about. Being a university lecturer, Professor Glover understood this perfectly, and he probably had some dull students like me. Here then, in part, is what he had to say in evidence about the presence of the foreign seminal fluid in the deceased victim.

> TIMOTHY DAWSON GLOVER, SWORN AND EXAMINED: I am emeritus Professor from the University of Queensland and an Honorary Professor in the University of Leeds in the United Kingdom. That's St. James University Hospital. I'm a biologist by training, and I have a PhD degree, doctor of philosophy degree, and doctor of science degree from the universities of Edinburgh and Cambridge, respectively.

I asked him to relate his teaching experience, explain the nature of his work and deal with his area of expertise:

> PROFESSOR GLOVER: Yes, sir. I've been actively engaged in research in reproductive biology for the last 35 years. I specialised in the maturation and the survival and the degeneration of spermatozoa, and in 1975 I was appointed to chair here the Comparative Anatomy at the University of Queensland, and I retired from that chair in December of last year. Before that I was a reader in the University of

Liverpool in the United Kingdom and Director of the Ford Foundation Unit of Reproductive Biology at the University of Liverpool. I have been a consultant to WHO on male fertility in Queensland and have been an Associate Scientist with the Queensland Fertility Group, as well as past president of the Australian Fertility Society and immediate past president of the Australian Institute of Biology, and for the past 13 years I was also consultant seminologist in the Queensland Fertility Group here in Brisbane.

The readers may sense an element of name-dropping here when presenting the qualifications and experience of experts. That was always true, and, in this case, it was thought that there was a need for further elaboration, so he was asked:

MR LAKSHMAN: What group is the Queensland Fertility Group?

PROFESSOR GLOVER: It is a group which specialises in human fertility and has particularly concentrated in the last few years on in vitro fertilization.

He was then asked whether he had published anything in this specialised field. It appeared that he had published a few:

PROFESSOR GLOVER: Yes, I published about a hundred papers on reproductive biology on different aspects, including chapters in textbooks. But my special field has been in the decapitation and degeneration of spermatozoa.

MR LAKSHMAN: What do we understand by these two expressions you just mentioned?

PROFESSOR GLOVER: Well, decapitation of spermatozoa is a manifestation of the aging of sperms. When they get older, they first of all tend to coil their tails from having straight tails, and the next phase is that the tails and the heads become separate. It is a manifestation of age. It takes rather

# CHAPTER 6

a long time to achieve in the body and is very, very difficult to achieve outside the body. If you try artificially to knock the sperms' heads off, it's an extraordinarily difficult thing to do, but yet the body manages to do it. Therefore, it has some very strong enzymes and various other phenomena to achieve this decapitation and make sperms age slowly, but nevertheless it achieves that end after a period of time. So, the various things in the body that we perhaps have not really been able to identify produce this effect that we aren't able to do outside the body, and I think that decapitation and age and degeneration of spermatozoa could all be used synonymously

MR LAKSHMAN: When we speak about the loss of tails, just what are we to understand by that, what actually happens when you speak about loss of tails?

PROFESSOR GLOVER: Well, the actual mechanism of the loss of tails is uncertain. All I can say is that it denotes an old sperm that's been hanging around for quite a little bit of time in the body. Now, the ease with which a sperm will degenerate, age, or become decapitated does depend upon the environment in which it finds itself. And we have to say, sir, that the vaginal environment is very hostile to spermatozoa. And so, I could perhaps be helpful if you gave me the opportunity to describe the series of events that occurs after intercourse to the spermatozoa in the vaginal environment and indicate how it is that they become decapitated. Would you give me that opportunity?

    The eminent expert was warming up to the subject and was invited to continue. What he was about to say was not in the witness statement, so I had little idea where this digression would lead. Expert witnesses, unlike ordinary witnesses, have great freedom to range far and wide. Often, until they have given what they want to say, the tendency is not to constrain them. Counsel at the bar table rarely object, and trial judges rarely interrupt until the speech is over. With expert witnesses, it is sometimes difficult to know whether their evidence is seminal until they launch into the subject matter of their expertise. In this case, it was important. He continued:

> PROFESSOR GLOVER: Well, after sexual intercourse has taken place, sperms are deposited in the vagina, but because the vagina is a hostile environment, they are protected by a gelatinous substance in the ejaculate. Now this gelatinous substance eventually liquifies but is there just long enough to ensure that the majority of the sperm get into the cervix, or the neck of the womb. When sperms get into the cervix, they are happy because the cervix is not an adverse environment, and of course they are able to reach fertilisation.
>
> But there are a number of these sperm that never get into the cervix. They remain behind, perhaps 20 to 30 percent, and after the gel of the semen have liquified, they are exposed to the dangers and hazards of the vaginal environment. And as soon as that happens, then of course they start to disintegrate, because they are exposed to the low pH vagina condition; that is, the vagina is acidic, and sperm don't like acidity.
>
> They are exposed to body temperature, and they don't like body temperature either, because mostly when they are stored in the male in the scrotum, they are positioned in a position that is below body temperature. So, when you put them up to body temperature, they tend to disintegrate. In addition to that, the vagina has lots of bacteria which, as soon as those sperms start to disintegrate, will make matters worse by increasing and augmenting the degeneration, and you may also have a few enzymes involved.
>
> Now, when these sperms in the vagina disintegrate, that gives a signal to the body to send in what we call phagocytic cells or phagocytes, and those phagocytes are like the cleaners. They bring a vacuum cleaner. They come in to gobble up the remnants of the sperms. And this is a process which is known as phagocytosis. And of course, when that happens,

## CHAPTER 6

then of course the population of the sperms will gradually decline in that particular area. But this is a slow process. Some of the disintegration happens after about two hours of intercourse, so that you'll find some decapitated sperms, say, just arbitrarily about 20 per cent after about two hours. But it's a slow process. So that even after 10 hours you still only have about 40 per cent of them. And what I would like to remind people is that particular sample of sperms which I was asked to examine showed between 90 and 100 per cent degenerated spermatozoa.

He told the court that it was on 24 August 1987 that he was approached by Detective Chapman and Detective Sergeant Pease at the University of Queensland when he was given two slides of a vaginal sample taken on the date of the murder. There were always some humorous even if unintended results:

> MR LAKSHMAN: And again, Professor, in the type of work you do, are you involved in microscopic examination of material of this nature?
>
> PROFESSOR GLOVER: Yes, I am. I'm involved with it every day.
>
> BY HIS HONOUR: Pretty hard to do your work without doing it, I imagine?
>
> PROFESSOR GLOVER: That's so.
>
> MR LAKSHMAN: And so that when you examined them, I take it that you used a good microscope at the university and so on?
>
> PROFESSOR GLOVER: Yes, on Friday we examined these specimens under oil immersion using a Zeiss photomicroscope, which is a very good quality microscope. In August of 1987, I had a more cursory look at the specimens.

Now, after all that mental foreplay, the intention was to get to the substance of the evidence, and Professor Glover continued:

PROFESSOR GLOVER: There were not many sperms, but of those sperms 88 per cent were totally decapitated. Now, there were a few with tails on them, but, you see, if you look at these in detail, one finds that of those 12 per cent that had tails, about 8 per cent of them only had half tails. The rest of the tail was eaten away. So consequently, we can only really say that there were 4 per cent sperms with complete tails.

MR LAKSHMAN: What could you say to the proposition for example that 20 per cent of the spermatozoa were intact or some such proposition?

The reference to 20 per cent in the question was due to other forensic scientists having assessed that at least 20 per cent of the spermatozoa were intact, a number that appeared too high for the conclusion being sought for the prosecution.

PROFESSOR GLOVER: Well, I think unless you're well versed in semen analysis, unless you're really doing it every day, it's rather like horse-riding, I suppose. Unless you do it every day, you don't get so good at it. And I think that often people don't realise that if you want to see whether a sperm is disintegrating or not, you have to look very closely. You have to look at its mid-piece, and you have to look at its tail, and if you looked at these sperms, even those that under, say, times 40 appear to be intact, in fact when you looked under a high magnification times a hundred, they were not intact. So, I think that would be an understandable comment but an overstatement.

MR LAKSHMAN: Now, doctor, what effect has death on the body process? Would you explain that to the jury?

PROFESSOR GLOVER: Well, I think that the picture that we see here, I think that post-mortem changes, post-mortem conditions, can probably be disregarded here, because all the processes which I have outlined are vitiated at death, barring bacterial activity. The body temperature falls ... acidity of the vagina changes. Any enzymic activity immediately stops. The phagocytes cease to function, and the only thing that will continue in a slow gnawing sort of way would be the activity of bacteria. But if the body was stored at low temperature, even they would cease to be very active. I mean, that's why we put things in a fridge, because you slow down the activity of the bacteria. So, I don't think that this picture is likely to have been modified very greatly, sir, by post-mortem effects. I think it happened before death.

Now Professor Glover gave the opinion on which the Crown heavily relied. The substance of his evidence:

PROFESSOR GLOVER: Well, I gave the opinion, when I was asked this, that these sperms in my view would have been 24 hours or even up to 36 hours old before the deaths of the individual. Because I cannot emphasise too strongly the semen disintegration here, the deterioration of the sperm. It really is a terrible mess and so obviously they have been there for an awful long time. I think they have been hanging around for quite a considerable time. Now if you consider that after 12 hours you can still recover normal intact sperms, not 30 per cent of them, but 50 or 70 per cent normal, intact sperms, not sperms with tails on them that have disintegrated and Swedish work has shown, and I have it before me here that that is the case, then you could not possibly get a picture like this in my view under about 24 hours at least and probably 36 or even more.

In this case, the panties of the deceased woman were found next to the body and the question was whether Professor Glover could comment on any findings of spermatozoa on the panties. It so happened that none was found, but I was not aware of that, and as Professor Glover was returning to England the following morning I thought it best to deal with this matter whilst he was in the witness box. The defence objected to Professor Glover dealing with the matter without a proper foundation for his qualification to comment on articles of clothing. This produced some light moment in his evidence as I sought to establish how much time he spent with women's panties and whether he was an expert in all this! The trial judge frowned and appeared bemused.

> MR GRIFFIN: Your honour, I don't know whether my friend has established sufficient expertise of this doctor to give this sort of evidence. It seems to me that it is evidence that resides in another area of expertise.
>
> MR LAKSHMAN: May I lay a foundation. Doctor, is that an area where you can comment and if so why? In other words, what experience or studies or …?
>
> PROFESSOR GLOVER: Yes, it is an area on which I can comment because at least on two or three occasions per week in the infertility clinic that we run in Leeds I am involved with interpretation of personal intercourse tasks in the examination of infertility.
>
> MR LAKSHMAN: What is the significance of that when it comes to your area of expertise? What do you look at and why is it that you will be able to comment on the presence or absence of seminal material on a woman's clothing or underpants?
>
> PROFESSOR GLOVER: Well, because we are involved not only with the examination of sperms after intercourse has taken place and their distribution in the female tract over a period of time, but of course we're also associated with donor insemination and artificial insemination by a husband so I mean I can only briefly say that we are sort of messing about with this area all day long.
>
> MR LAKSHMAN: I think there is sufficient foundation that the learned professor shows that he has been messing around …

# CHAPTER 6

The trial judge seemed alarmed at the prospect of a detailed examination of the expert witness on his experience with women's panties generally and said:

> HIS HONOUR: I'm prepared to accept it. I don't want a demonstration.
>
> MR LAKSHMAN: I'll ask you to comment on whether or not one would expect to find evidence of seminal material, necessarily, after intercourse, on the articles of clothing, particularly panties?
>
> PROFESSOR GLOVER: My considered judgement on that would be that it would be possible but is certainly not axiomatic. If a male has a fairly large seminal volume, then I suppose it is possible to beget a dribble and stain from the vaginal orifice shortly after intercourse, but it is by no means necessary. Intercourse can perfectly easily take place without semen running out at all. After all, the deposition of semen is fairly cranial in the vagina and [in] normal coitus, semen is deposited close to the cervix and although there's no doubt that semen can dribble out and does on occasions, I wouldn't say by any means that it's axiomatic. I think it would be totally unacceptable to make that point.

It was clear that in the absence of some significant concessions arising out of the cross-examination of this expert witness and in the absence of some powerful rebuttal evidence from the defence, the jury would accept that whoever was the donor of the foreign seminal material, it had nothing to do with the murder of one of the deceased. The prosecution now dealt with the only other major problem. Apart from the witnesses who gave varying fleeting glimpses of the possible assailant and despite the very positive identification of Harding in his progress towards the property where the murders were committed, there was still not a single witness who could put him on the property, let alone in the house.

## Kirsty Payne: witness for the prosecution

The police had always appreciated that Kirsty Payne was the only one, apart from the killer, who held vital clues. She was present when her mother was raped and killed and could give clues, no matter how vague, about what happened in that slaughterhouse. At the very least, she could describe the killer.

Kirsty had witnessed or was present in the vicinity during the attacks on the two victims and could now, some two years after the event, tip the scales of justice balanced so precariously. Kirsty could provide information to enable the police to trace the killer. As already stated, in the early stage of the investigation, it was never thought that a child in these circumstances should be called to give evidence. Kirsty was only five, and this was not a case of a child standing on a footpath and witnessing a car accident but of a tender fragile, mind being tested to the limit to provide details on the brutal killing of her mother. The evidence of identification was good but pointless because the jury had to be satisfied beyond a reasonable doubt 1) that it was the accused Harding who was seen in the vicinity of the rural property, and 2) that he was later in the farmhouse. The witness who had seen a man answering Harding's description at the gate was not able to identify him from the photographs shown to him. Even if it could be shown to be Harding, then it was not a crime to act suspiciously or to be found loitering near a murder scene. So close and yet so far. There was insufficient nexus to the actual crimes committed, and the seminal fluid was a red herring and a near disaster for the prosecution.

There was nothing in the several detailed scientific examinations of the crime scene to connect the accused to these crimes. There were no traces of blood or other material found in the washing machine at his residence and no fingerprints at the scene or in the stolen vehicle, and the murder weapons had not been found. The motor vehicle had been stripped, the panels removed, and everything examined, but no fingerprints had been found in the bedroom or the immediate vicinity of the attack. If it were a crime of opportunity, the assailant would not have

## CHAPTER 6

taken gloves with him on the off chance that he might need them. No fingerprints and no scientific findings linked him to the murders. There were some shoeprints, but these could have come from anyone wearing similar shoes.

The police had been told in several discussions that it was extremely unlikely that the prosecution would be prepared to use the child's evidence but would rely entirely on circumstantial evidence, if possible. I was assigned to examine the evidence and decided that it would be impossible to secure a conviction without further evidence. The decision to call Kirsty was not easy. The soul-searching was not unique to this case because there were always cases in which diametrically opposed forces were at work. This happened to be just one of the countless solved and unsolved crimes in which police struggle to find answers and seek assistance from various professional disciplines in society. The police had been sitting on the available evidence for twelve months, and there was growing public pressure and anxiety for a resolution. The usual rumours were circulating that such a fiendish attack might happen again, and there were concerns for the safety of the child. These were the important factors that led to a more determined effort to resolve the issues. The killer knew that the child was alive, and there were extensive media reports that the child had described the assailant to the police. The investigators were determined to do whatever it took to bring the vicious killer to justice but were also well aware of the constraints and problems with a young witness.

The Crown prosecutor entrusted with a case has some discretion both on the question of the adequacy of the evidence in a criminal trial and how the prosecution conducts its case. In this case, the child became a vital witness in the most critical and weakest area in the prosecution case. The defence was certain to subject the evidence to the most rigorous examination, and the prosecution could not call a witness of tender age to give evidence and then complain merely because the opposing counsel was doing his job properly. There seemed to be no choice in this matter but to call the child as a vital material witness for the prosecution. There was no point in proceeding with the killer seen at the gates, as even that was not certain from the conflicting descriptions of the possible suspect given by witnesses who had varying windows of opportunity to see a man sometimes running and sometimes walking in the locality. The prosecution was certain that it was the accused but could not be certain that all the varying descriptions given would be accepted by the jury as a clear description of Harding. What if the jury thought that he was not properly identified as being at the actual scene of the murder, which was the house? Or that the prosecution had failed to establish conclusively that Harding was the perpetrator of the crimes with which he was charged?

The attitude of the defence to the calling of a witness of such tender age to give evidence was predictable and anticipated. Moreover, there was a sound legal basis for their objections. The various possibilities open to the prosecution depended on a ruling on the admissibility of such evidence. This now became the centre of focus. The weight to be given to the evidence of a little child in a criminal matter that carried a mandatory life sentence was the central issue. The objective, sober and contrary view was that the prosecution should not use a child as cannon fodder in a cynical tussle with the defence. The likely attitude of the presiding trial judge in such circumstances was not known, and the legal landscape was sparsely populated with cases where trial judges had allowed evidence from little children in criminal trials. There were some precedents but few and certainly none dealing with a child of such tender age as the sole witness on the critical questions of identification and commission in a murder trial. The child's evidence had to be corroborated in some material particular, but there was ample evidence to support Kirsty on the identification, provided the trial judge was satisfied that she had the capacity and could be regarded as a relevant and credible witness. There was the possibility that some two years after the event she had blotted out of her mind most of the salient details of the brutal rape and killing, and many objective persons thought it cruel that Kirsty should now be subjected to searching questions that could revive the events and force her to re-live them, and all this in the very hostile environment of a criminal trial.

# CHAPTER 6

It was difficult to be objective and detached, and this posed a personal problem. Rosemary and I, as well as many of our friends and neighbours, had little children at the time. The idea of putting one of them in a witness box did not sit well with us. There might have been some cases on these matters, but in those days for some of us who were frequently in court and grew up in an age before lawyers 'ogled on google', it was not easy to study everything, and I could not find an exact precedent.

For the uninitiated, 'precedents' are cases counsel use to bore trial judges silly until they submit and accept the point of view of one party to the exclusion of the other party. It is one area of advocacy in which if several cases sufficed to prove a point it was thought preferable to refer to twenty or more and for good measure give a list of all of them to the opposing counsel, not so much to assist him but to demoralise him, and to do that only after everyone has settled down for business in court. That seemed to be the practice in my time. Counsels were not obliged to give any list of cases to be used during a criminal trial, although such lists were exchanged when appearing before the Court of Criminal Appeal.

The possible consequences for the child were considered in a broader context. The general position as far as witnesses were concerned was that in the early days in the fifties when I was a student and later in the sixties and seventies, the legal system was not remotely concerned with the feelings of witnesses or with the possible traumatic effect on victims who gave evidence no matter how deleterious the consequences. Justice had very little to do with feelings and emotions and was blind to such matters and remains blind in most situations. Children were mostly not affected because it was rare to see them in court, except as victims. I had prosecuted several trials in which infants had been murdered and the feelings of parents, close relatives and friends had mattered, but nothing was done to shield them from intense public scrutiny.

However, things were different by the time of this trial. There were now provisions for children to give evidence under carefully regulated conditions and the Children's Act at that time.

I discussed the matter of the capacity of a child of such tender age with several forensic psychiatrists who had previously given evidence in cases that I had prosecuted, but these were cases that dealt with the criminal conduct and behaviour of adults, and some were cases in which insanity was raised and vigorously contested by the prosecution. As usual, there were many factors to consider, and the reliability of a child of five in such circumstances of severe trauma surfaced again and again. There was a need for experts familiar with little children to help gauge, fathom and chart the course that should be followed. However, some very serious minds thought that there was no need for expert advice to instruct the jury on such matters as memory and appreciation of concepts or to show that little children do not appreciate the significance or relevance of some matters. It was true that there was no need for much imagination to form a view on how a child might respond when confronted with the killer in the court. I thought that the prosecution should not take anything for granted and needed to demonstrate the strength and reliability of a child's evidence by reference to clear expert testimony on both the capacity and reliability of this particular child—and to do this to the satisfaction of the jury.

There were intense discussions and serious reservations expressed. Like many men in various professions who consult their wives or soothsayers, but not necessarily in that order, I decided to consult my wife Rosemary who was a social worker with extensive experience. Rosemary had completed a degree course in Social Studies in 1963 at the University of Queensland at about the time I finished Law. We had many family friends who were social workers, and some had gone on to make significant contributions in this relatively new field. The legal fraternity was slow to recognise the immense impact of professionals in social justice and related fields, although by the time of this hearing, social workers and others in related fields were increasingly being consulted in criminal matters. The prosecution sought assistance, but there were strong objections to the very idea that a child of such tender age should be confronted with the killer and compelled to recall painful events. There was little or no support for the idea from the social workers,

## CHAPTER 6

who were more concerned with the living, just as the prosecution was more concerned with the dead and the battered. I recalled that when I graduated, some seasoned, crusty, testy and battle-hardened legal practitioners referred to social workers as 'bleeding hearts'. They probably had a point!

The prosecution now turned to specialists in child psychiatry. Fortunately, the child in this case had been examined by a psychiatrist soon after the murder, so there was ample background material available.

Kirsty had been seen several months after the murders and again early in 1988 and immediately before the trial by Dr Maria Hanger, a psychiatrist who worked at the Royal Children's Hospital, which was a teaching hospital at the time. Dr Hanger was a consultant who worked with the Child and Family Therapy Unit at the Royal Children's Hospital. It so happened that Dr Hanger had specialised in child development and had extensive clinical and teaching experience and could address a broad range of problems associated with a child required to give evidence in court. She was eminently qualified to speak about the capacity of a child of tender age to give evidence and had delivered many papers on the problems facing a child in a court of law. She had delivered papers on the subject at various medico-legal conferences in Australia and overseas as well. The evidence of the child was so vital that the prosecution intended to call expert evidence dealing with the issue of the capacity and reliability of a child of tender age in the context of a criminal trial where witnesses were expected to be subjected to rigorous cross-examination. These were not civil proceedings, which were thought at the time to be, well, more civil.

The Crown also approached Dr Helen M Connell, a recognised eminent authority on the subject. I had spoken to her on several occasions about this case and met her briefly when she came to court to assist the prosecution. I was curious and fascinated by some details in Dr Connell's background such as that she had graduated in Medicine from London University in 1945 when there were few women in the professions and when I was still a child. I noted from the background material that she was elected a foundation member of the Royal College of Psychiatrists in the United Kingdom in 1972 and elected to the fellowship of that college in 1982. Dr Connell had extensive experience with children first as a developmental paediatrician and finally as a children's psychiatrist and was appointed Associate Professor of Child Psychiatry at the University of Queensland from 1970 and taught there until her retirement in December 1987, just a short time after these murders were committed. Professor Connell was also the author of a standard textbook on child psychiatry and had over seventy publications on the subject. Shortly before the trial, she had delivered papers on forensic child psychiatry, which included important sections on the use of children as witnesses in court proceedings. Why so much time devoted to the qualifications of these witnesses? Well, it seemed that in the absence of some very persuasive evidence dealing with both the capacity of a child of such tender years and the reliability of expert assessment, the critical evidence for the prosecution would be rejected and not go before the jury. There was also the risk that the defence would rely on other experts who held contrary views and then seek to exclude such evidence. The prosecution had to prepare for that possibility as well.

This concern as to what might happen in court was not so fanciful because during the trial Mr Justice Moynihan, after extensive legal submissions, first ruled that such evidence was admissible and that the Crown could lead this evidence dealing with capacity from the two experts. But he also gave some indication that the debate on the subject was not closed, and that he was prepared to reconsider the matter, if necessary, during the trial. To the prosecution, this was a signal that the preliminary ruling on the admissibility of expert evidence was not settled, and it was likely that that ruling would be reversed. In the end, shortly before the child gave evidence, the trial judge ruled that, whilst the evidence from the two expert witnesses was admissible, he was not inclined to allow this evidence because of the possibility that the jury was likely to use it for some other purpose such as to buttress the credibility of the child. He declined to allow the prosecution to call the experts, and they were not called. The determination of the question of capacity was a matter for the trial judge. He ruled that the

## CHAPTER 6

child's evidence was admissible and that other issues, including the weight to be given such evidence, were a matter for the tribunal of fact, and there was no need for experts.

In a criminal trial, nothing happens in a vacuum and, although the ruling to exclude expert evidence was binding, the boundaries when dealing with the capacity of a child as explained by the experts helped in the examination and cross-examination of the child. The defence was provided with the statements of both experts. From the extensive discussions that followed in the absence of the jury, and from the lengthy legal submissions, both counsel and the trial judge were acutely aware of what the expert witnesses would have told the court. It certainly influenced the way the case was conducted by the prosecution. Every suggestion made by these two experts as to how a child should be dealt with was followed both by counsel and the trial judge. This then is a brief account of what the jury did not hear from the experts and a summary of what the expert witnesses were going to say:

Dr Marika Hanger summarised the position with a very young child as follows:

1) Children as young as three can recall and accurately provide information. The sharp distinction between children and adults was made clear: children were not 'miniature adults' but were 'growing organisms, constantly developing, not only physically, but also emotionally, mentally and socially' and a 'person who gathers information from a child should bear in mind the child's developmental level and adjust his interviewing technique accordingly'.

2) Young children had good memories but 'tend to remember more the significant events rather than the peripheral detail ... while they can quite accurately recall what was done to them, or to significant others and who did it, they may not remember the furniture in the room' and 'with the passage of time these peripheral details fade even more. In young children, motor memory is much better than verbal recall' and 'children were better in showing what happened than telling about it'.

Children taken to the site or scene of some event or episode would point out things. If it were not possible to take them to the scene, then a small model of the site was a valuable recourse.

3) Concepts of time, space and particularly distance were poorly developed, and abstract concepts were also a problem with children. There was a need to elicit information to see if the child understood the concept and to guard against assuming that the child would have understood it. There was a need for simple short questions introducing only one idea at a time. Young children did not understand irony or analogy and had a shorter concentration timespan.

4) Children should not be expected to deal with 'evaluation' questions. They have difficulties with 'why' questions and should not be expected to deal with these. 'They don't reason from observation; they do not understand contradictions and will accept false explanations. They do not understand cause and effect'.

5) Young children had good memories of significant events and were able to give useful information in court.

Dr Helen Connell said:

1) Children can retain clear memories of events, but it had to be realised that what was meaningful and important to a child did not necessarily have the same connotation for adults and vice versa. Up to the age of 3 years, it is difficult to know how much a child can remember. Studies have shown that after the fourth year, children could give useful information in court.

2) Gaps and omissions could occur in evidence, not because of forgetfulness but because younger children had difficulty in describing (in words) their experiences. Children must be allowed to recount their experiences in their own way. The thought processes of a five-year-old differ greatly from those

## CHAPTER 6

of adults. Concepts such as 'death' or 'violence' had little meaning for a young child.

3) Events that produced intense emotions in the child made a greater impact than trivial happenings and were more likely to be clearly remembered.
4) Children do not intend to deceive (and this applies especially to the younger ones) but can be influenced by parents or other authority figures to suppress facts or repeat falsehoods. Many children had rich fantasy lives, but most appreciated the difference between reality and fantasy under questioning.
5) The child's mind is continually developing and expanding. Events that occurred at age five would be described, say, two years later (as in Kirsty's case) by an individual whose intellectual and language attributes had made considerable progress, but the events described would remain as those experienced by a five-year-old.
6) The courts can be very frightening to children: questions directed towards the child have to be appropriate to his or her level of comprehension and not as posed to adult witnesses.
7) These observations were relevant to a child of average intellectual ability whose mental age was commensurate with his or her chronological age.

Dr Connell endorsed Dr Maria Hanger's assessment on the evidential capacity of a normal child of Kirsty's age and was prepared to give evidence in the trial. Dr Hanger had already given the opinion that Kirsty was 'developmentally a normal child'.

The question of capacity was initially a question for the trial judge to decide, but the exclusion of the expert evidence was a setback for the prosecution. It was all very easy to say that the jury would be familiar with the ways of children and capable of making a judgement for itself. If it was all so very easy, why did experts such as those proposed to be called spend their lives studying and writing about it?

Kirsty was living with her father in Toowoomba and attending school there. Before making a final decision, I wanted to meet Kirsty. It was thought more congenial to meet her in informal surroundings and not at the Crown Law Office in Brisbane or the police station in Toowoomba, so I travelled to Toowoomba with Detective Sergeant Robert Pease to meet and talk to her one afternoon after school. Kirsty, accompanied by her father, arrived at the motel where I was staying, and the clearest memory that I have now is how little she was for a witness. We talked about general matters dealing with school and sport, and I found her to be comfortable talking to me. I was impressed with her short, precise responses to my questions. She was completely at ease and even lit up a bit when I told her that she would have to miss school for a day or two as I wanted her to come to Brisbane to see my office, the workings of the court, and the courtroom. I think she had spoken to Dr Hanger on several occasions and felt quite comfortable with the idea of travelling to Brisbane. I do not recall any other trial in which there was so much time devoted to one witness. I did not discuss the evidence for some very good reasons.

The other suggestions by these expert witnesses were followed by the prosecution in its preparation of the case and there was intense activity directed to practical matters. In every case, there are contributions made by people who are never acknowledged and who never give evidence. They remain in the background.

One such person was Thomas Eric Howe, who was a sheet-metal worker by trade. He had manufactured or cobbled items required by the Police Department for various purposes. He undertook to make an exact scale model of the farmhouse, including the swinging door in the bedroom, which Kirsty had mentioned several times, and the water tank outside the house. He went to the property to take exact measurements, and he did all this at the weekends in his spare time. The model had no roof. When giving her evidence, Kirsty used a pencil to poke and show what she observed and where she was in the house.

One afternoon, before the start of the trial, I came out of court from another trial in progress. As arranged, Kirsty arrived with detectives

## CHAPTER 6

Pease and Chapman. I was still robed and wigged, and Kristy giggled at my formal penguin attire. She was shown the formal courtroom, which the bailiff had opened for this purpose. I noticed that she was not overwhelmed by the surroundings. She showed interest in where the jury sat and, in fact, ran her hand several times on the front panel of the jury enclosure and, when invited, sat on the chair usually occupied by the Crown prosecutor. She even went up to see and pat the judge's chair and … she probably sat on it as well. Kirsty wanted to know where the 'man would sit', and that was the only time she appeared slightly tense and agitated, but that was all she asked about the man when I pointed to the dock. I recall Detective Chapman assuring Kirsty that he (Chapman) would be in the back of the court when she gave evidence. He was dressed in a suit and not in uniform, being a plain-clothes detective. He stood on his toes in a boxer's pose and told her that everything would be all right. I had put the wig on the table, and Kirsty poked and examined the horsehair. She confirmed what I had been told earlier by Dr Hanger and said that she liked drawing and wanted to know whether it would be alright for her to draw when giving an account of what happened on that day.

I formed the impression that the court would be dealing with a confident child unlikely to be overwhelmed either by the formal surroundings or the task of recounting what had happened. She would be able to tell the court how she had tried to help her mother, who was on the bed and bleeding profusely. How, after failing to revive her mother, she had kissed and patted her and said that she would ring for help. And how, on finding that the telephone had been ripped out of the wall, she had decided to go get help. She was worried about the man's threat to hurt 'Simi', the Arab stallion on the property, and had wanted to save the horse.

I saw Kirsty on several occasions, but I personally never interviewed Kirsty on the evidence she might be capable of giving. I never asked a single question about what happened on that day. It was proper for the Crown prosecutor doing his work diligently to interview witnesses of critical importance to the case, and this was one such case, but I had decided that, whilst the recollection of details was important, the prosecution was seeking only one vital detail: clear, reliable, and uncontradicted evidence that it was Harding who was in the house minutes before the victims were murdered. Once Harding was in the house, the rest followed from the overwhelming other circumstantial evidence. The whole case hinged on proper identification in the house of murder. This was put succinctly by a junior clerk assisting me in a comment directed to a police officer who was interested in the outcome of this case. He expressed it in language somewhat like that used in some presidential election, but perhaps before then. He said:

'It is identification, STUPID.'

However, the reliability of the evidence could be tested because immediately after the murders Kristy had given an account that contained a description of the assailant and several weeks later had picked Harding out from a number of photographs as the man in the house. This was taped and was available to the defence to show any prior inconsistency in her account. She was only five at the time of the murders and so the two accounts she gave had some serious inconsistencies in the

Model of the murder scene for use by a five-year-old, the only surviving witness.

descriptions. These were legitimately used by the defence during the cross-examination. It was common practice to discuss the evidence to be given with the witness before a trial, but in this case, I had asked the police not to question the child or show her any material or photographs again. One of the first questions by the defence counsel was whether before the start of the trial the police had shown Kirsty any of the

## CHAPTER 6

photographs used for identification some two years earlier and whether any effort had been made to couch or to help refresh her memory. When this was put to Kirsty, even without thinking she said 'No'. Kirsty was not shown anything until she came to give evidence in court. I had told the police that any shadow cast on her evidence would compel the trial judge, no matter how reluctantly, to exclude her evidence.

The risks of interviewing impressionable young children were obvious. The danger was that she might preface her evidence with a muddled statement suggesting that she was repeating in court what she had been told by the police or the Crown prosecutor. A child could not be expected to separate her account from any hearsay material. Had she been shown photographs before the trial, she could have made some such statement as: 'The policeman showed me some photographs and said was this the man you saw in the room and I said yes. Then the policeman said do you know such and such, and I said yes'. This sometimes happened even with adults, even though the only thing the police might have done was to show photographs and invite comment. Despite there being no suggestions put by the police, there was always room for suspicion. Police were frequently attacked in the witness box for doing precisely that—and mud sticks.

There is no substitute for experience, and I was acutely aware of the problem because something akin to that happened to me in a rape trial in which I ran a severe risk of being censored and perhaps even worse. I have a vivid recollection of what happened in that case because in the fifties and sixties there were no gang rapes or none that I had heard of, and this rape trial happened in the seventies. I have no recollection now of the names of the accused, but three young men were charged with raping a fifteen-year-old girl in brutal circumstances and because she had come from a broken home and had lived in a hostel for wayward children, she was an easy target for defence counsel.

Being only 15, she was under the age of consent, which meant a straightforward case of 'unlawful carnal knowledge'. However, that was a lesser charge than rape, and I wanted to convict these young men of rape.

These were three very experienced trial lawyers who did their best to thwart me. The trial was in the Supreme Court before a seasoned and highly respected Mr Justice Lucas. That I remember clearly!

As expected, there was an unrestricted and vigorous attack on the character and other doings in the past of the rape victim, which at the time was all permissible and legitimate. This happened during the period when judges told the jury that when a woman said no, she probably meant yes and if there was no recent complaint then that could be some evidence of consent and if there was a recent complaint that was no evidence of lack of consent. It was said that a recent complaint was evidence of consistency in the conduct of the victim, but it certainly did not mean that she had not consented and that it somehow went only to her credit. The jury was always told that it was dangerous to act on the uncorroborated evidence of the complainant, and this was the prevailing attitude in the community to victims of rape and sanctioned by decided cases and other statutory provisions. There were some aspects of criminal responsibility and onus of proof in our laws from which the authors of sharia law would have found solace and useful hints in the decided cases in Queensland. Certainly, a female victim was not required to produce three or four eyewitnesses in support of her case, but once the evidence was tortured, emasculated and distorted it was almost always an extremely difficult task for the prosecution, especially with the jury being told several times that the uncorroborated evidence of the complainant was dangerous to act on and that the absence of a recent complaint might be some evidence of consent. However, once women began to be selected for jury service and female barristers began to appear regularly in our courts, the tone and substance of the debate shifted and by the time I retired it was difficult to find many male barristers repeatedly haranguing the jury in those terms, and the trial judges stopped almost completely from reminding the jury that when the victim said 'no' she probably meant 'yes'. Those few who did were met with stony silence and a look of barely disguised contempt. A look speaks louder than words. The prosecutors who appeared regularly in the criminal courts all had experienced ceaseless and unwarranted

# CHAPTER 6

attacks on the character of female rape victims. The real problem in the cases of young, wayward but vulnerable female victims was that they did not know the requirement of the law dealing with recent complaints and were the frequent targets of abuse. These cases were tough and vigorously contested and with four counsel at the bar table, as in this rape case, objections came thick and fast. These verbal jousts were mostly relatively friendly 'jaw-jaw' and 'yo-yo' affairs. There were times when the exchanges were mild and friendly and to the uninitiated silent observer the vision would have been decidedly comic with counsel sometimes yo-yoing to their feet and sometimes doing a slow Mexican wave with their bodies as they rose to their feet almost in unison. Sometimes during adjournments, they were seen hurriedly filing out of court seemingly doing a 'conga', all lost in various states of mental disarray. Occasionally, one saw four or even six men of serious mien, darkly attired, rising in unison, doing a slow Mexican wave with their bodies as they headed for the exit. When the exchanges were heated, the body language changed and all could be seen jerking up to their feet like marionettes or like darkly clad bikies kick-starting motorbikes, objecting and being objectionable. When at rest and in relative calm, some large bodies could be seen heaving and tossing, splayed over the bar table like groupie walruses found slithering on ice seemingly completely at ease with their lot of having to defend cretins not worthy of their talent and time. Or so they appeared to the jaded eyes of the regulars in the gallery.

I once approached a middle-aged, rather dishevelled man with his face peppered with tiny cotton-wool wads covering shaving mishaps, who was seen in the gallery frequently during criminal trials. I wanted to know why he got so much pleasure from watching the proceedings because he was observed sometimes chuckling and sometimes smiling and sometimes bursting out in laughter. I asked one of the police investigators in court to make some inquiries, and he did that but said to me with a friendly smile that it would be 'best if you spoke to him, he is probably a crank'. I could not understand why he would take such perverse interest in these cases and could not resist the temptation to ask him personally. Generally, the unwritten rule in court for counsel was to never speak to strangers sitting in the gallery. This man was delighted to talk to me and had no hesitation in reassuring me that it was not the gory details he was interested in, nothing of the sort. He chatted about his interest in cases for some time but told me that he was laughing at '… the stupid antics of youse blokes' and went on to say '… fancy youse all getting paid for it too'. It is best not to seek public opinion on such matters during a trial.

The young complainant in that rape trial was subjected to extensive cross-examination and pressed to reveal whether she had discussed her evidence with anyone before appearing in court. She agreed that she had been interviewed in my office and that she had asked to see what she said in evidence in the lower court during the committal hearings. She told the court that my clerk had given her the depositions and that she had looked through the whole of them including the evidence by other witnesses. This looked like a case of a young girl being tutored to dovetail her evidence with that of other witnesses and the defence sensed that it had struck gold. Mr Justice Lucas, who was sober and sombre in criminal trials, frowned at such a flagrant breach of practice and perhaps reflected on the possible consequences for the prosecution. The prevailing practice then was that a witness could be interviewed and could have access to what the witness said in the lower court and could discuss the details with the Crown prosecutor, but the idea of a witness trawling through the whole of the depositions was a serious departure deserving of censure.

I did recall seeing the complainant in my cramped office sitting with my experienced instructing clerk and reading from the depositions. I had no idea what she might have read, and, unfortunately for me, my instructing clerk was not in court when all this happened. I had no time to seek clarification but was certain that she could not possibly have read some 500 pages of material in the hour or so that she was waiting in the office. However, it was possible that she had seen material parts and that was sufficient to establish the point being made—namely, that she had been given a chance to doctor her evidence. When stuck, it is

## CHAPTER 6

almost always best to bite the bullet. I handed the whole of the lower court depositions to the witness and invited her to show the jury what she had read. It appeared that she had read her own evidence, and when the clerk was absent, she had flipped through the pages in the way she demonstrated to the jury and had not read anything. When she had said that she had gone through the whole record, she meant she had flicked through the pages. When asked to read a few sentences of her own evidence, she struggled with it because she could not read quickly and took a long time. So much for the skilful cross-examination and repeated concession by the witness to a question which was in some such form as: 'Now, are you absolutely certain that you were allowed to look at the whole of the depositions and you went through the whole lot of it and looked through the lot?' Answer: 'Yes'. The complainant came across as naïve, untutored and honest, and as the accused did not give evidence and perhaps also because she was subjected to such persistent attack, the jury believed her, and all were convicted. So, in Kirsty's case, the solution was not to talk to her about her evidence, but there was no doubt that the family members had discussed the case with her, and she might have spoken to the psychiatrists the Crown intended calling.

On the morning Kirsty gave evidence, the trial judge invited both counsel and Kirsty to his chambers and spent some time chatting with Kirsty. The judge also accompanied her to the courtroom and explained what would happen in court. Kirsty had a good look around the judge's chamber and seemed confident when she met the trial judge. When the judge spoke to her, she smiled and seemed comfortable with him. She certainly liked the defence counsel, Milton Griffin (now a District Court Judge), who was considerate and spoke to her quite softly. During the hearing, she was so relaxed and comfortable talking and discussing matters with Milton Griffin that I was slightly apprehensive that she might agree to unlikely propositions put to her in the cross-examination. But there was no attempt made to confuse or muddle her with clever questions save the searching questions to show that as a child her evidence had a few weaknesses.

The appearance of the little witness for the prosecution transformed the court and changed the dynamics and the relationship between the opposing counsel at the bar table. The changes suggested by the various experts were followed and, whilst to the regular observers accustomed and inured to the severity of the design and architecture of a courtroom these may not have appeared significant changes, they did make a deep impact on the conduct of the trial. The architecture of the courtroom changed, with austere functionality yielding to comfort and homeliness. These were small changes but had a marked effect on the little witness. The furniture was tossed around, and sitting arrangements altered. A small table and chair were placed just in front of the Bench but a bit to the side close to the jury so that Kirsty could sit and do her drawing when giving evidence. Just in front of her on the table sat the scaled model of the farmhouse approximately at eye level from where she sat. The model was placed so Kirsty could reach out on the table and point to the various rooms in the dwelling and not only describe but 'show' the jury what had happened. When she chose to do so or was directed by me, she got up out of her chair and walked around the table. She pointed at and looked at the model and then looked directly at the jury and give her account. During her evidence, she did both. She was not required to sit in the witness box, and as she wanted to be next to a family friend, another chair was placed so a family friend could sit next to her.

Kirsty did not want to see the 'man'. It was never contemplated that that should happen. A suitable barrier or curtain was placed so that the accused and the child were not forced to confront each other. The arrangement was such that the accused could see her if he wished, but she could not see him at all. The court bailiff, who just happened to be sitting near her, was dressed in a formal-looking uniform like a policeman or some 'official' and she liked that. The trial judge gave leave to both counsels to move into the well of the court as required without any procedural constraints, and the usual formal deference to the judge, such as the constant reference to 'Your Honour', was dispensed with. My instructing clerk was permitted to sit in the witness box to take notes of what Kirsty was pointing out or to move about and follow her when she

# CHAPTER 6

was on her feet showing the jury something on the model. She pointed to the various rooms frequently and poked with her coloured drawing pencils in different areas of the house. Sometimes she was absorbed in her painting.

It was agreed that as I led her through her evidence, there would be no interruptions to her train of thought. The usual practice of identifying and putting on record photographs and other exhibits used and the requirement of putting on the court record the areas that she pointed to on the model of the farmhouse were kept to a minimum. The jury members were rapt but tried not to look or stare at her. The very experienced court reporters assigned to deal with the apparent confusion with exhibits flying from hand to hand and back to Kirsty and then back to me melted into the general court scenery and were unobtrusive as they went about their business. I intended to use photographs that were in the exhibit, and no attempt was made to refer to or identify these in the usual way. Notes were kept and the court record dealt with later. I stood next to Kirsty just in front of the trial judge with my back to him so I could see the model and see what she was describing, and the defence counsel was at liberty to move to any position he chose. Within reason, all formality was dispensed with; we were not required to wear our wigs. But there were unstated but clearly understood limits to the relaxed atmosphere in court and counsel were aware that the liberty to move or sit anywhere they pleased did not imply permission to sit on the Bench with the trial judge and nor did the trial judge give such permission.

The change in the atmosphere in the 'battlefield' that is the criminal court was such that during the course of the evidence the transcript was peppered with the trial judge telling Kirsty to show something to 'Vish' (for Vishal) and sometimes directly addressing me as 'Vish' and telling Kirsty to 'show it to Milton'. I was calling the defence counsel 'Milt' and sometimes 'Milton' like in the good old days when he was with me in court.

Kirsty really appeared quite little for the age of seven. Of slight build with straight, sandy brown hair, she was soon deeply engrossed in painting and quite oblivious to the apparently hostile surroundings and to the many people sitting in the gallery intently watching her. Criminal trials are public hearings, and no one can be excluded save for good reason. The gallery was full of professional people, the media and spectators.

As she painted and talked to me, the conversation had occasional references to what she was doing:

> MR LAKSHMAN: Now you like drawing, what sort of things do you normally draw?
>
> KIRSTY: Houses.
>
> MR LAKSHMAN: What else?
>
> KIRSTY: People, grass, and trees.
>
> MR LAKSHMAN: And trees?
>
> KIRSTY: And trees.
>
> MR LAKSHMAN: And what are you drawing at the moment?
>
> KIRSTY: Grass.
>
> MR LAKSHMAN: What would you be drawing next?
>
> KIRSTY: A house.

We were not used to such succinct and precise responses from witnesses in criminal trials!

Kirsty then gave an account of the movement of the two women on that morning. When it came to her evidence of the stranger appearing at the gate of the property, I saw that she had her head down and seemed to be moving her hand furiously, still painting. As it was thought best to distract her from the painting at this stage, so there was no confusion in the critical area of her evidence, this exchange took place:

> MR LAKSHMAN: Do you still want to draw, or would you want to talk to me now? What would you prefer, draw and talk or just talk to me?

# CHAPTER 6

> KIRSTY: Draw and talk.

She went on drawing when giving her evidence of what happened in the house.

> During the cross-examination by Mr Griffin, she was still drawing. After asking Kirsty some questions about the colour of the hair of the assailant and about his features, he noticed that she was not looking at him but drawing as she answered. He asked:
>
> MR GRIFFIN: What are you drawing there? Is that grass?
>
> KIRSTY: Yes.
>
> MR GRIFFIN: Are you going to put some trees in there as well?
>
> KIRSTY: Yes.

During the re-examination, I noticed that the jury and others in court were trying to see what Kirsty was drawing on the sheet of paper, and so there was this exchange:

> MR LAKSHMAN: ... Everybody probably wants to know what you're doing there. You might just tell us what you have done. You have a house there?
>
> KIRSTY: A house, some trees and some grass and sky and some sun and now I am doing some flowers and a path.

The trial judge then took up the role of art critic from counsel at the bar table and said:

> HIS HONOUR: Can I have a look at the picture now? [drawing handed to him]. That's pretty good. Pity we didn't have some green pens and some other colours for you.

Kirsty just nodded and put out her hand to get her drawing back and went back to drawing.

When Kirsty had finished giving evidence and walked past the bar table, she put her drawing on the table for me and later told the police that she wanted me to keep it because I had asked her to do the drawing. She said that she wanted me to have the picture, and I kept it in the proverbial 'shoe box' in our home. For decades it lay there, and perhaps it is still there.

Earlier in the trial, when telling the jury what had happened that day, Kirsty got out of her chair and, using the model and a photograph of the front of the farmhouse, she showed the jury where on the property the man was when first offered a lift. She said she was in the front seat with 'Mummy' and that the man sat just behind her in the back passenger seat. This man said that he wanted to see one of the horses and to ride it. When they got to the house, her mother left her at the house and went to the paddock to show the man the horse. Kirsty told the court that earlier in the morning she had been given an injection for a foot injury and was feeling sick at Donna's place. She said: 'I went upstairs and had a tablet with some cordial and lay down on the lounge'. A short time later, she went looking for her mummy and asked Donna 'Where is my mum?'

When told by Donna Tidy that her mother and the man were still in the paddock, Kirsty went to look for them and saw her mother and this man petting one of the horses. When she was back in the house a short time later, she recalled that she came out of one room, which she pointed to on the model, and said: '…I saw Donna was lying on the floor and the man [was] holding her up and he said to me: "Donna just slipped over the dog."'

She did not hear Donna speak. It was likely that her throat had been cut and she was being held up on her feet when the child appeared suddenly, disturbing the assailant, who then explained that Donna had just slipped on the dog. Kirsty saw a lot of blood on the floor at the feet of Donna. When found wandering sometime later, she kept repeating that she knew that 'Donna never slipped and fell' and kept asking these strangers whether they knew where Donna was. She told the court that she never saw what happened to Donna after she saw the man holding her up and did not see where Donna went. There was no evidence

## CHAPTER 6

that she ever saw the body of Donna, which was lying just outside the house.

Earlier, before the attacks, Kirsty was told by the assailant to go into a room and shut the door, and this was Donna's bedroom. In an account she gave to one witness she said that the man had pushed her into the room and hurt her shoulder. In court, Kirsty got out of her chair on several occasions and pointed to the room she was sent to and said in evidence: 'I came through that door and peeked through that door … saw this man walking in the hallway.' It was thought highly probable that the assailant was not aware that the little child was watching him. This was because the bedroom door through which Kirsty said she 'peeked' was a swing door, and she had opened it just a little. The slight opening of the door went unnoticed by the killer busy with his work. Pointing at the hallway on the model, Kirsty said that at one stage she: '… saw him coming down the hall. I went back into that room'. It appeared that the murderer, occupied by the frenzied attack on the women, and perhaps in a hurry to get away, had completely forgotten the child. The police did not doubt that the child was in great danger at that stage and that the killer would have had no compunction in killing her had he remained a little longer and taken stock. When Kirsty saw him walking in her direction in the hallway she quickly went back and hid in the room again. It was shortly after that she heard her mother screaming. She told the jury that the scream came from the area where her mother's body was found on the bed.

She never saw the man actually attacking her mother. When she 'peeked' again, she saw the back of the man as he went out of the house and described his movement on the model: 'He went through there [pointing], through there [pointing], and outside [pointing].' And in her account, she also said that: 'After I heard the car going, I went outside to see where he was going and I saw him taking Mummy's car and he was going out the gate, so I ran back inside and saw Mummy lying on the bed.'

Kirsty went on to describe how her mother was completely naked and bleeding profusely but not talking to her. She said: 'I kissed Mummy and then I ran outside to get the horse. I went up the driveway. I opened the gate and started walking down the road.'

I was curious to learn why she took the horse because in court she described how she had to stand on some tree stumps so she could reach up to untie this very large horse, and all this effort took some time while she was trying to escape from the scene to get help. She was later found walking and leading the horse down the road quite some distance from the house. She was not riding the horse. She could have just run away from the house and not spent all the time finding the horse. In the meantime, the killer could have easily returned to deal with the child. So, I wanted to know why Kirsty spent so much time securing the safety of the horse and said:

MR LAKSHMAN: Why did you take the horse?

KIRSTY: Because that's the horse Mummy always rides.

Then she gave her evidence of identification of Harding from photographs she had been shown a month after the murders. This evidence was persuasive because she simply had no difficulty recognising the man she had seen. She kept on repeating that that was the man; it was his face and eyes and that it was a black man.

The most telling evidence of her certainty that Harding was the man came during the cross-examination when she was taken through some features in her descriptions that also fitted in with other dark men in a series of photographs she had been shown. When shown the photograph of Harding and asked what possible distinguishing features there were to set Harding apart from other coloured persons of similar build in the photographs, Kirsty looked intently at the photograph of Harding for a long moment. As if talking to herself and not to any particular person in court, she said: '... the eyes, the eyes ...'

Kirsty had remembered the look in the eyes of the murderer and had not forgotten. There were no other eyewitnesses or any other evidence on the essential question of identity. The weak circumstantial case, which had been vanishing down the gurgler, was saved by Kirsty's eyewitness account.

The accused did not give evidence and did not call any evidence. He was convicted on both counts of murder and given a life sentence on each. On his sentencing, the court was informed that he had a criminal record in New Zealand and that he had worked in Brisbane and had a taxi licence. It also came out that, a few days after the murders, he was busy driving female passengers late at night as part of his job. There was the usual public outcry about the failure to check the backgrounds of misfits from other parts of the world who applied for jobs, and I was told by police that the ladies of the night working in that area were outraged about workplace safety. The politicians assured the public that this would never happen again, and the public, reassured, went into its default position of rest and slumber until the next time.

Harding appealed to the Court of Criminal Appeal. He was represented by Mr Griffin and I appeared for the Crown. The appeal was dismissed. Kirsty faded into the vastness of our continent, and the police were satisfied that all the hard work they did was not in vain.

At the time, I mentioned to some of my colleagues that in an ideal system of criminal justice, at least in serious cases, the accused should be compelled to give evidence. Had that avenue been available then, the prosecution might not have been compelled to call a child to give evidence but could have taken a chance with an extensive cross-examination of the accused. The defence is never obliged to indicate the course it would take until the close of the Crown case, and in this case, it was not possible to proceed without Kirsty's evidence.

This was a case in which the Crown lacked the opportunity to cross-examine the accused, who had repeatedly lied about his movements and could not explain where he was during the missing few hours before the murders were committed, and there were other significant omissions in his account. However, the judgement not to call evidence was a sound one from the defence's point of view. The defence had to grapple with many complex issues.

There were those who thought that the evidence of a very young child should not be used in serious cases such as murder, which carried a mandatory life sentence, because it was possible for a child to be confused or mistaken. The answer may be that Kirsty's evidence was not challenged by other evidence, and its reliability was thoroughly tested in the cross-examination. The prosecution is not entitled or given the opportunity to make an adverse comment on the failure of an accused to give evidence. If Kirsty's evidence was not reliable, all the accused had to do was walk just three or four paces to the witness box and swear that the child was mistaken and that he had not murdered the two women. The trial judges always had the right in appropriate cases to comment on the failure of an accused to give evidence, but in most cases, this was done to reinforce in the minds of the jurors that no adverse inferences could be drawn from the failure of an accused to give evidence. However, normal jury members are down-to-earth, practical people capable of drawing an adverse inference from the failure of an accused to give evidence.

When the Crown case is compelling and the evidence overwhelming, then the question hardly matters because a reasonable jury would almost always convict whether the accused gave evidence or not. It does matter when the Crown case is just there but not quite there for the jury to be convinced of the guilt of the accused. There is no way to measure human conduct using an objective scale, but supposing the jury concluded that 'We are 90 per cent sure he is guilty' or 'We are almost sure he is as guilty as hell' or 'We are almost there and really quite satisfied but not satisfied beyond a reasonable doubt, as explained by that old codger on the Bench', what should we do? Just let him get away with bloody murder when we are 90 per cent sure that he must have murdered them? The jury is not expected to have such muddled thinking after being given such lucid directions on what constitutes the test of 'beyond a reasonable doubt'. I, in common with some other lawyers, had absolutely no idea what exactly it meant, apart from the well-settled and repeated mantra. Some judges have tried in vain to explain what 'beyond a reasonable doubt' might mean only to find the logicians and the keepers of the gate in the appellate jurisdiction descending on them like a ton of bricks, and one might look in vain for what the term really means from these sages from on high. The practice was to use mantras such as 'beyond a reasonable doubt' and terms such as 'honest and reasonable' or 'intention' and when asked to explain simply indulge in tautology so that if the jury wanted to know what the term meant the trial judge merely repeats what they said before. So, the jury may be told on redirection: 'As I have said, reasonable doubt is a doubt founded in reason. Look, the term needs no further explanation. It is so simple: reasonable doubt is reasonable doubt.' There was one recent case in which this happened.

## An aside about Simi

When the jury inspected the murder scene, many of the members wanted to meet 'Simi', the horse, and pet him. I recall that Simi reared and neighed, and the court reporters wanted to know if that was evidence and whether they were required to take all that down on record. I think someone in the defence team (probably Milton Griffin) quipped to me that if the Crown were desperate enough to call a little child to give evidence, then it was only a matter of time before the prosecution would be seeking to call the Arabian stallion as a witness. There was some light-hearted discussion on the reliability of evidence coming literally from the horse's mouth and the problem of swearing in such a witness as there was a Bible but no Q'uran in court. There were enough difficulties in the presentation of the Crown case without some such added burden, so I dismissed the suggestion.

## *Hypothetical circumstantial evidence cases*

In some cases, identity is not a critical issue. The only question is whether there is sufficient evidence on which a jury might convict. In other cases, the evidence lurches, ebbs and flows in many directions. Finally, other facts and circumstances support what was initially a weak case on identity.

For example, a man answering the general description of X (the accused) is seen at the scene of the crime, but nothing more is known about the identity of the assailant. All that is known is that he is tall (180 cm), heavily built, has broad shoulders and answers to the description of either Tongan, Maori, Fijian, Indian or Chinese. The victim was raped, murdered and left naked, and the only item found was an empty blue handbag. X denies everything and says that he never met the dead woman. Police acting on some information or hunch search X's house and find women's clothing like the victim had been wearing and some jewellery. He explains that these things belong to his girlfriend. Police check and the girlfriend confirms that she spent time with him in the house. That could be enough for the police. But then they find spots of blood on the underwear, and it is of rare blood grouping like the dead woman and not the girlfriend's. But there could be scores or hundreds of people with similar blood grouping in the district.

A strange man is seen burying something on a farm, and again the witness gives a vague description of the man. The police investigate and find a carving knife with a black plastic handle and traces of blood, which turn out to match the rare blood type of the deceased. More articles of clothing, including a dress very similar to the one the deceased had been wearing, are found. But hundreds of similar dresses were sold that year. The police get lucky and find several credit cards with the name of the deceased and the car keys of the missing woman. Now we know that even though there is no name tag on the dress and, despite the fact hundreds were sold that year, this dress is likely to be the dress the deceased was wearing when she was killed. (Let's make it easy for the poor police.) There is also a well-preserved boot mark on some clay soil with a good imprint of the sole of the boot. Now, these items would leave little doubt about their connection to the murder, and the identity of the deceased is already known. The connection of the items found to the actual murderer is now taking shape, but his identity is still not established.

There is another police search of X's house, and this time the police are looking for specific items because they have more clues. They find a set of knives, but the carving knife in that set is missing. X is shown the knife found buried at the farm and says he has no idea what happened to his missing knife. However, there may have been thousands of similar knives sold over the years. Is it a mere coincidence that the police have found a knife of the same type, shape and size that X has? Is it a mere coincidence that an article of clothing found in his house has the same rare blood grouping as the deceased woman's? X said he had never met the deceased. The police search and find a pair of boots in the garage with a similar sole pattern. The boots look as if they have been washed. X says that they are his, but that he has never even been near such a farm. There are hundreds of similar boots in the district. Police examine the boots and find some clay soil on one boot like the clay found where the items were buried.

They take possession of what X was wearing on the day of the murder, but the articles of clothing have been washed, and they find nothing. They go back again and this time they are looking for something else. They take all his articles of clothing in the house and are no longer interested in what X was wearing on the date of the murder. One pair of trousers on examination reveals grass seeds and seeds from weeds found only in the area where the articles were buried. X has no explanation for this. Someone may come forward with a story that on that night he was driving past the murder scene and saw something etc.

## *R V BARRIE JOHN WATTS*: MURDEROUS HUSBAND AND WIFE TEAM (1988)

In this case, I will spare you most of the details I have given about the search for evidence by the investigators to convict an accused. I am writing this case in tribute to the murdered young victim whose memory has haunted many people, including me, for some thirty-five years. Even now, you only need to mention the name of Sian Kingi and people will tell you that they still remember this case. It has nothing to do with how the prosecution conducted its case. It has a lot to do with the memory of this child and how she must have fought her killers.

Sian Kingi was just twelve years old. She was born in Auckland, New Zealand, and was living with her family in the vicinity of Noosa, a resort area just north of Brisbane. This little schoolgirl was described as a lovely young person with many friends of her age. Late in the afternoon of 27 November 1987, after school, she was riding her bicycle to meet some friends and then going back home. From the evidence collected, the prosecution could show that she was abducted in broad daylight from near a shopping complex in Noosa whilst proceeding home on her bicycle. The abandoned bicycle was found at about dusk at Pinaroo Park.

Sian Kingi

The family had thought that she might have been delayed for some reason, but with approaching dusk they began a frantic search and found the abandoned bicycle in the park. When the alarm was raised, the police searched the area but found nothing. This was followed by a search by a large contingent of police and the local people with no sign of Sian Kingi. It was eight days later that her body was discovered in a secluded forested area some twenty kilometres from where she was abducted. This was near Tewantin.

The deceased child had been abducted and subjected to savage brutality and terror whilst in captivity. The defenceless, terrified child was subjected to a sustained, senseless attack. During her terror, she was raped, sodomised and stabbed. She was viciously stabbed seventeen times and her naked body left there for vultures to feed. The partly decomposed body was found by someone who detected an odour whilst driving a 4WD vehicle in the forest.

The only clue was that a white vehicle of some description was seen in the area. This, coupled with other sightings, led to a composite fit of the car, which was then found in a remote part of New South Wales. They found the owner, Barrie Watts, and his wife Valmae Faye Beck. Both denied being in Queensland and there was nothing found in their possession or on their person to connect them to this murder. The police separated the husband and wife and grilled them separately for

# CHAPTER 6

a long time until eventually the wife confessed that they had abducted the child, that her husband had raped and murdered her, and that she was just a bystander. Of course, when I say the police grilled them for a long time, that is my choice of words because, in my long experience in prosecution, I never came across a police officer who admitted to grilling a suspect!

The accused and his wife were both charged with murder, and the prosecutor who was given the prosecution brief decided to separate these two trials and try Valmae Fay Beck on her own. The separation of trials like this is undesirable because sometimes each blames the other, and both are acquitted. When the accused appear in the same court charged together, the jury can see more clearly what might have happened.

However, Valmae admitted to being at the scene of the crime, and there was other evidence of her complicity. When you have a confession, a conviction is easier. Valmae Beck was convicted and sentenced. The accused, Barrie Watts, made no confession and denied committing any offence.

It is usual for the prosecutor of the first trial, who is familiar with the evidence relevant to both accused, to do both trials. This prosecutor did not, and through either accident or design, I was lumbered with a case with no independent witnesses to prove anything.

I decided to call the convicted wife of the accused as a witness for the prosecution because the rule that spouses cannot testify against each other does not apply in serious criminal trials. So, calling Valmae Beck, the wife of the killer, was unavoidable. When she was served with the summons by one of the investigators to appear in court, he came back with glee written on his face and said: 'Mr Lakshman, can I tell you what that bitch said to me when I served her with the summons?' I had heard of other cases when serving police officers were abused by convicted criminals, and I must say I did not mind hearing about it, so I said yes. He said: 'Valmae said to tell that black bastard [expletives deleted] wait till I get my hands on him.' It served me right for wanting to hear what she said. However, it is not a very bright idea to abuse a prosecutor who might try to think of all the ways he could make the life of this witness more miserable in the witness box! I did.

The investigators, having failed to get any admissions of complicity in the crime, then put them in separate cells but got an order from the court under the then Invasion of Privacy Act to place listening devices in the cell. This recording was played in court and lasted some six hours and the sound was good. The trial judge allowed the jury to have in their possession a transcript of what was heard on the tape. On conviction, the defence appealed on two grounds—that such tape-recorded material should have been left to the jury because parts were not audible and that it was unfair to give a record of the tape to the jury on an application of the prosecution. For example, the jury never takes the transcript of the trial whilst deliberating in the jury room.

The Appeal Court rejected this and dismissed the appeal. The police were keen to solve this murder, so they put an undercover officer in an adjoining cell where he spent some time shouting and abusing the police to gain the confidence of the accused. The undercover officer spent some eight or ten days in jail, but the accused made no admissions. Sometime later, this officer had to be discharged from the police service because he had suffered a lot from the stress of this task.

However, whilst in custody awaiting trial, the accused was subjected to constant abuse by other prisoners. On one occasion, a prison officer saw him crying. Now, this is the evidence as recorded in the material put before the Appeal Court. The witness said:

> I spoke to the prisoner and I said what are you crying for? He said he was sick of being hassled. I asked him what he was in jail for, and he said something about a murder ... which murder? ... accused said: 'the one at the North Coast'.

And he told the officer he was talking about the Sian Kingi murder. The prison officer said to the accused: 'Surely you would expect some shit put on you for that.' The accused said: 'But I didn't do it' and the officer said: 'What do you mean you didn't do it?' And the accused said: 'I just fucked her, but I didn't hurt her.'

# CHAPTER 6

He told this prison officer that his wife killed the child. This was the only piece of damning evidence linking him to the crime and the murder scene. The defence counsel strenuously objected to the reception of this evidence and argued that his client was in custody and under pressure and this evidence was highly prejudicial to his client. The evidence was allowed, but that was not enough.

The prosecution called his accomplice Valmae Beck, as a witness for the prosecution. The risk here was that she could have turned hostile and refused to answer any questions, and as she was being called by the prosecution, the rule was that the party calling a witness could not cross-examine its own witness. These are problems that only lawyers would understand.

I had already been informed about her attitude to me. Sure enough, when called, she was openly hostile, giving me some problems. She kept looking at the members of the jury in defiance and seemed angry when she looked at me to answer questions. I decided not to start asking questions about the actual murder but asked her instead about her children and their ages and what they did and her relationship with them. Her attitude changed because she wanted to tell the jury how much she cared for her children. I let her talk about each one of them, what work they did, and about their school and so on. I allowed her to go on and gave her many opportunities to tell the jury whatever she wanted them to hear. None of this had anything to do with the murder case, but the very experienced trial judge allowed me to continue with this approach. She became relaxed and perhaps thought that the jury wanted to hear her life story.

Then I asked her whether she could tell the court what she did on the morning of Friday 27 November (the date of the murder). Without any further prompting, she told the jury about her activities that morning. She said she and her husband went to various shopping centres and had coffee, and then they thought it would be fun to go to Noosa. On the way they saw two young women on separate occasions. She mentioned that the accused liked both the sheilas they saw and tried to chat with them. She said he wanted to see if he could pick up one of them and take her for a drive.

When she reached Noosa in her account, I wanted to know what they did. The question was to the effect: 'When you got to Noosa, what did you do?' She then told the jury that they were just looking around and had nothing much in mind. She described some of the shopping complexes in the vicinity. You will notice that up to that point, I had not asked her any questions about the murder.

Then, seeing that it was now or never, I said to her something to the effect: 'Do you remember seeing the deceased?' You see, I had a copy of her signed record of interview, and she had confessed to her involvement in the crime of murder, and she had been convicted and sentenced. The purpose of the prosecution was to get an account from her under oath that would implicate this nasty, brutal killer before the court.

When I asked this witness that simple question, what happened next was witnessed by me, the trial judge and the members of the jury. She appeared to go into some sort of a trance or whatever you would like to call it. She seemed to be looking in my direction but straight over my head, and she had a glazed look. She went on to describe how the little girl was dragged off her bicycle and how she screamed all the time; how they went into this secluded forested area; how the little one pleaded repeatedly with this monster (that is what the police called him): 'Please don't hurt me. Please don't hurt my hair. I am going to a party. I just got my hair done. Don't hurt my hair' and so on. The witness described, in detail, how the accused stripped this child and raped her several times and how he sodomised her and repeatedly stabbed the child, and she went on to give other small details the prosecution knew nothing about.

The jury listened in stunned silence and later returned a verdict of guilty in a relatively short time. I asked the trial judge to recommend that this prisoner should serve a full life sentence. I think he spent some thirty years in prison. He appealed, but his appeal was dismissed. I also remember this case as one in which I did so little to secure a conviction. This case was all about how hard the police work and how the ordinary men and women on the jury perform their duty.

## CHAPTER 6

# *R V DE JACKSON*: **HEADLESS BODY (1991)**

This was a murder case that received such wide publicity that there was an outcry that the accused could never receive a fair trial in Queensland. I had many murder cases, but I had never done a case like this and could find little help for the problem I had. I will tell you the problem after I relate what happened. I will again remind you of the type of readers I am writing for—those who want to experience the trials and tribulations of those who pursue violent criminals. Again, I am just one of thousands.

The accused, Geoffrey Paul de Jackson, who was a Cook Islander, seemed to have settled well in the city. He spoke well and had a relatively sophisticated social background and a habit of wining and dining at hotels such as the Hilton. He had lived in Sydney and other cities and was charged with murder.

I appeared as Crown counsel to prosecute the accused on this charge of murder. I told the jury that one Cynthia Kay Verdich was murdered by the accused and that her decapitated naked body, wrapped in a plastic bag, had been found in a nearby Ashgrove quarry. When the body was found in the quarry, dozens of police dressed in ordinary civilian clothes descended to search for the missing head. It was never found.

It was common in those days for some people to frequent such places to collect abandoned items such as tables, chairs, and furniture that had been dumped there, sometimes in the dead of night. On this morning, the treasure hunters watching from some distance saw the strange sight of many other hunters milling around.

They were not to know that these were police investigators who, in the normal course of their duty, were searching for a human head. The area was cordoned off, and the public was not told what the police were doing. One seasoned investigator said that he wondered what would have happened if one of the fortune hunters had poked a stick and lifted it only to be greeted with the macabre spectacle of a head with the tongue sticking out!

The case for the prosecution was that early one morning in May 1991 Cynthia Kay Verdich was murdered by the accused. The naked decapitated body, wrapped in green plastic rubbish bags, was found in a quarry in Ashgrove, an inner-city suburb in Brisbane. A sharp instrument such as a knife or machete was used to sever the head from the body. The head of the deceased was never found.

The Crown intended to rely on a substantial body of evidence and asked the jury to infer from all the facts and circumstances proved that the accused was the perpetrator of this crime of murder.

The prosecution relied on some seventy witnesses in an endeavour to show what might have happened to the victim. This included glimpses of the victim, the clothes the deceased was wearing, and the sighting and movement of the accused. In circumstantial evidence cases, the prosecution attempts to build its case drip by drip and the evidence is spread over a long period, and all this is served to the jury like spaghetti; and the jury is asked to make sense of it all.

The deceased was the owner of a house in Paddington, but she had been living in Sydney for some time and had returned to Brisbane in June of 1990. Subsequently, the accused, who had formed a relationship with her in Sydney, followed her to Brisbane and began living with her. The deceased had left her five-year-old daughter in Sydney. It appeared that she had very little to do with her neighbours in Brisbane. The neighbours had seen her and remembered what she wore (as the body found was naked), but none of them had spoken to her much or had ever been invited inside her house.

The deceased was described as well-groomed and striking. She had slim features and mostly wore black dresses. She was aged 41 years. In the early stage of the investigation, the police had no photographs to show to some of these prospective witnesses and that was the reason for their seeking descriptions from these witnesses. The deceased was a virtual stranger to the neighbours in the district.

The accused made no admissions and told significant lies to the police. I gave the details of the finding of the body and outlined the evidence that convincingly pointed to the accused as the killer. The accused made no admissions suggesting that he killed the deceased.

## CHAPTER 6

The deceased was employed as a temporary secretary by the Australian Securities Commission, which made the police suspect in the early stages of the investigation that the killing had something to do with her work.

The prosecution intended to show that the accused when questioned about important details, engaged in a series of deceptions and falsehoods, all calculated to distance him from this crime. The evidence was led to show that a guilty mind tries to conceal evidence of an awareness or consciousness of guilt and that the varying accounts the accused gave betrayed his consciousness of guilt—that he knew that he had killed.

I must digress to tell you that this role of the prosecution carries with it some significant advantages. In many cases, some of the members of the jury have never sat in court. In my experience, they are overwhelmed by the formal surroundings, including the wigs and gowns, all floating in the air with this new mantle of 'judges of fact' cast over them. Judges indeed tell them very briefly what is expected of them, but the prosecution opening the Crown counsel lays out the battleground and the rules of engagement in the contest.

Prosecutors take advantage of the opening address to reassure the jury members that being 'the judges of fact' does not mean that, like the judges, they need to be learned in the law. They are not expected to use any new method or skill in arriving at their verdict. They are not expected to bring a new discipline into play. Their role should be no more alien to them than how they function in their daily dealings in their ordinary life.

I reminded the jury that the unfamiliar surroundings and the formal legal language we used in court would be explained to them. I also told the jury that they would be invited to make notes, but that the quality we admired most in the judges of fact was the desire to listen to and pay attention to the whole body of evidence. I told them that the whole body of evidence meant all the evidence they would hear until they retired to consider their verdict and not only the Crown evidence. I told them they must not make any final judgement until the whole body of evidence was before them. I never used the expression 'whole body of evidence' as meaning any evidence given by the accused.

This was because the accused does not have to give evidence, and any suggestion that the prosecution was implying that the defence could or should give evidence could abort the trial. Nothing must be said to suggest that the accused is required to give evidence. I told the jury that what they were about to do was what real judges learned in the law did every day. They, too, do not rush to judgement, waiting until everything is before them.

I have witnessed members of the jury looking relaxed and even smiling and whispering as the opening continued. I told them that no criminal trial was conducted in a vacuum and when they were told not to listen to reports but only to the evidence, this did not mean that they had to leave their common sense and life experience behind them. It was because of their collective common sense and experience that they were called judges of fact. Their role required no new logic, no knowledge of the law and no new tools.

In summary, I always, as the first speaker, said:
- listen to the evidence
- assess it in light of other evidence
- don't be gullible
- bring into play your understanding of human nature
- understand you are the repository of our society's values and culture and society's general sense of justice and fair play, and
- deliver a true verdict that accords with the evidence.

The idea was to infuse the jury with the conviction that they were perfectly equipped to deal with a criminal trial.

I told the jury that the deceased first lived in Sydney where she was known as a person who enjoyed a trendy lifestyle and had many friends. She kept a nice home she was proud of and intended to return to Sydney because she loved her little daughter. She was a very popular person with many social contacts.

The deceased met the accused at a nightclub on New Year's Eve in 1990, roughly a year before she was murdered. He was employed as a

# CHAPTER 6

storeman and bar attendant. He was 29 years of age and a native of the Cook Islands. I mentioned how he followed the deceased to Brisbane and was living with her in her new home. There was a brief period of good domestic relations followed by gradual deterioration, which culminated in the murder of the deceased.

The evidence showed that, apart from some casual work, the accused was unemployed and supported by the deceased; history is full of creatures that bite the hand that feeds them. The deceased was a kind and gentle person, but in the end, she asked him to leave. When he refused to leave, she made him leave her bedroom but allowed him to stay in a spare room until he found new accommodation. He continued to refuse to go. She told him that she would get her former partner to evict him. I believe that had she gone to the police and made a complaint she would be alive today. The day before she went missing, she went to see a real estate agent to put her house up for sale.

The evidence showed that by the time of her disappearance the neighbours were hearing yelling and shouting, and it seemed that he could be subjecting her to physical harm. I called many witnesses to deal with the various aspects I have mentioned.

On Sunday 19 May, the immediate neighbours heard some disturbance around midnight, including a prolonged argument. Then things quietened down until about 6 am when the neighbours heard a scream coming from the house, followed by silence. This was when the accused beheaded the victim. It was three days later that the decapitated body was found dumped at the quarry.

On Monday morning, a man living on his yacht moored at the City Botanical Gardens went to deposit some rubbish in a bin near the Edward Street Ferry. Partly concealed under other rubbish, he noticed a woman's black shoulder bag. Inside, he discovered personal items such as a diary and umbrella. He took the bag and put it on a fence railing, and when he returned in the afternoon it was gone. The evidence showed that the black bag belonged to the deceased.

Another witness who had seen the black bag saw the news on television and recognised the bag. The witness went to the nearest police station to report the matter.

Now the police linked the name on the driver's licence in the bag to the body found.

The bag contained other things too: a visa card, a cheque book and the address at Paddington. Extensive searches were carried out at the Edward Street Ferry because the police were not sure where the deceased was killed. They found a lady's wristwatch in a grassy patch, and this too belonged to the deceased. Some days later, a student who was on his way to college noticed something and found a gold ring. It was a small ring with a row of diamonds. He gave it to the lost property section of the Queensland University of Technology. That night he read in the newspaper something about a missing woman and a report of the finding of a bag somewhere near where he had found the gold ring. He immediately contacted the police. The ring belonged to the deceased.

A schoolteacher living in Bardon was in front of her house with her three-year-old daughter who for some reason kept pointing to something 'blue'. (I am sure she grew up to become a detective!) The mother investigated and thought the blue object must have fallen out of a car. She was carrying her little detective child in one arm and when she bent over to pick up the blue object, a hammer and large machete fell out. This blue object was a car mat from the accused's car. The mother and child also saw some brown material. She put her child down on the footpath and picked up the machete, a brown towel and the hammer, which had red marks on it. She put all these in a wheelie bin under the house. When her husband came home and saw the items, he contacted the police; he too was hearing and reading about the decapitated body of a woman.

The local police did not bother to respond, so the next day he put everything in a box and took it to the police station, but there were no police there. It was 9 am. I suppose the police were still in bed. He spoke to a civilian female public servant and left these vital pieces of evidence with her. There were many instances of local police doing nothing for

## CHAPTER 6

several days before contacting the main investigators. I often thought of them when writing about this case as being gormless and clueless.

I must explain how laborious this work is because, as I mentioned, some seventy witnesses were called and eight of them had something to do with all the items found near the Ferry. The Crown is obliged to call everyone who handled the incriminating evidence. Out of those seventy witnesses, five were called to deal with what was found in the gutter by the schoolteacher with her baby. I have mentioned elsewhere that there is nothing glamourous about most of this boring work I did. There were ten witnesses called to tell us something about the house and ten who heard all the screaming during the night.

I will now tell you the problem I had in dealing with a headless body and then give the whole evidence. Then you can give your verdict. What I am going to outline to you is almost exactly what the jury received.

Now, for the problem with a headless body. There are many cases in which bodies are buried or only skeletal remains are found and there is never much problem. In this case, the defence counsel objected to the Crown showing to the jury what the deceased looked like. Juries like seeing the face of the victim. Why was the defence objecting? Why did the trial judge rule that the prosecution could not show any photographs of the face of the deceased to at least some of the vital witnesses?

I had anticipated the defence argument but had dismissed it because I thought the defence had more problems than what the face of the victim looked like. What was the problem? The headless victim had been stripped naked before the body was dumped. It had no rings or jewellery, no body marks such as tattoos. She was slim, and her hairstyle was purported to be different from one of the photos I was going to use. Above all, the photo was nothing like how the neighbours had described the deceased. The argument was that you could show a photo of many women, not only the deceased, and they would go with the body found. The Crown did not have the missing head to compare the photo with, and the judge ruled that he would not allow it for that reason.

I have mentioned that none of the neighbours had met the deceased and whenever the deceased came out, she wore a black 'slinky' dress and had a black handbag and long black hair and when asked to tell the court whether they could point to someone to show what her face and body looked like, most of them said that she looked like Morticia from *The Adams Family*, which was screening every night on our television screens. They even said that they called the deceased Morticia. I would like you to check YouTube and see even today what the victim looked like. I told the court I had seen Morticia. The defence counsel said he had seen Morticia. The trial judge sheepishly announced that he had seen Morticia and what she looked like too. Thereafter, both counsels at the bar table, themselves attired like characters from *The Adams Family*, said things like 'Tell the court what Morticia did next'. In fact, both counsels in the address to the jury sometimes slipped into using the name Morticia instead of the real name of the deceased. Something like: 'Well, members of the jury, you just heard from witness X what Morticia did next.' I remember telling my instructing clerk something to the effect that how could the prosecution lose this murder case with a witch on its side! However, murder trials are serious, and this really happened, and it happened for a reason.

I will now give you the salient features of the prosecution case and as I write I have before me a typed copy of the actual address I gave to the jury some thirty years ago. So, in a sense, this is a voice from the past and a long-forgotten tale. I told the jury the following:

The accused was the last person to see the deceased alive. Shortly before her disappearance, the accused was engaged in a violent argument with the victim, and the victim was heard screaming. Suddenly everything went silent because the accused had used a machete to sever her head.

1. There were signs of a struggle in the kitchen of the dwelling, including blood splashes under the ledges of the kitchen table, as well as on the floor. There were signs that blood had been wiped off surfaces, but blood patterns were still there. There were some items like knives and forks in the sink with smears of blood on them. I pointed out that the Crown had even produced the sink itself for the jury to see. (I must tell

the readers that years later I used to tell my friends that this was the only case I did in which the prosecution threw in everything, including the kitchen sink!)

2. The deceased's blood type was somewhat rare. In the method used in scientific testing, it occurred in about one in 4400 persons in the community; that is, it represented .02 per cent of the population.

3. There were swabs taken from the kitchen cupboards and other areas that screened positive for blood. This is not conclusive but is indicative of the presence of blood traces. The areas where these were found will be canvassed later. There was a bloodstain found on the telephone extension cord on the kitchen floor. The blood was consistent with that of the deceased. She was attempting to get help. There was blood on the back landing at the top of the steps. Again, all this was consistent with the deceased making attempts to flee.

4. There was blood found in the boot of the car that the accused had access to and used that morning. There was a coloured towel in the boot, which was extensively stained with blood with the rare blood grouping consistent with that of the deceased. The parcel shelf in the car had blood consistent with that of the deceased.

5. The police took possession of the carpet in the boot. There was a large area of approximately 100 to 200 cm, which was saturated in blood. This area showed what the police described as 'extensive bleeding', and the case was that the severed head and body were placed in the boot for disposal. The police squeezed some 100 ml of blood out of the carpet. It was of that rare blood type.

6. The machete that was found in Bardon gave only a weakly positive screening test for blood, but the preponderance of the evidence suggested that the machete was the murder weapon.

7. The hammer that was found had a visible bloodstain on the head near the claw consistent with the rare blood grouping of the deceased.

8. The brown towel had a bloodstain consistent with that of the accused. The examination of the brown towel yielded a long strand of head hair, and this was microscopically compared with the head hairs found on hairbrushes in the dwelling and found to be a good match. It was like the hair found on the body of the deceased.

9. A sample was taken from near the skirting board under the sink. This was examined by the government pathologist and the forensic scientist. A microscopic examination showed flesh tissue and bone. The flesh tissue was attached to the bone shards. The test showed that traces of blood were consistent with the deceased.

10. The items found in Bardon—the machete, the hammer and the towel—all came from the dwelling house. The towel was like other towels found in the house. It was known that there had been a machete in the house and that it was missing. The Crown urged the jury that it was the one found in Bardon.

11. The motor vehicle that was used in this crime belonged to someone else and had been lent to the deceased the previous evening.

12. The accused gave various accounts about his movements and about himself that were false, and this was known to the police. The Crown said that he was concealing facts, and this showed that he was conscious of his guilt. He told many lies about his relationship with the deceased, including how he came into possession of the car.

13. He never got in the witness box to give evidence. He was not obliged to do this, but we have known from time immemorial that when a man does not speak when you would expect him to scream his innocence, people suspect that he is hiding a guilty truth. There are many thinking lawyers familiar with the modern means of communication of information that know the world has changed, and it is no longer in the

interests of justice to give an accused this cocoon of silence. It should, and I think it will, go in our lifetime.

The accused was found guilty and sentenced to life imprisonment. He appealed. The appeal was rejected and his conviction on the charge of murder affirmed. The Appeal Court had nothing to say about Morticia Adams who helped the prosecution.

## *R V MENINGA*: THE SADISTIC KILLING IN THE PARK (1991)

This was the 1991 case of Beven Errol Meninga, then 20 years old and the younger brother of footballer Mal Meninga.

Bevan Errol Meninga was charged with murder, and I appeared as the Crown counsel for the prosecution. This case received wide publicity because it involved the killing of an eighteen-year-old female who was subjected to a savage attack, and it involved a close relative of a sporting celebrity. The trial lasted some three weeks.

You might think most murders are brutal, but even seasoned police investigators were shocked with what they found at the scene of the crime. The half-naked body had been subjected to severe blows. The evidence showed that the victim was mercilessly beaten with a tree branch. Her face had been subjected to such heavy application of force that the flesh was almost pulverised—the victim was barely recognisable. Whilst she was still alive, the assailant had rammed a stick into her vagina, which penetrated the back wall of the vagina. He then left her to bleed to death.

As the accused was the younger brother of Mal Meninga, the public gallery in the court was always full. Mal Meninga was a household name in Australia. Even in that period, he was a legendary rugby player and a role model for young Australians. He was highly respected. I did not follow rugby, but I knew as much. Every day, Mal Meninga was present with his family to support his brother.

Rugby is very popular in Fiji. When we were children, my brother and I tried to play it but settled on soccer instead. It was really a strategic move we made for our survival. You should have seen the size of the little Fijian children!

I will digress to remind you that it was sometime in 1942 that some 40,000 American troops landed in Fiji to save Australia. You might ask, what has that got to do either with football or the murder case? Well, I suppose when you get old, you meander and travel down memory lane; however, it does have something to do with both subjects. My brother and I had a deep discussion before we stopped playing rugby with the Fijian children. Gautam said that playing football with Fijians was like riding a bicycle into an American tank and that it was perhaps safer to take a chance with the tank. Our thoughts were like what they say in Australia about getting the Hail Mary pass when playing rugby.

Some Indians did not have much to do with Fijians, but my father was a teacher and trade union leader who wanted to give educational opportunities to Fijians. I have already given this account in my childhood adventure stories. I mentioned that my father opened a school for adults who had no educational opportunities in Fiji in the early forties.

My brother and I attended that school. See photo gallery for a college photograph of two very little students sitting with all these burly, surly students. One of the young men was Josefa Levula, who came to Australia with the Fijian Rugby Team a year or two before we came as students in 1956. Josefa Levula was a sensational player, and the story goes that the Fijians wiped the floor and left the Australian National Team for dead. Even after our arrival, we saw large posters of Josefa Levula plastered all over the place.

It so happened that I had first met Constable Mal Meninga (as he then was) on an earlier occasion many years before. He came to deliver statements to me dealing with a case in which he was not really involved. It was only because I was writing about murder cases that I thought about this earlier case. I think there was some confidential material and the Superintendent of Police wanted it hand-delivered to me. I think that was the case in which the wife of a federal Labor politician had been attacked in her home and had received some injuries; she was alone at home with her children while her husband was in Canberra.

# CHAPTER 6

The Member of Parliament happened to be Bill Hayden, who went on to become the Leader of the Labor Party and later the Governor-General of Australia. I first met Bill Hayden when he studied Law. He, too, attended the University of Queensland.

It so happened that Jim Killen, who was already a Member of Parliament, also attended law lectures, and Mr Killen and I became good friends. He also appeared as defence counsel in a few criminal cases I prosecuted. For some courses, we were all in the same year.

I did not have much contact with Bill Hayden, but I met him for the 80th birthday lunch for the Deputy Commissioner of Police, Norman Gulbransen, who was a much-respected crime fighter. Bill Hayden worked under him when he joined the police force. I think Hayden was a police constable while at the university.

Bill Hayden, who was sitting next to me, remarked that as a young constable, it was his good fortune to be assigned to work with Norm Gulbransen and not a corrupt senior officer. This lunch was during a period well after the corruption trial of those police officers, which lasted six months (mentioned earlier). If I had known that Bill Hayden would become the Governor-General one day, I might have cultivated him and kept in touch with him! But he was just a lowly constable then; also, he had such a whinging, whining voice! Whereas Jim Killen had a cultivated oratorical voice right out of Cicero and others in ancient Greece. I do not mean that he was a match for Cicero or Cato. It was his delivery system.

I was the prosecutor in the case, and the accused was charged with assaulting Mrs Hayden. I think the accused in that case had struck her several severe blows. On the very morning of the trial, he pleaded guilty and was sent to prison.

It is because of Mal Meninga's slight involvement in the Hayden matter that I always remembered meeting Constable Mal Meninga when he came into my office. I wanted to mention Josefa Levula to him but did not get around to it. After that brief meeting, I never saw him again until the trial of his brother, and now that I was prosecuting his brother on a charge of murder, it was not appropriate to speak to him.

This was a shocking murder case that the old investigators still remember. Over the years, I have seen reports of the prisoner seeking to be released on parole. The parole board declined to do it until 2014 when he had served twenty-one years in prison, a very long time.

This was not a complex case on the facts, but it took about two weeks before the jury retired. To understand why it took so long, you will have to follow the evidence. I will be repeating some types of evidence such as alcohol consumed and what the accused remembered and what he saw and where he went in detail, and I will tell you why soon.

The body was discovered quite early in the investigation. The evidence was that the accused was living with friends on the Sunshine Coast very near where the body was discovered. The accused told the police that he was unemployed, and he gave a detailed account of his movements that day, including meeting his many mates. He told the police that they all went to several places and had some drinks. Over the course of the afternoon and into the evening, he and his friends went from one nightclub to the next until finally going to the nightclub where he met the diseased, Cheree Richardson, who was known to him.

She was a striking-looking girl, aged about eighteen and much loved by her parents and friends. She, too, had gone with some friends for an outing to the Club Mooloolaba. Later that night, after leaving the club, they went to the residence of one of the mates where they all had 'a bong with some marijuana, sitting in the lounge room'. The accused

Cheree Richardson

told the police that none of them was affected by the drugs. They then decided to go to another nightclub and were there by about 3 am. In the first account he gave, he said that he left alone, and the deceased was still there on her own. This was not true. He told the police that he only found out that the deceased was missing the next day when his

CHAPTER 6

then-girlfriend told him that the parents were alarmed because she had not returned home that night. He told the police that he then rushed out to search for the missing victim.

He repeatedly told the police that the last time he saw the deceased was at about 3 am and that he had nothing to do with her death. The police discounted the false accounts he gave of other persons who might have molested the deceased and took his clothing and shoes.

He gave a vivid and extensive account of his movements during that afternoon and the evening. This showed that he had a good memory and had not been gravely affected by the alcohol and other drugs. He was able to remember and give minute details of both time and events. He remembered the names of many people he had met that afternoon and during the evening and the police checked and found them to be true. He also told lies to hide things that might implicate him. He hid in the bathroom ceiling to avoid detection before being questioned and gradually began to make those damning confessions of his actual involvement in this horrendous crime.

When giving his shoes, he told them that these were the shoes he was wearing that night. The forensic examination showed that the shoes had no blood or soil or other material on them to suggest that the accused was involved in the crime. The police later took possession of the shoes that he had been wearing that he had kept concealed. These had blood that matched the blood of the diseased. Several shirts also had traces of blood of the same grouping as the deceased in different areas of the shirts, and some long blonde hairs were found on these shirts.

He then made a full confession and admitted that he had killed the deceased. He confessed not once but several times. The police told him that he could have a solicitor present for the interview. He told the police that he wanted to make a full confession and did not want a solicitor to be present for the interview.

He gave a detailed account of what happened. He said: 'I hit her on the head, I just kept hitting her' and that: 'I stuck a stick up her vagina'. He had spoken to his girlfriend and had made similar admissions to her;

she, too, was called to give evidence. He told the police where in the park he had left the body.

He said: 'I remember I punched her to the ground' and that he had grabbed a stick from somewhere and 'I hit her and kept on hitting her'. He told the police that he had hit her repeatedly over the head; she was beaten badly on the shoulders as well. He repeated on several occasions that he had pulled her dress up and stuck the stick up her vagina. He told the police that the stick was a thick branch, 2 feet long, thick enough to be used as a cudgel, which he used as a small sledgehammer that smashed her head; the victim's face was almost unrecognisable. He denied having intercourse with her, and the prosecution did not suggest that she was sexually molested in any way.

He told the police that his father came from the Solomon Islands and that he had a grade 12 standard of education and could read and write.

He was given a chance to correct any mistakes in his account of events to the police, and he simply repeated the whole story. The jury heard all this in court. He told the police that he had given them the wrong pair of shoes because he suspected that the shoes that he had worn might have had blood on them, and they did.

He also punched her face very hard with his clenched fist. He was a strong, well-built man. The victim was light and slim, and he had punched this defenceless and slightly intoxicated girl. He told the police that he had no idea why he killed her but thought that she might have said something that annoyed him. I give all these details because of what happened next. In our criminal law, motive may explain some killings and the Crown might attempt to show such motive, but motive is not an element of the offence. An intentional, senseless killing without any motive would still be murder. This was a senseless killing without an obvious motive.

When the Crown case concluded after some twenty or thirty witnesses had given evidence, the defence opened its case and said that the accused would give evidence. The accused gave evidence and said that he was heavily intoxicated and had smoked Indian hemp with his friends and the deceased.

# CHAPTER 6

He told the court that he had no memory of what had happened that night and that what he had told the police he had made up just to please the police! He also said he got the details of what was supposed to have happened to the victim by reading the local newspapers as well as some interstate news. There was not much evidence that he read newspapers. The defence tried to tender newspapers, including some from Perth, so that the jury could read different accounts. The trial judge refused. When I cross-examined him, he gave a hedgehog defence—that he had had too much to drink; that he had no memory of what had happened; and that he suffered from blackouts. There was evidence that he had been involved in a car accident. It is near impossible to cross-examine someone who keeps replying that he has no memory.

The defence called specialist medical evidence to show that he suffered from a mental condition that diminished his criminal responsibility. The evidence showed that the accused had never received any medical treatment for any such thing. I called evidence in rebuttal from very experienced medical witnesses who told the court that there was no substance in the claim that he had any such mental disability. You will recall that he had given a detailed account of his involvement in the crime. There were no newspaper reports about the injuries to the victim's vagina. That was only known to the killer and the police.

You might say, and I think you would have if you were on the jury, that the accused made a full confession, and so he must be guilty of murder. Yes, the defence was saying that he did kill the victim, but on the medical evidence, he could only be convicted of manslaughter and not murder. You see, in most cases if a man is found guilty of manslaughter, he is imprisoned for only five or six years, and if he behaves well, he serves less than that time.

I am repeating some of this for the lay readers for whom I am writing. The defence had a brilliant strategy: to raise doubt about the accused's mental state. The defence had to prove nothing, whereas the Crown had to satisfy the jury that the accused had the intention to kill or to do grievous bodily harm before a jury could return a verdict of guilty on the serious charge of murder, which meant that the convicted prisoner would have to serve a life sentence.

The Crown was not prepared to treat this as a manslaughter case. I was disappointed when the trial judge ruled that he would leave the question of diminished responsibility to the jury. I had argued that that was a red herring and would throw an extra burden on the Crown and that there was no evidence on which he could leave that to the jury. So, the defence relied on its expert medical evidence and the Crown on its rebuttal of that medical evidence.

It so happened that the accused was awaiting trial in the correctional centre for three weeks after he was charged. He contacted the police and told them he wanted to give an interview. This time he told the police that another person was also involved in the killing of this victim and named him and said that this man had hit the victim with a branch, and he was there and saw it all.

He also said that he took the branch away from this man and threw the branch in the area. He said that he was holding her down while the other man was hitting the victim. Why tell the police this new version? There was no truth in this story. He said he was 'drinking and was stoned'—that is, he was very drunk and had no idea what was happening.

Now he was giving the sort of stuff that allowed the medical evidence to say he did not know what he was talking about and that he was very drunk. He said that he did not stop the other man because he was scared. However, the man he named was a very small man, and there was no evidence to implicate him.

When asked in the first interview whether he had a good memory of what had happened, he had said that he did. When the police asked him if he ever had blackouts, he said only sometimes but nothing serious, and that he had never had to see a doctor or get any medicine for this. Then, after three weeks in custody, he called the police to change his story. Why was he doing this?

When I turned up to prosecute on the date of the trial, the defence said that the accused should not be charged with murder at all but only

## CHAPTER 6

with manslaughter. This meant that if he got convicted, he could serve four or five years and get out of prison. But this was such a shocking and brutal killing that no way was the Crown prepared to let him get away with a lighter sentence. The defence said that he had no intention to kill because he was very intoxicated and had a toxic mixture of drugs in his system, which explained the frenzied way he had attacked her and the fact that he had not raped her.

defence counsel also said that he had such memory loss that the murder charge should not go to the jury, that the Crown should charge him only with manslaughter and not murder. He told the court that his making up the story about another man being involved proved there was an aberration in his mental condition. In murder cases, the prosecution must show that the accused has the actual intention to kill or cause grievous bodily harm, and the argument was that the Crown could not prove this case beyond a reasonable doubt on the murder charge. The defence also said that he was so intoxicated that he could not form the intention to kill; he killed but with no intention.

I will give you a summary of the law to show what we are talking about. The law provides that diminished responsibility reduces what would be murder to manslaughter. The jury must be satisfied that the accused at the time of the killing is in such a state of abnormality of mind as to impair substantially his capacity to understand what he is doing, or his capacity to control his actions, or his capacity to know that he ought not to do the act (killing).

The jury in this case refused to accept that he had any such abnormality of mind. It is the jury that considers the weight and quality of medical evidence, as judges of fact. In short, medical evidence is not the end of the matter.

He was convicted on the charge of murder. The Appeal Court rejected his appeal and confirmed his conviction. The Appeal Court said that there was no basis for the trial judge to allow the evidence given by medical specialists. The court also said that diminished responsibility should not have been left to the jury

Beven Errol Meninga spent some twenty-one years in prison, before finally being released on lifelong parole sometime in 2014.

## *R V WEISSENSTEINER*: BODIES NEVER FOUND (1992)

This story is like something out of fiction. It is a difficult story to tell because it is riddled with questions of law, and without reference to some laws, the story would be meaningless. I am writing for the benefit of friends and readers with no legal knowledge. The purpose is to explain what some of us do in my type of work. There is no glamour in this work. Most of it is arduous, tedious and thankless. I also want to address some matters to scholars and students of law.

In this case, I would like you, the reader, to play detective or prosecutor for me. I will give you the raw material we call evidence and I want you to tell me whether Johann Manfred Weissensteiner is guilty or not guilty. I hope you are ready to look at some boring evidence and pretend to play a part in the investigation. Remember, this is what investigators and criminal lawyers do for most of their working lives.

The first thing to remember is that there is no glamour in this field in our courts. There will be times in this story when I deal with legal issues and other questions of law. You might think that it makes no sense to you. There will be some comments that may make sense only to lawyers and not to laypeople unfamiliar with our legal system. You can just ignore these comments and go on to solve this case.

You start with the strange story where no bodies are found. The victims vanished not in some small part of a country and not even on a large continent like Australia; that would be daunting enough. The victims vanished in the deep, wide Pacific Ocean, which licks the shores of many countries, including Australia, Asia and America. How do skilled investigators solve such murder mysteries? Certainly not how fiction writers with imagination solve crimes.

This then is a story of a murder case that I prosecuted over three decades ago. In those thirty years, the case has not disappeared but still

# CHAPTER 6

haunts experienced criminal lawyers and the criminal courts in Australia, essentially on how to properly direct a jury.

In 2016, the High Court of Australia revisited this Weissensteiner case in another murder case called *R v Robert Baden-Clay*. It is essentially about what direction the trial judge should give the jury and what use the jury should make of the fact that the accused did not step out of the dock and walk to the witness box just a few feet away from the dock to say anything to contradict the case for the prosecution. We all know that no accused is obliged to give evidence and the prosecution has the onus of proof, but there are consequences. In the Baden-Clay case, the High Court was highly critical of the Appellate Court's lack of appreciation and understanding of the proper direction that should be given in such cases.

There are scholars in law and practising barristers who give lectures on the reach and scope of such a direction to the jury, and on the applicable underlying legal principles in support of such a direction.

I prosecuted Weissensteiner and appeared before the Court of Criminal Appeal when the convicted murderer appealed to get the conviction set aside. The court rejected the appeal and upheld the conviction.

The direction the trial judge gave to the jury was regarded as unusual. I learnt after my retirement, which was soon after this appeal, that the High Court decided that the direction given to the jury was sound. This decision was thought so stunning and brilliant that prosecuting counsel all over the country rubbed their hands together with barely concealed glee! There were litigants everywhere seeking such a direction, and as I write, it is still reverberating three decades later. It is also a tribute to Mr Justice Moynihan who presided over that trial and many other trials I prosecuted.

I read in some reports that the matter was considered by a committee in the House of Commons or one of its subservient committees. The British yawned and wanted to know what the fuss was all about. I suppose this is typical of the British when dealing with a former convict colony!

I believe it was also discussed in the House of Representatives and the Senate in America. I am not able to find the news report I read at the time. I believe America would have rejected the principles of law in this case because the American Constitution dealt with it.

I have not read criminal cases for thirty years, so I will not deal with the legal issues in detail, except in passing reference. Besides, I am no authority on what changes have taken place in law in the last thirty years. I will leave it to the scholars and professors who spend their whole life quibbling over such things! I do know that any student studying criminal law today must study the Weissensteiner direction to a jury. Although I was the Crown prosecutor in that case, I have never been asked to participate in these lectures and moot courts. I am bemused that the defence counsel is mentioned by name and I am called 'the prosecutor who appeared ...'.

However, back to the real story about which I am writing for my readers. I know that some lawyers may find it all somewhat boring. There is nothing much here for them. This is a story of how an investigation virtually languished for two years until there was a public outcry in England and Germany about the lack of interest in Queensland to solve the mystery.

I was asked to look at the evidence and have the conduct of the trial should the matter proceed. The investigators had a collection of evidence and had worked with great dedication and diligence.

I was now the assigned Crown counsel for this case, and thus I had general supervision over the method and direction of further investigations. There was a vast area to search, and the investigators were very good, but I had general supervision on matters such as the relevance of any data or evidence.

This was the practice in our office when the Police Commissioner or the Minister for Police approached our Solicitor-General in writing and sought assistance in some difficult cases. I must also tell you that some of the very senior Crown prosecutors liked a properly prepared brief and wanted to do the actual work in court. I, with others, did not like being burdened with such thankless tasks; so, we all tried to wriggle out of it if we could.

# CHAPTER 6

The preliminary proceedings for committal are generally handled by the police, but I was instructed to appear in person. There was very wide publicity given to the case in England and Germany because the victims came from there.

The searches and investigations involved police officers from Australia, Scotland Yard, Interpol, and Germany. The only thing needed to introduce some colour in the enfolding drama was to introduce an Indian Crown prosecutor who had come from the former British colony of Fiji to study in Queensland and had attended one of the most prestigious secondary schools in Australia at that time. This was Brisbane Grammar School. I graduated in Law and Arts from the University of Queensland.

I must tell you that it did sometimes happen that friendly classmate-cynics of mine quipped to me that the only reason I had a guernsey to appear for the Crown was not because of merit but because white society felt that it was about time the blacks were exposed to the real world! Ever since childhood, I always had an approach to dealing with comments such as this. You must have read in my childhood adventures in this book and noticed that I always had a sort of comic response to criticisms at home. I told these critics that just because white people were brought up under the class system in England did not make them an authority on the subject. I boasted that the Indians were among the first to invent the caste system, which made people more miserable than the British ever could. So there!

The story of a missing vessel in the vast Pacific Ocean is not necessarily so remarkable, nor the fact that it was never seen anywhere for some two years. However, the involvement of Scotland Yard and Interpol, not to mention the German and Australian police, ensured that the media would report everything with sensational care and consideration both here and in Europe.

It so happened that one day the relative peace and quiet of sleepy hollow, the small coastal town of Cairns, was suddenly broken by the arrival of press reporters from all over the country. These were closely followed by writers of crime stories and fortune-tellers, all wanting to contribute their bit to what they had heard or seen about a missing couple who were expecting a nuclear catastrophe and had gone into hiding somewhere in the Pacific with the avowed intention of not being found—and, indeed, were never found.

By the time I appeared for the actual trial, there were many witnesses prepared to say that this couple was very peculiar with queer, unbelievable ideas. The defence wanted the prosecution to call not some but all of them to say that the victims told them repeatedly that they were going to hide in the Pacific.

The prosecution had a duty and was obliged to do so. You do not have to have the imagination of a fiction writer to predict what the defence counsel would repeatedly tell the jury in his address: that the victims were still hiding and probably fishing and drinking coconut milk and that the poor man in the dock had nothing to do with their murder, and that the failure to produce the victims alive was more a reflection on the incompetence of the police. It was thought that the missing couple were weirdos, but this was simply not true. They were a nice couple who were very much in love.

The movement of the accused was interesting to the police, but the jury was never told much about Weissensteiner's background. He first arrived in Australia in June 1988 and went to Melbourne and Sydney. But in 1988, before coming to Australia, he went back and forth to the following places: Hong Kong, the Philippines, Malaysia, Thailand, and Indonesia. In one year, he made sixteen trips. The police were looking for clues and made inquiries far and wide.

The usual questions about whether the victims were dead or alive occupied them for some two years before the start of the murder trial. This is what detectives do in this type of case; they go plodding all over the planet, looking for clues. Why did he make these sixteen trips? These areas are notorious for drug dealers.

The various law agencies I have mentioned tried to find clues. So vast was the search that the police made inquiries everywhere, including on our large continent, Australia. This is the boring thankless, task police perform in the search for justice. I want you to soak in all these

## CHAPTER 6

boring details and join the search. You have the freedom to stop playing detective in this case and move on, but the police do not.

The accused landed in Darwin in July 1989, so we are now approximately six months away from the murder. It seemed that he was seeking an area where he could sponge on someone, and he found that someone in Hartwig Bayerl in Cairns.

I must digress to tell you that I remember going for a walk on the Esplanade in Cairns on a late afternoon, and this was virtually in front of the police station and near the court building. I was approached by a woman suitably dressed in a flowing floral dress with a bandana on her head. I had seen her in the court precinct, and she told me that she believed in flying saucers and could help the prosecution find the missing couple. It so happened that about that time in 1990 there were reports of a new book on UFOs, and there was a great surge in the number of true believers in UFOs. There were many sightings of aliens too!

I must say that I was despondent too because the prosecution case looked so fragile and paper-thin. I was sorely tempted to use some such fresh new approach! Lawyers have a habit of looking for desperate solutions when dealing with desperate problems. But unfortunately, the defence seems to have a virtual monopoly in that field in criminal cases. The Crown is prevented from using fantastical creatures as witnesses, but the defence is not. I know because I have cross-examined many such witnesses. However, I did wonder what would happen if I told the police to get a statement from my new surprise witness for the prosecution.

I know that Perry Mason would have approved! I have mentioned elsewhere in this book that the indentured Indians believed in soothsayers and fortune-tellers. Had they heard about UFOs, they would have embraced them too. Indian tradition is deeply imbued with cosmic events in the universe, and they are not averse to the idea of alien invasions.

This was not all. My instructing clerk told me that the place was buzzing with rumours, and worse was to come. The news gatherers and crime reporters from other countries were coming to town too. These people could write their reports and leave the country before we could start contempt proceedings. I should also mention that the cream of weird people in the areas surrounding Cairns was also coming to town to listen to the criminal trial. I can still picture this crowd, which seemed to appear from nowhere, floating around like fairy-floss and soap bubbles, in my mind's eye.

The coastal town of Cairns, even three decades ago, was a tourist town. It was mostly used as a point of arrival and departure of tourists who had gone there to explore the pristine beauty of marine life on the Great Barrier Reef. And according to some of the law enforcement officers, visitors came to snorkel and copulate on the distant deserted beaches.

I mentioned elsewhere, when dealing with my early childhood in Fiji, that my father did not want me and my younger brother to go to England to study because of the cold climate. He took a pencil and ruled a line from Fiji to Australia, landing near Cairns! However, there was no university in Cairns, so he settled on Brisbane. That was the first time I had seen Cairns on the map of Australia. My mother was tearful and thought that the White Australia policy would mean that we would be treated badly in Australia. But the experience of most overseas students testified to the protective care given to them by many Australian families. That was my experience too.

I must tell you this was not my first visit to Cairns. I had been to Cairns to prosecute criminal trials on many occasions. I sometimes went to these islands on police ocean-patrol boats. On one occasion, my visit was in relation to the murder of a young woman (see Knibb case). The police offered to fly me slowly over the beach where she was killed to inspect the shape and size of the beach. This was my first time on a helicopter, and the only memory I have of the experience is clutching my seat with both hands, closing both my eyes and gritting my teeth whenever the helicopter swayed from side to side, which was all the time. At the end of the trip, I told the police that I'd had a good look at the scene!

This was a story of a couple missing without a trace and with no direct evidence to show whether they were dead or alive; they had

## CHAPTER 6

been seeking shelter from some nuclear holocaust. There are countless islands and atolls in the open ocean, and the prosecution could not give evidence that the police had searched everywhere.

I must give you some details of who these people were. Susan Zack was an Englishwoman, some thirty years old and a pharmacist by profession. She was described as a talented and popular student who got her degree in Pharmacology with honours from the University of London. She graduated at the age of eighteen and worked in her profession in London for some time before deciding to travel with her college friend to Australia to work. For the first few years (1984–1986), she travelled extensively in South-East Asia, particularly in Malaysia and Singapore and then went to Sydney.

During this time, she was in constant contact with her family. She sent postcards and long letters to her parents and telephoned them. She also spoke to her 86-year-old grandmother on the telephone almost every week.

She was an ardent sailor who had cruised along the northern coastal parts of Australia and Papua New Guinea. She loved scuba diving and worked on board a diving boat to obtain a scuba-diving licence. So, she was unlikely to just fall overboard and drown. She missed her family and went back to London and worked there before returning to Australia in 1988 and gravitating to Cairns where she met Bayerl, who was an Austrian by birth. He was born in Salzburg, Austria. This extensive communication with her close, loving family ceased abruptly at about the time she went missing.

This background was just part of the evidence used to convince the jury that she had met with foul play. Her parents had gone to Cairns in 1988 because Susan had fallen in love with and wanted to marry Bayerl. They were also alarmed that she had withdrawn all her savings in various banks and even cashed her insurance policy. She had withdrawn large sums of money amounting to some $180,000 and spent most of the money refurbishing the boat and armour-plating it for the impending nuclear disaster. Susan paid $50,000 to purchase a berth in the Cairns Marina, and the refitting came to some $90,000. The prosecution argued that this was indicative of their intention to live in Cairns, not vanish and leave their yacht in the possession of the accused.

Bayerl sought approval from her parents to marry Susan. They gave it but wanted them to postpone the marriage. They had the impression that Susan was infatuated with Bayerl.

It was here in Cairns that Susan and Bayerl met Weissensteiner for the first time. He, too, came from Germany. Unemployed, he answered their job advertisement and started working for them on the yacht.

Eventually, the accused was charged with two counts of murder and one count of stealing a vessel. The case was put on the basis that sometime in the period between late November 1989 and the middle of January 1990 both Hartwig Bayerl and Susan Zack had been murdered at or near Cairns and their bodies disposed of either on land or at sea. The Crown would show that the bodies were probably disposed of at sea. It must have been some distance away; otherwise, the bodies would have surfaced near Cairns.

The accused was a calculating, cunning and evasive person. He had been observed near an inlet on Fitzroy Island (I sailed to see the place), and the police believed his behaviour was so suspicious that he might have cut the bodies in small parts and disposed of them in the shark-infested surrounding sea. It was inconceivable that in the hot climate he would have kept the bodies on the boat with people milling around the berth—so we thought, but we did not know. In all our efforts to find evidence, we missed a vital thread in the evidence and therefore this was never put to the jury.

After the trial, the police found out that many people who were saying goodbye to the missing couple were told that they were sailing alone. No mention was ever made of sailing out of Cairns with the accused. Why vital? Because the accused would have been left there to fend for himself without accommodation, money, or anywhere else to go. This could have been the main reason that he decided to kill them and take the vessel.

In this case, the Crown was unable to nominate the exact location of these unlawful killings. It sought to rely on a substantial body of

## CHAPTER 6

circumstantial evidence from which the jury could infer that the killings occurred in Queensland and that the accused was the perpetrator of these crimes.

What is circumstantial evidence? It is evidence of other facts and circumstances that, together, can be relied upon, not as proving the facts directly but proving facts from which the fact in issue may be inferred or deduced. Let me give an example. Supposing the fact in issue is whether A is responsible for killing B. Then supposing a witness saw A walking into a room. Another witness might say that he heard violent argument and noise coming from that room followed by the sound of a gunshot, and shortly afterwards A was seen leaving the room with a pistol in his hand.

In that example, from those few facts that were proven, the Crown would say that the jury as judges of fact could infer or deduce that A was responsible for the death of B. You might say: but hold on, what if there is nothing there and the victims have just vanished? Then what do you do? No one saw anything, and there was no sign of them. That is why you must play detective and prosecutor and follow the story.

It was thought likely that after such extensive searches and with police from various countries involved, something might happen. It did. The break came soon after the involvement of Scotland Yard and Interpol. The yacht was recovered at Majuro in the Marshall Islands with the accused on board and basking in the sun. The police swarmed into Majuro and surrounding areas and recovered the yacht. It had on it virtually all the worldly possessions of Bayerl and Zack.

The study of circumstantial evidence can be tedious, but I must give you a list of what was found because the prosecution relied heavily on what was found to prove the accused's guilt on the two charges of murder. No bodies were found, no evidence of how they were killed, no fingerprint evidence, and no evidence of any struggle or presence of blood.

In most cases, that type of evidence is often found at the scene of the crime, and sometimes there are witnesses who either saw something or heard something. That explains why you must embark with me on a journey to examine some boring-looking items to prove murder. It was different regarding the charge of stealing the vessel because the prosecution had in its possession the stolen boat itself as evidence. The police paid attention to every bit of stuff found on the vessel.

This is the list:
- a .22 calibre rifle
- a 7.62 calibre rifle
- a quantity of ammunition for both rifles
- a large quantity of female clothing
- male clothing identified as belonging to Bayerl
- a green coloured 2-man tent
- 2 backpackers—one orange and one black
- 2 sleeping bags, one blue and one aqua
- a quantity of cut and uncut opals and cutting equipment
- a large number of navigational charts
- old map of the world
- a Bible
- first-aid items
- female cosmetics
- two watches and a bracelet and assorted items of personal jewellery
- a precious black-opal pendant
- a dozen nappies
- maternity bras
- nautical charts showing all the ports he visited
- a map of mooring positions on Cairns
- admiralty chart showing all ports visited by Bayerl in Australia
- the boat called *SV Immanuel* … and so on.

The riffles and the ammunition and the camping gear and nappies were indicative of and demonstrated the complete lack of intention on the part of the deceased to part with the vessel and all their possessions.

Whilst in custody, Weissensteiner broke out and swam across to an island nearby and was dragged, wet and shaking, back into custody.

# CHAPTER 6

I thought it would have been poetic justice if the local sharks had consumed him and saved us so much pain and trouble in the pursuit of justice. The police had such contempt for this criminal that one of them said to me that even the sharks were particular about what they ate.

The accused had sailed the yacht thousands of kilometres through the Pacific, and he had no sailing experience at all. He had never sailed a boat in his life. The police interviewed him, and he gave some truly fictional accounts, which he kept changing. The prosecution proved that these were lies. He tried to distance himself, but in the process dropped hints and statements that allowed the investigators to conduct a thorough investigation and to follow all his movements in Cairns and his movements when he left Cairns. So, the prosecution could sheet his crime to Australia and prosecute him here.

I mentioned the problem before—namely, supposing he killed them in the Marshall Islands where we had no jurisdiction. In most countries, criminal law is territorial and that means the long arm of the law does not extend beyond the territorial jurisdiction. If an Australian is murdered in Japan, we can do nothing about it here. It is a matter for Japan.

I had long experience as a Crown counsel, and I knew that we were dealing with a cunning criminal who lied all the time. He would have left Trump for dead! What worried me most and gave me nightmares was the possibility that he would give evidence and tell the jury a story. Scenario 1: Bayerl had caught Weissensteiner naked in bed with Susan, and he went to get his rifle and in a struggle on the deck, Bayerl was pushed (in self-defence), and he slipped and went overboard, and Susan came out screaming and slipped and went overboard too. And supposing he said that all this happened on a dark and stormy night with gale-force winds blowing on the choppy seas and that he could do nothing about it, that he went into hiding because he knew that no one would believe him? I thought that in that scenario, the jury would have found it difficult to convict as he did in self-defence what you might expect. Even worse, the judge might have ruled that the State had no jurisdiction to try someone for murder on the high seas and discharged the jury. I would have argued in vain that the accused was lying.

But scenario 2 really terrified me because I was told that the accused was watching the jury most of the time to see their reactions. I very seriously thought that he might get in the witness box and give sworn evidence to the effect that he had fought with both of them and got the rifle and shot them both and dumped them at sea, pointing out that this happened on a tiny atoll in the middle of the ocean, and then said, 'To show I am genuine, I will plead guilty as charged, and what a pity I have no idea where it happened, but I can tell you it did not happen in Australia'.

He might have said that you all know that I know nothing about sailing, and I have no clue where it all happened. You can rest assured that the very feisty defence counsel would have gone on the warpath and won. The defence would have said that this was not a case of a clever criminal denying his responsibility but a contrite man willing to help. But alas! We could do nothing. I must tell you later what the defence did say to me immediately after the jury retired to consider its verdict. I think this would have caused some real problems for the prosecution.

Anyway, back to the case. The items found were the types of evidence used in circumstantial cases. In the light of the findings of these items on the boat, let us again talk about circumstantial evidence: what use can a jury make of these items? We know from experience that people draw all sorts of inferences from a story. However, in criminal trials, judges caution and direct the jury that to bring a verdict based on circumstantial evidence alone, it is necessary not only that guilt should be a reasonable inference but that it should be the only rational inference that the circumstances enable the jury to draw. You can skip all this and go on with the investigation.

The discovery of the boat and capture of the accused led to a further hunt for other tiny trickles of evidence to connect the accused to the crime, and no stone was left unturned. The result was that the Crown could establish with near certainty that he murdered the victims and that it all happened in Cairns.

## CHAPTER 6

When the vessel was seen leaving the berth, only one man was moving about on board. It was the accused who was seeking clearance and he gave a false account of the whereabouts of Bayerl. No woman was seen on the boat. The jury was asked to conclude that the victims would not have allowed the accused with no experience to pilot the yacht. This was not all, because more stunning and persuasive evidence was yet to come when the prosecution called the parents of Bayerl to give evidence.

They told the court that their son was deeply religious and had with him an old family Bible, which was found on board. This Bible was precious to the whole family. On one occasion, Bayerl had left it in Austria and flown back to collect it. The jury was told that he would not have left this Bible unless he had met with foul play.

The only memory I have of the cross-examination by the defence counsel was directed at Bayerl's father, whose full name was Adolf Hartwig. He was asked whether he had served in the Hitler Youth Movement. The jury gasped and the trial judge rolled his eyes! I think the father would have been fifteen or so years old during the war because I did ask him to give his date of birth. I suppose if I had some good legal foundation, the judge would have allowed me to call Stalin in retaliation!

Susan Zack was born in Chigwell Essex in England in 1959. Both she and Bayerl had travelled to Australia at different times and finally settled in Cairns. They were permanent residents. No passports were ever found, and extensive searches showed there was no official record of either of them leaving Australia.

Bayerl was not employed. At the time of his disappearance, he was working on his boat. A lot of evidence was given about this boat, which was called *Immanuel*. The lifestyle of both was described as somewhat unusual and even bizarre. They were living on that vessel moored in Cairns.

It is not widely known that in many cases the jury learns very little about the murdered victims, essentially because the history of the dead person is not an element; name and proper identity is all that is required unless it unfolds in the recital of other relevant and admissible evidence.

In this case, nothing much was mentioned in the trial about the early life of Susan who worked as a pharmacist in England for four years and then decided to come to Australia.

She was excited that one of her college friends, Jane Nicholls, had agreed to join her for a working holiday in Australia. This happened in 1984. There was evidence that Susan telephoned her parents frequently and sent cards and letters to her elder sister, who was ill at that time. She always phoned and spoke to her very elderly grandmother.

Susan found work in Sydney for a while and then in 1986 returned to England to see her family and that was the last time she saw her sister and grandmother. At about the time she went missing her elder sister died and then her grandmother died too. All contact ceased, and the parents became alarmed when their frantic efforts to contact Susan failed. They actually spoke to Weissensteiner at this time, who told them that the couple were on the Atherton Tableland, and it was then that he hurriedly left Cairns.

Their ageing parents in Europe were in despair, and it was mostly because of their persistence and perseverance that eventually a horde of police, both Australian and Scotland Yard (also Interpol), flew into action. The search for the missing couple and their sailing boat ranged far and wide and went on for almost a whole year before the first clues emerged. Some thought it was not that uncommon for boats to sink and leave no trace.

I am writing for my children and friends and other readers who are laypeople, so I must tell you what happens when someone is charged with murder. The Crown prosecutor presents an indictment in writing, setting out the charges and the document reads 'I was duly appointed to prosecute for Our Lady the Queen' and then the actual charge is written with great care. Our system of justice does not allow every lawyer to just turn up in court to lay such charges.

And no barrister, no matter how long he has practised law, can just turn up to present an indictment. He must have a commission to prosecute and the authority to present an indictment. The point of this exercise, among others, is that the charge of murder is so serious that

## CHAPTER 6

no one should go through such a traumatic experience without careful consideration.

This indictment is then handed to the judge's associate who, on the direction of the presiding judge, reads it aloud in open court. The courts do not allow spurious charges to be laid against a citizen. This is just part of the ritual we go through in such matters.

The charge must state when it happened and where it happened. The main reason for that is a suspect who leaves our jurisdiction generally cannot be tried here.

The importance of all this was that the two people had vanished, and extensive searches failed to locate them. No one saw them on the vessel. He was also charged with stealing and that was the subject of the third charge. So, in this case, we have two charges of murder and one of stealing a steel-hulled vessel.

Now, fortunately for me, I have kept a copy of this opening of the Crown case and a transcript of the actual trial for some three decades and can give an accurate account of what was alleged to have happened. Some sixty-five witnesses were called and there were documents, photographs and maps all over the bar table.

I told the court that the case for the prosecution was that between 1 November 1989 and 18 January 1990, Hartwig Bayerl and Susan Zack were killed, and their bodies were disposed of in or near Cairns or out in the Pacific Ocean with the result that no trace of the bodies was ever found. If the Crown satisfied the jury that they were killed in Cairns, then it did not matter where the bodies were disposed of. The gravamen of the offence was the unlawful killing, not where or how the bodies were disposed of. It was our case that he either killed them at or around the Atherton Tableland or the vessel on the berth, or within the territorial waters of Queensland. It was believed that he was unlikely to have thrown the bodies near Cairns where they would be easy to find.

I will now summarise the case for the prosecution and this involves repeating the main facts I have given, but the advantage is that you have the case stated in a compact, precise way and do not have to check all the details spread over the previous pages.

The court was told that the Crown was unable to nominate the exact location of these unlawful killings, but that the Crown would seek to rely on a substantial body of evidence and that the jury would be invited to infer from all the facts and circumstances proved that the killings occurred in Queensland and that the accused was the perpetrator of these crimes.

I told the jury that both victims had travelled separately to various parts of Australia and finally they met in Cairns and settled there. They were permanent residents, and no passports were ever found. There was no record of either of them clearing customs or any port authority. There was no evidence that they had left Australia.

This search was necessary to avoid any suggestion that they could have gone to some other part of Australia because, if so, Queensland would have no right to charge and try the accused here for crimes committed elsewhere. I hope that, so far, I have succeeded in showing that the law can be difficult for the uninitiated to understand. I told the jury that the police had made an extensive and thorough search.

Then I outlined the evidence to be given by some sixty-five witnesses. The opening lasted four hours or half a day. I outlined each vital and boring detail that you have read so far. I did not say that the prosecution case was fragile and paper-thin or that I wanted to consult flying-saucer experts to bolster the case.

I then outlined the evidence that showed that the lifestyle and attitudes of Bayerl and Zack could only be extremely unusual and bizarre and that both feared a nuclear holocaust. I told the jury that the victims had told many of their friends and acquaintances that they were going to hide in the Pacific where no one could find them.

You should have seen the utter surprise on their faces as they heard this weird tale! But you can imagine how both counsel at the bar table—each attired in a black funereal robe and with a wig made of horsehair stuck on their heads and used as some sort of a symbol of gravity and wisdom—rose to their feet with one hand stuck in the black vest pocket and spoke solemnly to the jury, which leaned forward to listen. You now have a vision of the high priests who function in our holy precincts called the courts.

# CHAPTER 6

I told the jury that the vessel was eventually recovered at Majuro in the Marshall Islands and was in the possession of the accused. It contained virtually all the personal possessions of Zack and Bayerl, including personal jewellery such as watches, gold chains, opals, bracelets. There were other personal items such as cosmetics and female underwear and several rifles belonging to Bayerl. Figuratively speaking, the prosecution intended to put in everything bar the kitchen sink. (Incidentally, in one murder case I did tender a kitchen sink—see the De Jackson case.)

I told the jury that the volume of the material detailed here showed a lack of intention to ever part with the vessel. The accused told the police on numerous occasions that the victims had given the vessel to him and gone into hiding somewhere in the Pacific Ocean, and he told the police it was their problem if they could not find them.

Susan was pregnant (hence the boat containing maternity bras and nappies) and had failed to keep an appointment with her doctor in Cairns on 24 November. From all the material, the accused was the last person to see the victims alive. On his own repeated admissions, he was the last person to see them.

The accused sailed the yacht thousands of kilometres through the Pacific despite having no sailing experience. I told the jury that the prosecution would show that the accused left Cairns in some haste and that he was the only person seen on board. What were the events and circumstances that led to his hasty departure on a boat that belonged to the victims who had spent so much energy and financial resources on it? He had absolutely no sailing experience. It must have been his desire to escape detection for the crimes of murder.

I told the jury that I intended to lead further powerful circumstantial evidence to contradict any alternative suggestions, such as that they were lovers and spent a lot of time in bed somewhere down in the boat whilst it was in harbour, and therefore they were alive but not seen.

It is an ordinary function of any experienced trial counsel to be ready to anticipate and effectively deal with problems that arise in the courtroom; otherwise, their chances of being engaged by the

Attorney-General or the Solicitor-General for such trials in the future are almost zero. This is not something special for just a few Crown counsels; hundreds work hard and have a high-performance level. It goes with the territory. I also mention this for the benefit of my children and friends who are highly educated and love reading. I want them to know that there was nothing special about me or my work. The public is often critical of police, but in countless cases, the police spend months and years trying to find the evidence that will lead to the conviction of vicious killers. I remember many cases in which I phoned them at midnight to tell them of some gap in the evidence, and this happened in the middle of a trial; and sure enough, they acted immediately during the night!

I told the jury that Bayerl and Zack had been missing for close to two years at the commencement of the trial and now as I write (2021) they have been missing for three decades. I remember at least on two occasions in this case the police from Europe urgently communicated with the Queensland police in Cairns and told them that the two victims were seen alive in Europe; I think on one occasion it was from Germany. I remember sitting on the back landing of our old colonial home, enjoying a buttered pumpkin scone when I had a call telling me that both were again seen alive and this time, they had witnesses. I knew already that people have seen flying saucers too. I told the police to tell them that we had proved beyond a reasonable doubt that they were dead and that all appellate courts in the country had agreed. The matter was dismissed with a quip that the next time they were seen the police might consider shooting them because they were legally dead. They have never been seen alive since. I never heard from the police again on this matter.

I gave the jury further details, including that the accused was seen on the island of Kosrae (then part of the Federated States of Micronesia) on 21 February 1990 and that the diseased went missing in January 1990. He was seen by Ingemar Carlsson, an engineer who was in Lelu Harbour Kosrae, but the Carlson sighting was not known to the police until about two years after the victims went missing. So, the police

# CHAPTER 6

now had direct evidence that, barely one month after the vessel had mysteriously left Cairns, it was seen on the Island of Kosrae, that the accused was alone, and that he had covered and concealed the name of the boat. Carlsson said that the boat could not be identified because it had no name. There were no signs of Bayerl and Susan on the boat.

I told the jury that the accused told Carlsson that he had bought the yacht in Cairns from an old man and the boat now belonged to him. He said that Kosrae was the first landfall since leaving Australia, but that he had wanted to land in Bougainville. He was prevented from landing there by some navy patrol boats. He also said that this was the very first time he had sailed in the boat and that he had never sailed before.

The accused said that he was leaving Kosrae and proceeding to Majuro in the Marshall Islands and then was going to Hawaii. Carlsson gave evidence that by the way the accused handled the vessel he could tell that he had no sailing experience. Carlsson had extensive sailing experience and thought it foolhardy for anyone to sail in January and February to Papua New Guinea; it was the cyclone season and very dangerous.

I told the jury that the immigration officer in Kosrae was told by the accused that he was a tourist, and he filled in the entry application form to that effect. Now all these sources of information began to pour in, and they were all talking to the chief investigator, Detective Sergeant Bruce Gray. The prosecution could establish that his first port of call was Kosrae and that he was alone.

I told the jury that the accused then gave an account of how in the following month of March he was in Kiribati and had cleared customs, telling them that he was on his way to the Marshall Islands, and he left that very day. He was back again in June 1990 and left in July.

This time there was contact with Cairns police, and the police learnt that the accused now was telling a different story and saying that they were alive and living in Kununurra and that they had gone for a holiday leaving him with the boat. I recall going to Kununurra a decade or so after my retirement, and I went to see this area.

The accused lived in Kununurra for a short time after he arrived in Australia, and so he wove a plausible story set in that place. The Australian Air Force was called to produce Airforce photographs showing that at the relevant time the place was in flames and no one could have lived there. Another lie. Again, he told one customs officer much later that both were still living in Cairns and he was going to take the vessel back to them in December of that year.

I told the jury that he met the editor of the local newspaper in Majuro, Marshall Islands and told the editor, Murphy, that he had left Australia with the owners and travelled to Bougainville on the yacht and that he saw Bayerl and Susan dropping boxes of arms. The jury was shown the vessel, which had been brought back to Cairns on a cargo ship. It would have been impossible to carry a large quantity of arms. The vessel was so heavily plated with steel sheeting that it sat very low in the water.

He told people that both had decided to stay in Bougainville, and he had gone to Port Moresby. All their personal belongings including the tents and backpacks were found on the yacht; he was instructed to go to Majuro and await contact. I told the jury that the only thing the accused forgot to tell Murphy was that they were going to swim across thousands of miles to meet him in Majuro! I told them that even in August of 1990 he was telling the local police that both were in Western Australia.

I must give you a break from this boring opening to the jury and tell you a real story. Everyone from very senior superintendents from Scotland Yard, Interpol and Germany and all the islands in the Pacific were willing to go to Cairns to give evidence for the Crown. Apparently, they all knew something about the Barrier Reef and beautiful Cairns. I did call every relevant witness including from the Pacific Islands and they numbered some twelve customs officers and police.

I mentioned that Scotland Yard assisted in searching for Susan in parts of England and made inquiries in Germany. It so happened that Mrs Zacks, who was very distraught, told the police in Cairns that the only person who seemed to care was a female low-ranked police constable and that she consoled her and conducted searches for Susan

## CHAPTER 6

and her contact even during that winter. But when I told the police that I needed to show the jury that she was nowhere to be found and I needed evidence that diligent investigations had been made in England, some very senior Scotland Yard Superintendents were prepared to drop their other tasks and come to balmy Cairns. The investigators told me what had happened, and I decided to call the policewoman. I spoke on the telephone with someone very senior in Scotland Yard who expressed surprise that we were proceeding with the case. They all thought it would be impossible to show that the victims were dead in a place totally unknown or that their boat had sunk in a storm. I told him that the prosecution required Constable Bryan. I had never seen a happier looking English constable turning up to give evidence. As mentioned earlier, after the trial, I was sent a special plaque from Scotland Yard in relation to this case.

I was staying in a relatively posh hotel in the centre of Cairns, and the police had followed instructions to arrange the same standard of accommodation for the islanders as that provided to the Airforce officers and the various witnesses coming from Western Australia. I remember that one morning the main investigator, Bruce Gray, came to see me because there was some question as to how these island witnesses might go in court giving evidence in English. I was required to ask non-leading questions. There was also a concern that they might find the courtroom wigs and gowns off-putting. Quite apart from that, I wanted to know how the Islanders were getting on. I'd had a lot to do with Islanders in Fiji when I was young. He told me that he noticed that the beds in the motel and hotel rooms occupied by the Islanders were very tidy and undisturbed. It turned out they slept on the floor because they did not want to disturb such neatly made beds!

The Attorney-General wanted to come and give evidence for the Crown. I was surprised because I had never heard of any Attorney-General in Queensland wanting to give evidence in a criminal case. We had no idea what time they got to work, and some cynics suspected that they mostly slept till ten!

I could not imagine that even in Majuro the Attorney-General spent his time following suspects around and giving evidence in court. I wanted proof of his statement and that it must be direct evidence. When I saw his telexed evidence, I burst out laughing and decided to call him for some nice dramatic effect in the trial.

This is a verbatim account from his final statement, and it had direct evidence too. It read:

> On the third of September 1990 I was standing on the beach and I had a clear view and I saw the accused being brought to the dock in a speed boat by five Islanders. He was handcuffed and lying on his stomach and dripping wet. He had tried to swim away from Majuro and escape from custody.

I think that his capture and incarceration saved us some money and time. He had not committed any crime there, and the police and the Crown were dealing with the American Embassy and our own Foreign Affairs Department to see how he could be extradited to Australia. This could have dragged on for months. Whilst in custody he told another inmate that he could never be charged because 'they have no bodies', and he then volunteered to return to Australia. The police acted quickly, and the next thing was that he was now in custody in Cairns. Ironically, the prosecution could not proceed because it, too, had nobody to put in the dock, and no one is tried in absentia.

This witness was the Deputy Attorney-General and Chief Prosecutor. He gave a brief history of that remote area of the Central Pacific that had the grand name of the Federated States of Micronesia. The area included the Republic of the Marshall Islands.

There was another group called Palau, Guam and Saipan. Some of us had heard of these islands during the war in the Pacific, so we sat there listening to the rest of the history he gave without any objections from the trial judge or defence counsel. He went on to say that after World War II, the Security Council of the United Nations put them under a trusteeship status under the guidance of the United States.

And as protective guardians should, the United States blasted the place with atom-bomb tests. He told the court that before 1979 the

# CHAPTER 6

Republic of the Marshall Islands was part of the Federated States of Micronesia, which included the island states of Chuuk, Ponape, Kosrae, and Yap. They all broke away from the Federation and formed separate states under Westminster-type governments. All this is captured in the transcript of the trial itself.

The Marshall Islands had a population of 45,000 people. What has this got to do with the murder trial? The Crown contention was that the victims were never going to Majuro to avoid a nuclear holocaust (the accused had said he was asked by the victims to wait there for them to arrive). The witness told the court that the United States conducted a minimum of 60 atomic tests, including the Bikini test, and a vast area of hundreds of kilometres was completely unhabitable. He told the court that, in addition, the United States used this area to test its missile systems.

He told the court that this happened in the Kwajalein Atolls. He said that the missiles were fired from California and travelled 4000 miles, obliterating large areas of ocean life. He said that the Americans also used the area for testing intercepting missiles in their spare time. He said visitors who had no business in the area, such as the accused, had to leave and then return later for a re-entry visa. This explained why the accused left and returned on numerous occasions. He told the court that he personally became interested in the accused 'because he was just such a strange occurrence'; that he was there and suddenly not there and was difficult to track down. He was held in custody for having a stolen boat, and he hired a lawyer to appear in the High Court to get him released. It was at that stage he tried to escape and swim away.

At this point, the spell about the destruction wrought by the Americans was broken when the defence counsel interrupted to say that he had nothing in his statement about American power in the Pacific. I told the trial judge that the purpose was that the accused was trying to escape and that it was extremely unlikely that the victims would go to a place like that.

After this quiet period, the interruptions and objections came thick and fast. At one point, the trial judge said: 'Mr Lakshman, don't ice the cake and light the candles. The jury is just as capable as I am.' We always follow a judge's intimations, and so I stopped icing the cake and lighting the candles.

In his address, the defence counsel repeatedly urged the jury to believe that they must have had some such arrangement. I was looking at the jury and, as the trial judge had observed, the Crown did not need any icing on the cake.

I addressed the jury first, and the defence counsel addressed the Crown case and told the jury that the Crown had gone on a fishing expedition and there was no evidence on which the jury could convict. It was significant for the Crown that whatever evidence was there was not contradicted by any other evidence produced by the defence. The trial judge gave a summing up to the jury, leaving all matters of fact to the jury, and the jury retired to consider its verdict.

The defence counsel then approached and told me that the accused wanted the boat back after the verdict. It so happened that during the trial the defence counsel, who was very experienced, told me many times that the prosecution did not really have a case. I agreed with him on several occasions that that was probably true. I wanted to keep him in his comfort zone and make him feel that he had convinced me. When I appeared before the Court of Criminal Appeal, some of the judges expressed surprise that virtually none of the evidence was challenged during the trial. One or two judges mentioned this in their judgements when rejecting the appeal against conviction.

When the jury was sent out to consider its verdict, and right in the middle of the ensuing arguments for redirections to the jury, a senior investigator approached me to tell me that the defence had told them that the accused wanted to get the boat back. I spoke to the defence counsel, who said: 'Too right he does.' And he told me that he would get an order from the court so the accused could get the boat back and was going to sail or sell it.

I remember vividly that I quickly got my instructing clerk to speak to the parents, and they were very upset. You know anything could have happened as far as the jury verdict was concerned, so I looked at the

Criminal Code dealing with the return of the property to the rightful owner.

We were still in the middle of arguments on redirection. This is when, while the jury retires to consider its verdict, both counsel correct errors and tell the judge what additional directions should be given. The bailiff came and spoke to the judge, who announced that the jury had reached a verdict.

This did not bode well for me because if the verdict was quick in lengthy trials that went for days, in most cases the verdict was an acquittal. The verdict was guilty on all counts. The news reporters rushed out of the crowded court as soon as the prisoner was sentenced to imprisonment for life. The parents wept and were relieved and had the satisfaction of knowing that this cunning criminal would spend a minimum of twenty years behind bars. Even the supporters of alien sightings seemed happy and cheered the police outside the court. I came back to Brisbane to prepare for the next long murder trial in Brisbane, which was to commence in the Supreme Court in Brisbane.

## *R V STAFFORD*: A CONTROVERSIAL CASE (1992)

I shall end with a case that I decided not to prosecute because I was not sure of the accused's guilt. It is an account of what transpired in the early stages and is a passing reflection on a strange and perplexing case with a tortured past.

It is strange and perplexing because I had initially advised that the accused should be prosecuted and had the conduct of the prosecution case. I then decided that he could not have committed the murder on the available evidence and told the prosecuting authorities that I was not prepared to prosecute the accused. In short, I declined to have the conduct of the trial. The case went ahead without me, and Graham Stuart Stafford was convicted in 1992.

The accused always maintained his innocence, but most charged with serious offences do. They deny any involvement, no matter how damning the evidence of guilt. In Stafford's case, he appealed against his conviction in 1992 and again in 1997, before the Court of Appeal finally overturned the conviction in 2009 and ordered a new trial. By that time, Stafford had served his entire sentence of 14 years. Then, in 2010, the Queensland Director of Public Prosecutions announced that there would be no new trial. As I write, there are dedicated people still seeking to prove that he was not guilty of the offence of murder.

The details of the case were as follow. A young female, Leanne Sarah Holland, aged about thirteen, was murdered and her mutilated body was recovered sometime later after an extensive police search. Graham Stuart Stafford, a sheet-metal worker and (at the time) the partner of her older sister, was charged with the murder. The murder received wide publicity because the victim was young, it was such a brutal attack, and there was some frustration with the perceived slow pace of the police investigation.

I was assigned this matter to deal with the ordinary issues touching on the sufficiency of the evidence in a case based entirely on circumstantial evidence. Stafford had already been charged and the committal proceeding was pending in the Ipswich Magistrates Court, and the police sought assistance at this stage. The police do not normally attend committal hearings even in serious criminal matters unless there are some special reasons for intervention.

This was a case in which the prosecution relied heavily on circumstantial evidence. As we have already established, there is nothing wrong with circumstantial evidence; indeed, it is how most cases are decided.

In this case, the police sought Crown intervention to deal with the usual legal issues on evidence. It seemed that the police brief had been compiled in some haste, although this was not immediately apparent, and there were unresolved evidentiary issues. But there was nothing in the case that would have prevented the prosecution from securing a committal for trial on a charge of murder. There was, in my opinion, a prima facie case.

The date for the committal hearing had already been fixed. Perhaps for some other pressing reasons it was thought best to deal with the evidentiary problems before the actual trial and to proceed with the committal hearings without delay. There had been many, much more difficult murder investigations based entirely on circumstantial evidence in which some of the evidentiary problems, especially of a scientific nature, were resolved after the committal hearings but before the trial.

There was nothing unusual in the suggested course of action as there was sufficient evidence to establish a prima facie case, which was the focus in the preliminary hearings. There was hardly a case based on circumstantial evidence that did not have some evidentiary or other problems, real or perceived, before, during and after the trial; and there were many cases that required further investigations before the actual trial. In short, there was nothing remarkable about this case; it was a case with ordinary problems.

The standard advice some of us gave to junior prosecutors was that, when doing a serious circumstantial evidence case, the prosecution should not only prepare to prosecute but anticipate and be ready to argue the routine standard grounds of appeal that were expected to be lodged on conviction. This was not to suggest that the grounds were frivolous or unsound but that there was a familiar pattern to such grounds of appeal in circumstantial evidence cases, which led to a total re-examination of what transpired during the trial. I have appeared in many such appeals and virtually every piece of evidence is subjected to scrutiny; it is like doing the whole trial again. The appellate courts deal with all grounds with rigorous thoroughness and the Crown is required to be prepared for all sorts of submissions.

There are several levels or stages in the preparation of any prosecution case. These comments are not a dissertation on how a case should be prepared but merely an explanation of the degree and extent of preparation required at different stages. No doubt someone with much greater experience or grounding had other methods that were less tedious and more productive. I belonged to the class of average lawyers who had found there was no substitute for tedious scrutiny of details; there is nothing of the glamour seen in fiction. In a criminal trial of this nature, give the hares a miss and settle on the tortoise every time. The details of the facts and circumstances relied on, no matter how minute or marginal, were routinely and repeatedly examined by experienced investigators. Some marginal facts that appeared paltry and seemed to have no bearing on guilt or innocence sometimes proved to be toxic and deadly to the prosecution case. This part of the task in preparation was just as exciting and memorable as studying an old shopping list.

The evaluation and assessment of evidence for committal hearings, including those matters with complex legal problems, was not in itself considered a difficult procedure. The police prosecutors and magistrates did this every day without encountering too many problems. The weight of the evidence could be assessed by a study of a properly prepared police brief and with necessary conferences with the investigators, and it was always acknowledged that in more complex cases that required Crown intervention the police should seek assistance at a much earlier stage in the investigation and certainly before the committal proceedings. This did not happen in this case.

The preparation for an actual trial, as distinct from a committal hearing, is necessarily a much more thorough exercise requiring a greater focus on the details. The ordinary things in a trial—such as a reasonable grasp of the relevant facts that are likely to be canvassed or that may be in dispute—receive a greater focus. Some understanding of other marginal surrounding facts and circumstances, no matter how peripheral and innocuous, was seen to be a good start. Innocuous and apparently worthless pieces of evidence could become noxious and lethal and could come back to haunt the prosecution or the defence or both—mostly both.

I was in the process of preparing the case after the committal hearings and was getting ready to proceed to the next level: trial by a judge and jury. I do not have the benefit of the exact dates and times in this matter because all this happened decades ago. I have read some media reports from time to time dealing with public disquiet on the matter, and I am aware that several attempts have been made to seek a review of this case.

I have retired and have no intention to enter any debate, nor am I required to make any comment. Observations and explanations in controversial cases should be left to those more familiar with the

## CHAPTER 6

evidence in the actual trial.

I declined to prosecute Stafford. End of story as far as I am concerned. The legal process is long over, and there is no prospect of any further prosecution. It was only because I happened to be reflecting on some past cases, and writing about them, that I thought of revisiting the Stafford case as well. I have never read the transcript of that trial or the subsequent appeal records and have no knowledge of what happened during those proceedings.

This is an account of why I decided not to handle the case personally due mostly to my own perception of the facts on the available evidence. I came to two seemingly contradictory conclusions: first, that there was a prima facie case and second that I was not convinced that Stafford was the offender. The question of guilt or innocence arises mostly when there is a prime suspect identified as an offender by the police.

On 4 December 1991, after the committal proceedings, I wrote a memorandum to the Director of Public Prosecutions. Generally, such communications are not a complete legal opinion for publication but are written under the pressure of work and are intended as notes for further discussion. It is a version of workplace communication between workers and lacks the elegance and completeness required in more formal legal opinions. However, cynics may say that that is too generous a reflection on those who do write legal opinions because these opinions are often cryptic, convoluted, disjointed, obtuse and unreadable; hurried and harried lawyers have little time to be elegant. I had serious reservations about the state of the evidence and the guilt of the accused. To avoid distortion, it is desirable to give the content in some detail. Fortunately, I found some notes and other material. I said:

> I refer to our brief discussion regarding this matter. Stafford has been committed for trial and the evidence is entirely circumstantial. There are features in this case that give rise to some doubt that Stafford is the offender in this crime.

I also said:

> I would like you also to look at the evidence so that we could have a discussion at some later date.

I was gradually concluding that Stafford was not the offender and gave the basis for my reservations about the case. I also wanted someone of at least equal experience and seniority to be engaged in the subject.

The reference to 'some later date' was not meant as a time at our leisure. This was just before Christmas, and we were all occupied with other matters.

> The victim was subjected to a very violent attack with a blunt instrument in which she sustained head injuries. One would expect extensive bleeding at the scene of the crime. On all available evidence if the accused is the perpetrator, the killing must have occurred in the dwelling house that he occupied with the deceased's family. There is no extensive evidence of bleeding in the house. The evidence of blood in the house may have little impact because the deceased lived there. And it would be expected if there was any bleeding in the domestic setting through injuries or whatever ... that may explain the presence of blood. There is no evidence of blood in the sink or drainpipes from the shower in the bathroom.

I had assumed or concluded on the evidence then available that the likely place for the killing was in the house, but the lack of evidence in support of that proposition was troubling. The problem in assuming something is that an assumption in such cases is provisional and is mostly guesswork and not evidence.

There was no other scenario on the table consistent with the rest of the evidence. The police had none, and any other theory as to the place of the killing of the young girl collided with the rest of the evidence, mostly as to time and place, which were known to the police. The prosecution did not consider the possibility of other scenes for the murder, nor the police investigating the matter. The Crown was not obliged to select any definite scenario at all. This happened in cases in which the body of the deceased was never found or not capable of

## CHAPTER 6

proper identification and when it was difficult to determine what exactly might have happened.

But in this case, it was thought that if the accused was involved, then the killing must have happened in the house. The timeframe or the window of opportunity did not allow for many different scenarios and that is how the prosecution viewed the evidence at that juncture. There was very little circumstantial evidence that the murder was committed in the house.

This was not like a case where the body of the deceased was discovered months later when incriminating clues were sometimes destroyed, giving rise to more speculative reasoning and conjecture on the part of the investigators and prosecutors. This was a case in which the body was discovered in a relatively short time and thus offered more prospect of tell-tale clues. However, there was not much found in the house if that was the scene of the crime. The police concentration in the search for evidence in the house was exhaustive and thorough because there was a genuine effort to make the crime stick provided the evidence was there. I was intensively inquisitive about the presence of incriminating circumstantial evidence in the house.

The rest of the circumstantial evidence linking the accused to the crime was also weak and tenuous. I said:

> There is blood in the boot of the car which belonged to the accused. It is a very small quantity and part of it is on a blanket which is normally kept in the back of the car. The blood on the blanket loses some of its force, again, because the deceased would have had access to the blanket (even if no witness can testify to that). A blanket is a mobile object which apparently was kept in the car. There is insufficient bleeding in the boot if the deceased was disposed of by being first placed in the boot of the car. This alone may not be of any significance.

There was not much reliance put on the hair of the deceased found in the boot because it was thought it could have been on the blanket from some previous association of the deceased with the blanket or that it could have got there in some explainable way such as leaning into the boot to pick up something because she had access to the car. The boot of a car is not like a safe deposit box; even neighbours sometimes might have reason to look into a boot to see what is in it, let alone a member of the family.

I then said:

> At the relevant times when she must be dead, she is seen by a large number of witnesses, particularly in the afternoon. Some of these witnesses have resiled from their earlier statements and some have not. It may be possible to discount all of them and this is a matter which needs some discussion.

It seemed to me that some eyewitness accounts could be discounted but not all of them. The Crown had an obligation to call all relevant credible witnesses even if they were likely to give completely contradictory versions of events. Having conflicting accounts or versions of events was never decisive or fatal to the prosecution in all cases, but sometimes these were important.

I dealt with the state of the maggot evidence and said:

> There is a maggot found in the boot of the car and there is no appropriate explanation for this. On all available evidence the accused must have disposed of the body long before the body would be in a necessary state of decay for maggots to form. It is difficult to pit a dead maggot as a Crown witness against witnesses who say that they had seen the deceased!

The statement was not intended to trivialise the evidence on which the prosecution relied to prove the probable time of death. The normal decay and the production of maggots in a dead body were relevant. It was thought strange that there was only one maggot, but strange things did happen in real cases. I had prosecuted several cases in which the prosecution relied heavily on the state of decay and the presence of maggots and had a passing familiarity with maggot evidence. The reliability of the scientific evidence based on the life cycle of maggots was never in question but was used in conjunction with other proven facts and circumstances. The fact was that the police found only one maggot and that was that.

The reference to the body being disposed of 'long before it would be in a necessary state of decay' assumed that if the accused had killed the victim in the house and had used his motor vehicle, then he would have attempted to dispose of the body immediately and not carry the body in the boot of the car for several days with the car left unguarded near the family home. The family members and his fiancée had access to the car and could have opened the boot with some other key or even with his own key. It seemed far-fetched to think that he would or might have a dead body in the boot with the possibility of having to drive around town with the sister of the deceased with him. There was no evidence of any odour or smell from the boot of the car. In the absence of some such evidence, it was thought by the police that this was because he had disposed of the body before there was any time for decay. It was difficult to explain the presence of a single maggot in the boot of the car, therefore. There was strong suspicion by some scientists I intended to call that the lone deceased maggot may have been planted.

The other striking feature, in my experience, was that most offenders in such crimes tended to distance themselves from the crime scene and any incriminating evidence. One would not expect a murderer or a suspect in a family setting to carry a dead body in the boot of their car for several days, for fear of detection. The family of the deceased had access to the car and could have opened the boot. In addition, there was nothing in Stafford's background, such as criminal history, to help decipher his motive or conduct. He had no convictions. That was neither here nor there because in some senseless killings it is difficult to discern a motive or explanation. Nonetheless, it was a feature that could not be summarily dismissed.

The suggestion of other possibilities, other than the house, as the scene of the crime was not considered by the prosecution at that time. Certainly, the Crown was not obliged to select any definite scenario at all, but no trial is conducted in a vacuum. As suggested earlier, this was not a case in which the body of the deceased was found months later with attendant difficulties. This was a case in which the Crown was obliged to give a reasonable account of where and how this could have happened. The Crown could have relied on one or several scenarios if necessary. The prosecution could not leave it to the imagination of the jury. If the accused was involved, it all happened in the house. That was how the prosecution viewed the evidence when I looked at the material.

I then went on to deal briefly with the obvious—namely, that if some of the eyewitnesses could be believed, then it would be difficult to prove that the 'maggot' evidence was reliable or even relevant. The absence of an appropriate explanation for the presence of a single maggot led me to conclude that the maggot evidence must be irrelevant to the involvement of the accused in the crime of murder.

The actual process of reasoning is now lost in the mists of time; entomologists who are enamoured of maggots may have good reason to remember a single maggot after several decades; prosecutors do not. It was generally thought that the police investigators had a deep aversion to maggots but in another context and a lighter vein. It was not uncommon in those days to hear some police investigators telling us, mostly in wilful damage and senseless vandalism cases, and especially when told that the evidence was insufficient to sustain a charge, that sooner or later they were going to 'get these maggots'.

The recollection and reasoning decades later may have some speculative elements in the reconstruction, but there was no question that the maggot evidence had to fit in with the rest of the known prosecution case and not the other way around. The prosecution case did not have to wrap itself around the life cycle of a single maggot. I was gradually forced to accept that the maggot evidence in the case was mysterious, unreliable and did not explain anything. This was one case that did not need a maggot; the maggot was the question, not the answer.

The uninitiated and even some legal practitioners who have never prosecuted would scarcely understand how painful, slow and reluctant a concession it was for a prosecutor to make that the maggot in the boot had no relevance to the guilt of the accused. The removal of the maggot as evidence destroyed one of the main planks in the prosecution case because

# CHAPTER 6

it was the only independent credible evidence of a connection or nexus between the accused and the deceased in the actual crime of murder.

There were no admissions in this case; no incriminating evidence such as blood on his clothing or other items or any clearly identifiable weapon. And without that maggot evidence, even the tyre tracks at the scene of the crime, which at first looked promising, were useless. Opportunity alone was not evidence and as the day progressed and the movements of the deceased and the accused were tracked and established, opportunity too was slipping through the prosecution's fingers—a case full of promise but little traction.

The problem for the prosecution was that there was no onus or obligation on the accused to show how the maggot got in the boot of the car either during the actual trial or in any subsequent anticipated appeal on conviction; there may have been dozens of explanations including those unknown to the accused. It was the prosecution that sought to adduce the damning piece of evidence and the prosecution alone had a duty to explain how it was part of the relevant evidence of guilt. There was no appropriate explanation for the presence of a maggot in the boot of the car.

In contrast to this case, suppose the following:
- the murder weapon was a carving knife and the injuries to the victim both in dimension and shape were consistent with the use of such a knife, and
- a similar knife from a set was missing from the house in which the murder was allegedly committed and was subsequently found in the boot of the suspect's motor vehicle covered with the rare blood grouping of the deceased victim, and
- a clear fingerprint of the suspect was found on the handle of the knife, and
- when questioned as to how the knife got in the boot of his car, the accused simply refused to answer or said, 'no comment' or said to the police '… your job to find out, you tell me' and lied about being in the locality at all.

Then not only would this be the most damning kind of evidence that the prosecution could rely on but the onus of giving an honest explanation, if there is one, would remain with the accused. Even on conviction and appeal, the court would seek that explanation from the prisoner and not the prosecution with the question: 'How does the prisoner explain the presence of the knife?' There was no such obligation on the accused to explain the presence of a maggot; a maggot is not in the category of a knife with a fingerprint. Sheet-metal workers may not have sufficient knowledge to explain the breeding habits and movement of maggots.

I had already decided that the house was not the murder scene and that there was no evidence of extensive bleeding in the boot of the vehicle, as one would expect if the body had been hurriedly removed from the house, and thus concluded that the maggot probably had nothing to do with the murder. And if that were all true, then it was extremely unlikely that the accused was involved in the killing at all.

Crown prosecutors look at the evidence in a case; they do not search for other possible suspects. It is no part of their function to play detective or to pretend to solve murder mysteries. I was simply not prepared to pit a dead maggot as a witness for the prosecution against eyewitnesses who had seen the victim alive. This was no ordinary maggot in the boot of the car; it was a red herring.

I went on to say:

> These witnesses were interviewed a few days after the event, so it is hard to say that they are mistaken and some of them knew the deceased very well. As I have said I have an open mind on this because it is possible that most of these witnesses may be mistaken as to the day when they made the observation. There is some evidence to support this view.

I decided that the maggot evidence was suspect, and the eyewitnesses would prevail or cast grave suspicion on the value of the maggot evidence. Ironically, lawyers are trained to have 'an open

## CHAPTER 6

mind' and to leave other possibilities open, at least on paper. Imagine the consequences for a lawyer's cherished professional reputation if he wrote that he did not have an open mind or that he would not allow for any other possibilities! Those with a more twisted cynical bent may say that in criminal matters legal opinions are highly qualified and are peppered with exit strategies—sometimes for the benefit of clients and at other times for the benefit of lawyers.

The combination of the facts and circumstances relied on by the prosecution did not seem to reach that 'critical mass' required in such a case. However, that was a matter of judgement. There is no reliable test of 'critical mass' in such cases and that term is not part of the legal jargon.

I recall dealing with the evidence of the tyre tracks found at the scene and had this to say in the memorandum:

> Some tyre tracks were found at the scene where the body was discovered and were similar to that of the vehicle driven by the accused. This evidence may have great significance because the accused had different sets of tyres at the front and the back of the vehicle. However, the police did not bother to take photographs of the tyres, but inked impressions of tyre treads were made and used for comparison purposes. There is further work being done on this aspect.

In cold print, this may sound too critical of the police investigation. I always respected the dedication and commitment of the police in difficult investigations and here I had not intended to criticise the individual police involved, some of whom were known to me as very good officers. It was more a reflection of my frustration with the state of the evidence, having regard to the nature of the case. The police had not taken any photographs of the actual tyres on the vehicle to enable comparisons for the purpose of opening the case to the jury.

I said:

> The time of death given by Bennett using the 'maggot

technology' would be sometime on Monday the 23rd of September. This is not an exact science. Further work would be required in this area.

I had appeared for the prosecution in many murder trials and at least in several of these cases the time of death was critical and the state of decay of the body and the presence of maggots and the life cycle of maggots and the relevant scientific evidence was important, but it was not an exact science.

In some cases, the time of the commission of an offence was critical. In other cases, the time of death did not feature at all. However, in cases in which time was critical and there was reliance on the maggot evidence, the police investigation had to be detailed and thorough. This type of evidence was always considered reliable on proper proof and mostly in conjunction with other reliable circumstantial evidence—and almost never in complete isolation. In one other trial I prosecuted it was even more critical; otherwise, the accused could not have committed the crime of murder.

Time and opportunity to commit a crime are always critical in such investigations. In this case, all relevant acts had to happen within a narrow timeframe or not at all. I concluded that on the evidence the most probable answer was not at all; this was allowing for the fact that human action is not robotic and precise as to time. I went on to deal with another aspect of the evidence and said:

> The accused has given an account of his movements and it is possible to show that some of the things he said were incorrect. The significant one being that on the date in question he had visited a doctor in the afternoon. The evidence would be that he had seen the doctor on the following day. However, there are not a large number of discrete lies to be found on the whole of the evidence.

There did not appear to be significant or many elaborate lies on which the prosecution could rely to show that the accused was trying to cover his tracks. No matter what the purpose, lies are generally admissible as part of the case. The prosecution does not have to pick and choose. However, lies told by an accused may be nothing more than lies and proof of lies has no evidentiary or probative value in these cases unless inferences can readily be drawn from such lies revealing a true consciousness of guilt. These must be relevant lies in the sense that the lies are designed to cover the suspect's criminal tracks or lies intended to create a distance from the crime committed, mainly to conceal guilt or for some other such reason.

The prosecution relied heavily on significant lies told by an accused to prove guilt and this was true whether the case was based on circumstantial evidence or not. There were very few such lies in this case. It was challenging, in this case, to find such lies for the purpose described. Mistakes and confusion alone would not be of any value. It is a curious fact that in the criminal courts lies are pointed out by way of examples, but no definitions are sought or given. The definition of a lie, if there be such a universal definition, is seldom discussed. This is curious and even strange because criminal trials are littered and showered in definitions, and lawyers relish definitions. And any attempt at definition is quickly reduced to a maze of confusion and tautological nonsense and can quickly become an exercise in circumlocution. A lie is something that is not true. What is not true may or may not be a lie. And lies come in all shapes and form: white, blatant, downright, malicious, mischievous and many shades in between.

In criminal cases, we are mostly concerned with intentionally false statements, but the category of lies is never closed. It may not be permissible to talk about the 'architecture' of a lie, but we seek out purpose-driven and purpose-designed lies; lies designed to conceal and not reveal some relevant fact in issue or generally to conceal guilt. Wisely, these things are left to the common sense of the jury.

On another aspect of the case, I said in the memorandum:

> The medical evidence suggested that the deceased was tortured and there are some burn marks on her body. I am informed by the police that the accused does not smoke. This

may or may not be of any significance, but it does not appear to fit the pattern of the accused's behaviour as known to us.

This was another striking feature because it did not fit in with the accused's known habits. In isolation, it may or may not have been of significance because in some bizarre cases it is conceivable that a non-smoker could use a cigarette for torture. There is no limit to aberrations in human behaviour. But there was strong evidence that the accused in this case did not have cigarettes or a lighter with him, and he did not smoke. This added to the improbability of the accused being the perpetrator or the actor in the crime.

This was in contrast with other examples of normal behaviour by the accused when his fiancée returned to the house and when he visited a friend in the early afternoon. There were some other small but significant things that did not fit any pattern of his known behaviour. The police were looking at a pattern of behaviour in a domestic setting; even contract killers in fiction are not as normal and as cool and composed as the description of the accused contained in the evidence.

I then dealt with the possible general implications of proceeding with the case with the evidence in that state and in passing said:

> I think in the light of *Chamberlain v The Queen* we would need to look carefully at circumstantial evidence of a scientific nature. Chamberlain's case set us back a decade and, if possible, no doubt, we would like to avoid the same sort of thing happening again.

The prosecution lived under the shadow or spectre of the Chamberlain case for a decade or more, but its influence was fading, and we had moved on. The case had reached a sort of cult status and sometimes the name was invoked as a signal or warning for some disaster on the horizon. It was perhaps not necessary to say all this in the memorandum to the Director of Public Prosecutions because he would have been all too familiar with that case, which was notorious for various perceived and/or real reasons. It was mostly noted for the failure on the part of the prosecution to deal properly with scientific evidence, but there were many other aspects of that case that led to the prosecution being repeatedly castigated and corrected in subsequent cases in the appellate jurisdiction. In short, the Chamberlain case created a nightmare for the prosecution. The courts placed severe restrictions on how the prosecution could interpret and use what are called 'primary facts' in circumstantial evidence cases, and it took time before these restrictions were removed.

I added in the memorandum:

> I have done many circumstantial evidence cases over the years and this is one of the few in which I find myself having some reservations as to whether the accused is the perpetrator of this crime. I may not entertain any such view after some discussion with you, but it would be desirable if you would be good enough to look at the material yourself and let me have your comments sometime next year.

The memorandum was written in December so the reference to 'next year' was simply January of the following year, 1992.

In a career stretching over some three decades, I had never declined to prosecute in cases perceived to be complex or difficult; most cases have complications of some sort. I was reluctant to prosecute because I had serious reservations about Stafford's involvement in the crime. The general details in the case did seem to fit in and the fitting of all the details in a precise way goes to the very foundation of circumstantial evidence cases. The problem here was that in some areas the evidence was vague and not precise; but in human affairs, one man's vagueness is another man's preciseness.

In circumstantial evidence cases, minute details are everything and here some areas lacked precision; the 'whole' was not honed and fine-tuned. A statement such as that may sound vague, but sometimes a case has a feel about it. This case lacked 'critical mass'. To my mind, it lacked the 'escape velocity' to take it over the threshold described in legalese as 'proof beyond a reasonable doubt'. It needed more preciseness, more detail and more flesh. There was a prima facie case, and the standard of proof required for that was lower. No matter how one looked at the case, there seemed to be a prima facie case; like the curate's egg, the case was still good in parts.

The somewhat vague expression 'critical mass' to a legal mind untutored in science (such as mine), when used about a criminal case, is intended to convey no more than the usual rule of thumb used by lawyers and expressed in so many ways to describe the total weight of the evidence required to move the evidence from the realm of mere possibilities to the world of probabilities in which we live and make value judgements. In these cases, the more the facts and circumstances fitted in, the more compelling the case because all discrete pieces of evidence came together through some undesigned coincidence, and when so braided and plaited together without human intercession, these discrete pieces of evidence combined of their own force and pointed to the accused as the perpetrator of the crime.

And that is at the heart of a circumstantial evidence case. There was some hidden, barely understood, magnetic quality to the pieces of evidence, some mutually attractive force that brought all the pieces together, and the operative message here was that it all happened independently of human intercession. Put more bluntly, it happened without human interference or not soiled or muddied by human hands. That was the attraction of the circumstantial scientific evidence in most cases of this nature.

The mute 'silent witnesses' in a circumstantial case appeal to the legal mind as these pieces of evidence seem to fall naturally in place and all telling and relevant evidence point in one direction only—namely, the guilt of the accused. Trial judges were generally painstaking in detailing to the juries the true nature of reliable circumstantial evidence and were in the habit of reciting something like that as part of their summing up, perhaps with greater elegance and preciseness and certainly with greater authority—occasionally, only with greater authority.

The reliability of circumstantial evidence as a powerful tool in

# CHAPTER 6

the search for meaningful explanations, the discovery of truth, and the sheeting of criminal responsibility was never in doubt; circumstantial evidence seemed to have much greater force and certainty than the evidence of eyewitnesses because it was not subject to the usual human bias and frailty.

There is greater public awareness on these matters because of the general interest in the popular (and exaggerated) television series now available. The real specialist forensic pathologists and scientific teams in our courts could only drool and dream about the trail of clues found with monotonous regularity in some good television series.

There is considerable force in the view or notion that silent witnesses never lie and never die and remain mostly at the murder scene and/or with the dead body and sometimes travel with the suspect until he is caught. The problem, as always, was the possibility that the human mind interpreting these pieces of evidence could be mistaken or blind to other potential conclusions. The safeguard lay in the protection afforded to the accused on conviction in our judicial process itself. The trial judges in appropriate cases subjected any dubious evidence to a critical evaluation, and counsel grimaced at what was happening to their brilliant submissions.

There was no question that, from the prosecution's perspective, the criminal justice system tended to favour the accused and sometimes the courts entertained and were open to all forms of submissions, whether the evidence was relevant or not, and many days were spent on needless, useless and futile legal arguments.

The next phase of the history of the case is from a combination of what was in the memorandum and the actual discussions I had on several occasions with the Director of Public Prosecutions.

In the Stafford case, the course I took seemed to be a departure from the general practice in the office. It is not a function of Crown prosecutors to decide what case they will take and what case they will refuse to take. The opinion of Crown prosecutors on the question of guilt is of no relevance whatsoever. The only exceptions are when a conclusion reached is that there is no case to answer or there is some acute public policy reason. For example, there is no good reason to prosecute a grandmother, charge her on an indictment for stealing minor items to feed her family, and subject her to a trial by jury.

In this case, there had to be some clearly identifiable deficiencies that would enable the case to be taken away. I had advised at first that there was a case to answer and that the matter could proceed, but even that was subject to the resolution of some of the issues and matters raised both in the memorandum and in the subsequent discussions. I had known Royce Miller QC, Director of Public Prosecutions, for several decades. He was also a Crown prosecutor in an earlier incarnation, and we all shared court experiences. He also served as a District Court judge. He was a conscientious and careful lawyer with extensive experience in criminal matters, and he was also a professional colleague. Miller treated the matters raised very seriously and agreed that there was a need for further clarification. However, he concluded that the case should proceed to trial because there was a prima facie case, and the whole matter was left within the safeguards available in the judicial process in which the evidence is subjected to rigorous scrutiny before an experienced trial judge.

The underlying reason for such consensus may be found in the fact that at least some of the matters raised and canvassed in the memorandum went to the question of the weight of the evidence, which is a matter for the jury, and not to the question of admissibility or relevance, which is mostly a matter for lawyers and judges to be determined in an actual trial. The course adopted seemed appropriate at the time; lawyers do cases, not quality control. This may seem like an abdication of responsibility but is simply a fact, a by-product of the British idea of trial by combat. In our courts, we know this as the adversarial system.

This was not the end of the matter. The question of who might conduct the trial was discussed. At one point, the Director of Prosecutions seriously considered appearing in the matter personally. It was not a good practice for a senior legal officer to simply hand over a prosecution case with problems to a relatively junior legal officer, but for whatever reason, he considered appearing in the case personally. However, I

# CHAPTER 6

expressed reservations about the suggested course of action and thought that his personal intervention in the trial was unnecessary. The case was assigned to a competent and experienced Crown prosecutor, and I discussed the content of my memorandum with him as well. I had no further interest in the matter.

It needs reiteration that prosecutors, and perhaps lawyers in general, do cases, not causes; they are engaged in combat, not crusades. In a sense, the adversarial system is designed for short, sharp and sometimes brutal contests, not for long campaigns. The outburst of legal energy in criminal trials is spasmodic and sporadic. Often, a short time after a trial, some of us have no exact memory of what happened without recourse to the transcript of the trial!

The primary function of prosecution is to prosecute—a role designed for combat, not quality control. The role of quality control is ultimately the function of the courts and particularly the appellate courts. This is because once a verdict is given in our system of justice, even judges who sit in criminal trials have a very limited scope for corrections and changes.

Trial judges respond and act in dynamic situations and when giving rulings on points of law they are compelled to act rapidly, decisively and pragmatically, and they do not have the luxury of giving some sort of a 'reserved judgement' with the jury in tow. That luxury is the privilege of the appellate tribunals; navel-gazing is not the basic tool of trade in criminal trials as these are more a theatre and are about the quick and the dead. A dramatic statement, yes; but true.

A common feature in criminal trials, appreciated by lawyers but not by outsiders, is that the contestants are bound by strict rules of engagement, which deal with the conduct of the trial, and well-established procedures determine the code of behaviour by the parties. On occasions, criminal trials descend into debating sessions, and experienced judges are quick to point out that their courts are criminal courts, not moot courts.

The account given of what transpired in the early stages of the Stafford case may be of little significance to the debate surrounding this case now, but this is a recollection of my involvement in that matter.

The complication arose because of a judgement formed on matters that some would regard as clearly within the province of the judges of fact and should normally be left to the jury.

Ideally, informed comments should only come from those with familiarity with the evidence in the actual trial and subsequent appeals. The opinion in the memorandum is merely evidence of the fact that on the material then available I formed a view on the evidence and is perhaps evidence of little else. It is possible that new material came to light before the actual trial.

There are many avenues for review in our system of criminal justice and sometimes the defence is given too many bites at the cherry. Part of the problem is that, given sufficient time and repeated mulling over past events, lawyers can change the whole trajectory of the evidence that was given in an earlier trial and reach entirely different conclusions. Then there is the further complication that the search for the truth is sometimes not the central but merely an incidental objective in the delivery-system of criminal justice. The exercise is sometimes like a game of chess and the best players win. It is perhaps the only profession in which making white appear black is lauded, and greater rewards accrue to those armed with nothing more than sophistry.

The art of persuasion is a powerful tool, and sophistry is an essential ingredient. It is difficult to imagine advocacy without sophistry. The word is not used in any pejorative sense because the sophists were a respectable team of thinkers and debaters in ancient Greece, and Socrates had a difficult time dealing with them and could have lost some of the debates had he not taken a high moral ground.

It is common knowledge that there is not much point in debating with moralists. Sophistry is in our professional genes and it would be an extremely dull world in the legal profession without it; any prohibition in the use of sophistry would sound the death knell for our cherished profession and would be a disaster. Natural justice, as interpreted in the current climate, declares that everyone is entitled to eke out a living, whether or not their services are essential and required.

I would not like to comment on the current position in the Stafford matter for the reasons given. However, in a hypothetical case in which, say, a child is murdered, and the only suspect is X, and the facts are somewhat similar, and the weaknesses in the case are also somewhat similar, then the police even now would charge X with murder. The police would be accused of dereliction of duty if they failed to charge X. It is also highly probable that a magistrate looking at the evidence would commit X for trial on that charge, and if the magistrate failed to do that, he would be subject to public criticism. The appropriate prosecuting authority would still advise that there was a prima facie case, and a properly instructed jury could still return a verdict of guilty. There would be no absolute certainty of an acquittal.

There is no final solution. It is a process of constant compromise and negotiation with the principle of uncertainty, and there is no escape from errors and mistakes. There is really no solution save the tired old and ignored call for eternal vigilance against apathy, and the need to guard against total reliance on any single system of logic no matter how soothing and how attractive it might be to lawyers. There is no substitute to the occasional purgative, or an enema delivered through public criticism to test and cleanse the legal system, and there are various civil-liberty institutions that play an extremely useful and thoroughly distasteful role—that is, thoroughly distasteful to the establishment.

The problem in the Stafford case has more to do with a design flaw in the adversarial system itself than with anything else. It may have little to do with individuals who honestly attempt to make the system function and assiduously follow all the proper rules in the quest for justice. In the absence of any better system, society must accept some of the failings.

The Chamberlain and similar cases are more the exceptions than the rule and whilst these can never be excused, justified or simply explained away, the fact remains that in most cases true justice is delivered. The only remedy in such cases may be to acknowledge the wrong done and compensate. Even that is poor consolation to those who have suffered. Compensation is only a sop for the collective conscience, to soothe the feeling of guilt.

It has been said many times and in different ways that a redeeming feature of a good functioning civil society is its ability to accept responsibility, adapt and change and then move on and not spend inordinate time contemplating the debris of the past. Cosmologists and sages remind us that we inhabit a transient universe and may not have been created in the image of some divine being after all. And that we may not be the inhabitants of the best of all possible worlds.

In such cases, there is the age-old tendency to sanitise and explain away such faults. All this is captured and expressed so nicely in the phrase: 'To err is human, to forgive divine'. Try telling that to someone such as a political prisoner who is incarcerated in a solitary cell for several decades! The sentiment expressed in that quotation may be seen to be absurd and a piece of nonsense because the opposite sounds even more profound: 'To err is divine, to forgive human'. The more we learn from cosmologists, the less likely we are to place all our faith in the notion of some divine forgiving principle. The universe may be an unforgiving, godless, senseless creation, and it is humanity that must make some sense of it and learn to forgive the divine. Change the previous expression to 'To err is divine, to forgive is human'. It sometimes feels good to put god in lower case.

This is the final case I wanted to mention in detail in these pages. In 1992, I gave away my working life, and for the next forty years, I travelled the globe and did not read any law books. These days I mostly garden, and in the true Australian tradition, I always complain and whine about everything. I am truly Australian now. My children and grandchildren have thought that my wife Rosemary married me because I was a good gardener. I always thought that was such a romantic thought because I had read *Lady Chatterley's Lover* when I was about eighteen.

I prosecuted many of the cases mentioned here during the three or four years before I retired. However, I had worked in the service of the Crown for close to thirty years and did many more such cases. This is not unique. Most Crown counsels have large workloads. You will be pleased to know that I have finished with this exercise!

# CHAPTER 7: A FINAL REFLECTION

Rose and I were sitting on our open back veranda, as we often do on late summer afternoons, especially in steamy heat. We were surrounded by greenery—trees, creepers and pot plants—and were appreciating the rainy days. I was describing the gory details of criminal trials, and Rose went through the motions of shivering dramatically. She said:

'All those terrible court cases. I don't know how you can even think about them. I can remember you would come home and say, "I'll be up all night. I have 400 pages of depositions to read". Then you'd have a big dinner because you wouldn't have eaten any breakfast or lunch. But then you'd say you might as well see a bit of the news on TV before you started your work. Ten minutes later you'd be asleep. After a while you'd stagger off to bed.

'The next morning we'd hear the 4.38 am train go through Wilston and you'd jump up and start reading. I was so worried how you would get through it all but so relieved I didn't have to do the work you did. It was all so confronting. And what about our poor little beautiful children? You could remember all these terrible cases, but you could never remember their birthdays. Well, you were always away on circuit to Mt Isa or Charters Towers or some god-forsaken place miles away from anywhere whenever one of them had a birthday party.'

She rambled on:

'You know, the reason you survived when you came here, and the White Australia policy was still in full swing, was that you had this amazing sense of indomitable superiority. You were imbued with your knowledge of the ancient history of India going way back to a time when the white colonial masters of Fiji and Australia were probably savage Britons living in their smoky huts in England. Also, you had been educated at primary school by those great old Irish nuns, so you had an understanding of the Christian Bible, whereas nobody here had a clue about Indian religions. You were happy to debate with anyone.

'Then, of course, there was the brass pot! Mum bought it at an auction and used it as a flower vase. As soon as you saw it, you recognised it as an Indian holy man's begging bowl. You were adamant that it must have been stolen. He would never have sold it, you said. You could even read his name engraved on the side. You said the reason you had come to Australia and we got married was all just to get this brass bowl back into an Indian family. It all had to happen!'

My final thoughts are that there are millions of workers and thinkers who work and toil and leave no trace behind. We are here like glow worms and fireflies that produce luminescence for a fraction of a second in cosmic time and then leave without any trace.

I am reminded of Thomas Gray's immortal lines: 'Full many a flower is born to blush unseen and waste its sweetness on the desert air' and 'A flower that smiles today, tomorrow dies, all that we wish to stay, tempts and then flies'.

This Lotta my wife speaks of belonged to a holy man or Sadhu in India. His name is inscribed on it in Hindi: *Harnam Das Sadhu*. Rosemary's mother bought it for Rose when she was about 12. I always quipped that Rose was destined to marry an Indian so this Lotta would find a Hindu resting place!

I have written my story because I was one of eleven children whose ancestors were, as I related, indentured labourers, which was a type of modern slavery introduced by the British in some of their colonies. My father was a freedom fighter who worked tirelessly for the future of

# CHAPTER 7

Indians in Fiji. I had never attended a secondary school or sat for any formal examinations such as Junior or Senior Certificate before coming to Australia in June of 1956. In Brisbane, I graduated in Arts and Law and embarked on a career in the law that was almost ended before it began when I was threatened with deportation. I won that battle and was later entrusted with important political trials. I also prosecuted many high-profile murder trials despite once being told that an Australian jury would never accept an Indian barrister. I appeared before the High Court in some matters, something many more brilliant barristers than I have not had the opportunity to do. Ironically, I appeared for the Public Service Department in several appeals for promotion of very senior appointees. To think some on the Public Service Board had once worked hard to dismiss me from the Service! With satisfaction, I have witnessed the dismantling of the White Australia policy.

I want my children, grandchildren, friends and you, the reader, to know that everything is possible, and we need not blush unseen on the desert air.

These things are now in in my distant past. Today, I see a new world virtually unknown in my generation. With revolutionary advancements in medicine and science, we are now on the cusp of an evolutionary tectonic tilt. Homo sapiens are in the process of being replaced by new silicone man, who may be better able to conduct inter-galactic journeys lasting thousands of years. The homo sapiens may be lost in the cosmic sidereal dust, leaving no trace behind.

www.ingramcontent.com/pod-product-compliance
Lightning Source LLC
Chambersburg PA
CBHW020625220526
45464CB00001B/28